D. H. Lawrence

The Rainbow and *Women in Love*

A CASEBOOK

EDITED BY

COLIN CLARKE

MACMILLAN

First published 1969 by
MACMILLAN AND CO LTD
Little Essex Street London WC2
and also at Bombay Calcutta and Madras
Macmillan South Africa (Publishers) Pty Ltd Johannesburg
The Macmillan Company of Australia Pty Ltd Melbourne
The Macmillan Company of Canada Ltd Toronto
Gill and Macmillan Ltd Dublin

Printed in Great Britain by
WESTERN PRINTING SERVICES LTD
Bristol

CONTENTS

ACKNOWLEDGEMENTS

D. H. Lawrence, Prologue and Foreword to *Women in Love* and *The Collected Letters of D. H. Lawrence*, ed. Harry T. Moore (Laurence Pollinger Ltd, the Estate of the late Mrs Frieda Lawrence and the Viking Press Inc.; © 1962 by Angelo Ravagli and C. Montague Weekley, Executors of the Estate of Frieda Lawrence Ravagli; © 1932 by the Estate of D. H. Lawrence and 1934 by Frieda Lawrence; © 1933, 1948, 1953, 1954 and each year 1956–62 by Angelo Ravagli and C. Montague Weekley, Executors of the Estate of Frieda Lawrence Ravagli); George H. Ford, 'An Introductory Note to D. H. Lawrence's Prologue to *Women in Love*', from *Texas Quarterly*, VI (Spring 1963) (University of Texas); John Middleton Murry, *Reminiscences of D. H. Lawrence* (Jonathan Cape Ltd and the Society of Authors as the literary representative of the Estate of the late John Middleton Murry); John Middleton Murry, *Son of Woman* (the Executors of the John Middleton Murry Estate and Jonathan Cape Ltd); Mary Freeman, 'Lawrence and Futurism', from *D. H. Lawrence: a basic study of his ideas* (University of Florida Press); Roger Sale, 'The Narrative Technique of *The Rainbow*', from *Modern Fiction Studies*, V (1959) (Purdue Research Foundation); S. L. Goldberg, '*The Rainbow*: Fiddle-bow and Sand', from *Essays in Criticism*, XI, no. 4 (1961) (Mr F. W. Bateson); G. Wilson Knight, 'Lawrence, Joyce and Powys', from *Essays in Criticism*, XI, no. 4 (1961) (Mr F. W. Bateson); *The Deed of Life* (Oxford University Press and Princeton University Press, © Julian Moynahan 1963); H. M. Daleski, *The Forked Flame* (Faber & Faber Ltd and Northwestern University Press); *Double Measure: a study of the novels and stories of D. H. Lawrence* (Holt, Rinehart & Winston Inc., New York; © George H. Ford 1965); *The German Tradition in Literature, 1871–1945* (Dr Ronald Gray and Cambridge Press).

GENERAL EDITOR'S PREFACE

EACH of this series of Casebooks concerns either one well-known and influential work of literature or two or three closely linked works. The main section consists of critical readings, mostly modern, brought together from journals and books. A selection of reviews and comments by the author's contemporaries is also included, and sometimes comments from the author himself. The Editor's Introduction charts the reputation of the work from its first appearance until the present time.

What is the purpose of such a collection? Chiefly, to assist reading. Our first response to literature may be, or seem to be, 'personal'. Certain qualities of vigour, profundity, beauty or 'truth to experience' strike us, and the work gains a foothold in our mind. Later, an isolated phrase or passage may return to haunt or illuminate. Where did we hear that? we wonder – it could scarcely be better put.

In these and similar ways appreciation begins, but major literature prompts to very much more. There are certain facts we need to know if we are to understand properly. Who were the author's original readers, and what assumptions did he share with them? What was his theory of literature? Was he committed to a particular historical situation, or to a set of beliefs? We need historians as well as critics to help us with this. But there are also more purely literary factors to take account of: the work's structure and rhetoric; its symbols and archetypes; its tone, genre and texture; its use of language; the words on the page. In all these matters critics can inform and enrich our individual responses by offering imaginative recreations of their own.

For the life of a book is not, after all, merely 'personal'; it is more like a tripartite dialogue, between a writer living 'then', a reader living 'now', and whatever forces of survival and honour link the two. Criticism is the public manifestation of this dialogue, a witness to the continuing power of literature to arouse and excite. It illuminates the possibilities and rewards of the dialogue; pushing 'interpretation' as far forward as it can go.

And here, indeed, is the rub: how far can it go? Where does 'interpretation' end and nonsense begin? Why is one interpretation superior to another, and why does each age need to interpret for itself? The critic knows that his insights have value only in so far as they serve the text, and that he must take account of views sharply differing from his own. He knows that his own writing will be judged as well as the work he writes about, so that he cannot simply assert inner illumination or a differing taste.

The critical forum is a place of vigorous conflict and disagreement, but there is nothing in this to cause dismay. What is attested is the complexity of human experience and the richness of literature, not any chaos or relativity of taste. A critic is better seen, no doubt, as an explorer than as an 'authority', but explorers ought to be, and usually are, well equipped. The effect of good criticism is to convince us of what C. S. Lewis called 'the enormous extension of our being which we owe to authors'. A Casebook will be justified only if it helps to promote the same end.

A single volume can represent no more than a small selection of critical opinions. Some critics have been excluded for reasons of space, and it is hoped that readers will follow up the further suggestions in the Select Bibliography. Other contributions have been severed from their original context, to which some readers may wish to return. Indeed, if they take a hint from the critics represented here, they certainly will.

A. E. DYSON

INTRODUCTION

I

SIGNIFICANT commentary on *The Rainbow* and *Women in Love* may be said to begin with Middleton Murry's *Son of Woman*,[1] published in 1931, a year after Lawrence's death. Though he has little belief in the importance of either of the novels as achieved art (on the other hand he did admire *Sons and Lovers* and *Aaron's Rod*[2]), Murry has a sharp if partial and distorted comprehension of the tensions which are at work within them and which, in demanding to be ordered and controlled, help to determine their form. It is true that there is earlier commentary that is far more favourable and more balanced than his. Despite some virulent reviews and the public prosecution of *The Rainbow* Lawrence always had his devoted readers, and very occasionally critical comment was offered in a tone of appropriate and 'decent respect'.[3] Catherine Carswell reviewed *The Rainbow* in

---

[1] For an account of the reception of *Son of Woman*, see 'A History of Lawrence's Reputation', in Armin Arnold, *D. H. Lawrence and America* (1958).

[2] See *Son of Woman* and also *Reminiscences of D. H. Lawrence* (1933), where Murry reprints those of his reviews which had concerned Lawrence.

[3] For the phrase 'decent respect' see Lawrence's letter to J. B. Pinker, 16 Dec. 1915 (the 'book' in question is *The Rainbow*):

Tell Arnold Bennett that all rules of construction hold good only for novels which are copies of other novels. A book which is not a copy of other books has its own construction, and what he calls faults, he being an old imitator, I call characteristics. I shall repeat till I am grey – when they have as good a work to show, they may make their pronouncements *ex cathedra*. Till then let them learn decent respect.

(*The Collected Letters of D. H. Lawrence*, ed. Harry T. Moore (2 vols, 1962) I 399.)

October 1915 and later, in *The Savage Pilgrimage*, recalled how baffled she was but how disposed to admire:

Early in October I reviewed *The Rainbow* for the *Glasgow Herald*. . . . After *Sons and Lovers* it puzzled and disappointed me. I had been expecting a master-piece of fiction, and this did not correspond to my notions of such a thing. Neither did I understand the book. But the processional beauty, the strangeness, the magnificence of the descriptive passages, which passed far beyond anything in the earlier novels, gave me enough to admire and praise whole-heartedly. No other writer could have risen to such heights or plumbed such depths, and I said so as well as I could at considerable length. But I had no grasp, and I found it a hard review to write.

Amy Lowell, Paul Rosenfeld and Louis Untermeyer were early admirers in America. In an article in the *New Republic*, 11 August, 1920, Untermeyer praised Lawrence highly and called *The Rainbow* 'the best novel between 1910 and 1920'.[1] Francis Brett Young, for whom Lawrence had some contempt, as one might expect, spoke of him in 1925 in a 'Note on D. H. Lawrence' as 'the only authentic literary genius, in my opinion, of the generation to which we belong'. Concerning *The Rainbow* he said:

Many critics have considered it dull and inchoate; for myself – I would say that its first hundred pages contain more beauty than Lawrence himself or any other living novelist attained. . . . [It is] a work conceived by a spirit almost puritanical in its earnestness and austerity, as far removed from pornography as the Old Testament itself.[2]

There are brief, thoughtful observations on both *The Rainbow* and *Women in Love* in Herbert J. Seligmann's *D. H. Lawrence: An American Interpretation* (New York, 1924), a sympathetic discussion by Rosenfeld of what he takes to be Lawrence's novelistic virtues and weaknesses in *Men Seen* (New York, 1925)

[1] Arnold, *Lawrence and America*, p. 166.
[2] Ibid., p. 169.

and a conscientious analysis of *Women in Love* in Stephen Potter's *D. H. Lawrence* (1930), a monograph completed not long before Lawrence's death and published soon after it. An essay by F. R. Leavis also appeared in the year of Lawrence's death, in the *Cambridge Review*. It was expanded and published as a Minority Pamphlet in the same year and finally reprinted in *For Continuity* (1933). At this date Leavis's view was that *The Lost Girl* is Lawrence's best novel. In *D. H. Lawrence: Novelist* (London, 1955; New York, 1956) he was later to remark:

And learning to recognize the success and the greatness of *Women in Love* – I speak for myself – was not merely a matter of applying one's mind in repeated re-readings and so mastering the methods of the art and the nature of the organization; it was a matter, too, of growing – growing into understanding.

It is not surprising indeed that these early studies have very little now to offer the student of Lawrence's art. Potter, for instance, tells us again what the choric comment in *Women in Love* has told us already; but he is unable to get beyond this.

Gerald dies, Birkin does not die. Immortality is a question of character. Birkin has roots; he has the power to recreate himself out of the elements into which, as part of the corruptive process of modern life, he too is disintegrating. *Women in Love* describes the process of his renewal.

There is indeed no commentary before Murry's that helps us in defining the imaginative logic of either of the novels with which we are concerned – and Murry's commentary helps us almost despite itself.

In August 1921 he had reviewed *Women in Love* in *The Nation and Athenaeum* and had voiced a violent disgust. There is a sense in which this novel finds a virtue in corruption and mindless sensuality – the 'awful African process'[1] – and Murry is aware of

---

[1] From the chapter 'Moony'.

this to the point of horror. What he shows no awareness of is Birkin's effort to become whole through *incorporating* corruption; it is this, rather than a quest for corruption itself, that is a major motif in the novel. A dark river of dissolution rolls within us as well as a silver river of life, Birkin assures Ursula (in the chapter 'Water-Party'), and the implication throughout is that if we are to ride the dark river we must at least admit to its existence. Yet this, of course, is to state the issue too simply, for the novel dramatises nothing if not an explicit horror of dissolution and corruption. Indeed, there is an effect of double exposure: Birkin both embraces corruption and stands off in disgust, the unstained observer.

For all his distortions, then, Murry brings us up sharply against the question which any serious reader of *Women in Love* must come to terms with, a question expressed as follows by George H. Ford in a passage reproduced at greater length later in this book:

... if the 'dreadful mysteries, far beyond the phallic cult' associated with the beetle-faced statue are represented in one scene as degenerate and in another scene (with only a slight shift in terminology) as redemptive – when Ursula is transfigured by her discovery of a 'source deeper than the phallic source' – how is a reader supposed to respond to what seems a total contradiction?

But it is odd that Mr Ford should go on at this point to say:

Of the many critical discussions of *Women in Love*, the only one which I have encountered that even raises some of the questions that I have been trying to grapple with here is that by Eliseo Vivas.[1] Vivas' conclusion is that Lawrence introduced a contradiction which is seemingly not resolved, because the novelist has pictured Birkin as rejecting 'the African process' and then shown him as, in effect, succumbing to it.

Murry had developed substantially this argument almost thirty

[1] See Eliseo Vivas, *D. H. Lawrence: the Failure and Triumph of Art* (Evanston, 1960; London, 1961).

years before; it is not clear that the pages in Vivas's book to which Mr Ford refers represent much more than a footnote to *Son of Woman.*

II

There is no space to chart in detail the declining course of Lawrence's literary reputation during the thirties and forties, or the subsequent renaissance of interest so closely associated with the name of F. R. Leavis. There is a useful summarising account of all this, and of the relationship between the Lawrence revival and the New Criticism, in Mark Spilka's Introduction to *D. H. Lawrence: A Collection of Critical Essays* (Englewood Cliffs, 1963).

At this present date Leavis's services to Lawrence studies hardly need stressing. For over three decades he has waged war against misconceptions that retarded a recognition of Lawrence's distinction and stature: the notion that he is remarkable for intuitive powers rather than powers of intelligence, that his only theme is sex, that his genius is above all 'lyrical', that he is characteristically angry and lacks a sense of humour, that he surrendered quite simply to the primitivist illusion, that he fostered the spirit of something akin to Nazism and, most relevant to the present discussion, that he rarely or never produced finished works of art, and lacked the novelist's power to create characters or individuals. Murry had written in his review of *Women in Love*: 'We can discern no individuality whatever in the denizens of Mr Lawrence's world.' This view was persistently advanced in Lawrence's lifetime and throughout the thirties and forties (indeed, it still is in some quarters) and it was Leavis, insisting on Lawrence's 'power of making human individuality livingly present'[1] – a power apparent, he argued, not only in the *Tales* but in *The Rainbow* and *Women in Love* – who laboured most to dispel it. How necessary the work was may be judged from the following quotations, the first from Edwin Muir's *Transition:*

[1] F. R. Leavis, *D. H. Lawrence: Novelist* (London, 1955; New York, 1956) p. 182.

Essays on Contemporary Literature (1926) and the second from
Nathan A. Scott's 'D. H. Lawrence: Chartist of the Via Mystica',
a chapter in *Rehearsals of Discomposure* (New York and London,
1952), both of them sympathetic studies, the latter appearing
about the time Leavis was contributing his essays to *Scrutiny*.

There seems nothing which [Mr Lawrence's imagination] cannot
enter into, either in nature or in the instinctive life of men and
women. It recoils solely before most of the things in which the
imagination has till now found its inspiration: the conscious life
of mankind, ordinary relations and problems, the tragedy and
comedy of life as we know it. Mr Lawrence has deepened these
for us, but he has also dived beneath them so far that in effect he
ignores them. And that is because he is on the side of the instincts,
and against all the forms, emasculated or deformed, in which
they can be manifested in a civilized society. His view of life is
one-sided in a magnificent and obvious way, like the instincts, or
like nature.

When we come to *The Rainbow* and *Women in Love* we no longer
encounter characters who are recognizably living personal en-
tities, contributing each to the other's destiny in the sense to
which we are accustomed by the narrative conventions of the
English novel from Fielding to Forster and Maugham. The chief
characters – the Brangwens, Anna Lensky, and Skrebensky of
The Rainbow, Birkin, Gerald Crich, Ursula and Gudrun of
Women in Love – are now mainly larger-than-life embodiments
of a poetic mood; they are all vehicles used to project the vision
of a Darkness, beyond the fragmentariness of human existence,
in which the disunities of human life are negated and overcome:
they are all servants of the Mystery that lies beyond the 'phallic',
automatons of Lawrence's imagination.

Scott's book was not primarily a work of literary criticism; nevertheless his view that 'Lawrence's men and women desire, basically, a mutual immolation, a total eclipse, an utter lapse from
Day into Night' was representative, and underscores the value
of Leavis's work.

More than any other single critic Leavis has established the claims of *The Rainbow* and *Women in Love* to be great artefacts, and the peaks of Lawrence's achievement. At the same time he has demonstrated how each of them mediates a moral-religious vision of experience, communicated through a fully realised imaginative rendering of life. In his essay on *The Rainbow* in particular he has emphasised Lawrence's 'steady religious passion', his moral centrality, his inwardness with a living social tradition.

We are shown how Tom Brangwen's problem has been created for him, the problem of satisfying desire in a less simple way than that of mere animal response to crude instinct; how, that is, he has become so different from a Norman peasant – or any character – of Maupassant. . . .

But it is not the drift of *The Rainbow* to exalt this order of things – the order presented by the immemorial life at the Marsh and the 'close intimacy of the farm kitchen' – as finally adequate, the supreme fulfilment of life; the theme is rather the transcending of it. We watch the struggle towards self-responsibility in the individual – self-responsibility and a wider scope, things which entail a freer play of intelligence and a direct part in the intellectual culture and finer civilisation of the age, the finer contemporary human consciousness. But the impulse to this development, as well as the vigour for it, comes from the life that is to be transcended.[1]

But if Leavis has done perfect justice to this aspect of *The Rainbow*, he has done so at the expense of other meanings that are no less important. Neither here nor in his reading of *Women in Love* does he show any interest in the demonic Lawrence, or in Lawrence's deeply ambivalent treatment of the theme of corruption. Indeed it is implied throughout *D. H. Lawrence: Novelist* that Lawrence spoke in a quite unequivocal fashion for life and

---

[1] Leavis, *D. H. Lawrence*, pp. 105–6. The substance of the chapters on *The Rainbow* and *Women in Love* originally appeared in *Scrutiny* (see XVII 203–20 and 318–30, XVIII 18–31 (for *Women in Love*) and VIII 197–210 and 273–87, XIX 15–30 (for *The Rainbow*); reprinted 1963).

growth as against mechanism and disintegration. And this mis-
conception has done much to disable Lawrence criticism since.

However, since the publication of Leavis's *Scrutiny* essays a
tendency to recognise the socially subversive and demonic
Lawrence – Lawrence the outsider – has at least begun to be
apparent. In 1955 there appeared Mary Freeman's *D. H. Lawrence: a basic study of his ideas* (Florida) which has perceptive
remarks on 'the sensuous acceptance of social decay' in *Women in
Love* and on the paradoxical way in which corruption in that
novel generates life.

While denouncing the shames and brutalities of society, Birkin
achieves some satisfaction from recognising them as marks of
degeneration, from freeing his own life of outmoded moral
compulsions, and even from tasting with raw senses the hitherto
forbidden. . . . What has been regarded as ugly takes on a lurid
beauty; what has been considered ethically evil takes on sensual
good; what has been in essence death gives a flame of enhanced
perception. . . . If the lotus has its roots in the mud, it has its
flowers in the sun.

As she puts it in the chapter reproduced below, 'need to absorb
decay in an acceptable view of life became the dominant motivation in [Lawrence's] writing at this time', that is, at the time of
writing *Women in Love*. (Given this fact it is not surprising,
incidentally, that Lawrence should be fascinated and repelled by
Dostoevsky. Clearly both of them are indebted to that Romantic
tradition which Mario Praz and others have explored; and,
equally clearly, neither is contained by that tradition. The
Romantic agony – the quest for the god of death and the divinity
in pain – is both lived through and *placed* in *Women in Love*.[1])
In an article on 'Lawrence, Joyce and Powys', the relevant pages
of which are included in this anthology, Wilson Knight observes
that in *Women in Love* Lawrence tries 'to blast through . . .
degradation to a new health'. And in a more recent study, *The
Art of Perversity* (Washington, 1962), Kingsley Widmer has

[1] See Mario Praz, *The Romantic Agony* (2nd ed., 1951).

explored the demonic and nihilistic implications of Lawrence's shorter fictions. Unfortunately, as Mark Spilka observes in a review, Widmer 'favours shock-vocabulary' and 'antisocial toughness' and 'plays too glibly with the ambiguities of perversity'.[1]

More directly relevant to the purposes of the present anthology is an essay by Mark Kinkead-Weekes entitled 'The Marble and the Statue: The Exploratory Imagination of D. H. Lawrence', published in *Imagined Worlds*, Essays on some English Novels and Novelists in Honour of John Butt, ed. Maynard Mack and Ian Gregor (1968) pp. 317–418. This essay traces the evolutionary process by which the final versions of *The Rainbow* and *Women in Love* grew out of earlier versions, and indicates how the 'argument' in each novel is related to certain of Lawrence's non-fictional writings, particularly the 'Study of Thomas Hardy' and 'The Crown'. Especially valuable is the stress laid on Lawrence's discovery of a virtue in disintegration and corruption:

. . . the *Study* was positive, an account of the proper conditions for human growth, while *The Crown* is an attempt to diagnose disintegration.

The move from the world of the *Study* and *The Rainbow* to the world that would produce *Women in Love* can be detected in the third essay, 'The Flux of Corruption'. The first two essays are largely a rewriting of the *Study* in new terms. . . .

In 'The Flux of Corruption', however, Lawrence begins to analyse the process of disintegration which, he now sees, must always follow consummation if the theory is to be truly dialectic. . . . The flux of corruption seems terrible to us, caught as we are in the perspective of time; but in itself it is not evil. It is necessary.

Altogether, this is a scholarly and suggestive contribution to Laurentian studies.

Finally, in an essay on 'The Savage God: Conrad and

[1] See 'Post-Leavis Lawrence Critics', in *Modern Language Quarterly*, XXV 212–17.

Lawrence' (in *Critical Quarterly*, Spring 1968) K. K. Ruthven has endeavoured to set *The Rainbow* and *Women in Love* in the context of late-Romantic primitivism.

Recent studies of the idea of Decadence in the nineteenth century have shown how the *fin-de-siècle* sentiment originated in an awareness of imperial decline, a general feeling that Europe was played out, a sense of impending doom; and as for the corresponding fascination with the primitive, we have known for some time that the Romantic refusal to treat logic as the only valid activity of the mind was in many ways vindicated by the findings of Frazerian anthropology and Freudian psychology, both of which in different ways defended the integrity of the prelogical, analogical or illogical qualities of the mind. Particularly conducive to the development of savage primitivism were the reports of anthropologists who describe societies from which modern European prohibitions are absent. . . .

Perhaps the whole phenomenon of savage primitivism is simply Decadence in its most ferocious form, and if so then the books I want to discuss as examples of the genre – Conrad's *Heart of Darkness* (1899) and Lawrence's *The Rainbow* (1915) and *Women in Love* (1920) – are *fin de siècle* in so far as their subject-matter is basically *fin du globe*. . . .

In 1915 and 1916 Lawrence took a renewed interest in the Decadent theme that Europe is in the final stages of its decline. This is hardly surprising, seeing that war in Europe had turned *fin du globe* prophecy into fact; but what is peculiar to Lawrence's treatment of this theme is the way it merges with the ancient belief in resurrection. *Fin-de-siècle* pessimism is qualified by *nouveau siècle* optimism (Lawrence was after all writing a decade and a half after the nineties); the destruction of the old is necessary for the emergence of the new, the dying phoenix must destroy itself before it can be reborn. . . .

All this helps explain the phoenix-like fate of the people in Lawrence's novels, people who 'die' in some extreme humiliation and then find themselves reborn, not in heaven but here on earth, after undergoing various degradations in the course of which their connection with the old world and the old values is systematically eradicated. These degradations, it turns out, are degradations only in terms of the old values; looking back from the vantage point of the new life they see that the so-called degradations were really stages in their emancipation, the ultimate degradation being in fact synonymous with the final act of liberation.

Clearly, Lawrence too was searching for the heart of darkness, for the African experience that could revitalize refugees from a declining and falling European civilization. And the primitive, he knew, would be ferocious as well as vital. . . .

There is a welcome emphasis throughout the article on Lawrence's fascination with 'what civilisation excludes', and upon his conviction 'that the act of exclusion has severed us from sources of great vitality'. What is wanting is the complementary emphasis: a due recognition that in the world of *Women in Love* vitality is threatened, above all, by the dissolution entailed in just this act of exclusion. For degradation is not, as Mr Ruthven's reading would suggest, a process that Birkin and Ursula altogether emerge from renewed. If at one level it is suggested that a phoenix-like resurrection is possible, what is more pervasively suggested is that the processes of dissolution and renewal can never, in fact, be dissociated; or, more accurately, that there is after all only the one process, the ambivalent process of reduction. Accordingly, we find that every intimation that Birkin and Ursula are liberated, or 're-born', is undercut or obscurely qualified.

Over the last decade Lawrence's work has been discussed more than ever, and it is not unusual to hear the opinion expressed that we suffer from a glut of critical commentary and exegesis. Yet if his work has in fact been more commented on than the work of other great writers of our century it should still go without saying that there is always room for further perceptive criticism. In his Preface to *The Dark Sun* (1956) Graham Hough, referring to his debt to Leavis, writes: 'I owe most to his chapters on *The Rainbow* and *Women in Love* which indeed leave little for a later hand to add.' But if the immense distinction of these novels is admitted it must be admitted too that as subjects for discussion they are inexhaustible. And surely – due recognition having been given to Leavis's pioneering analysis[1] – the truth rather is that interpretative study of Lawrence's work has left a great deal to do. The assumption that *Women in Love*, in particular, calls for no further exegetical attention, that we have seen all around Lawrence at his most subtle, complex and comprehensive, will not go unquestioned by those who have read the novel repeatedly and wrestled with its difficulties.

COLIN CLARKE

[1] It was hoped that excerpts from Leavis's book would be included in the present anthology, but permission rights were withheld.

PART ONE

The Author on the Novels

LETTERS TO EDWARD GARNETT
AND OTHERS (1913–20)

After Lawrence finished *Sons and Lovers* late in 1912, he began writing a novel he at first named 'The Sisters'. This later fissioned into the books that became *The Rainbow* and *Women in Love*. *The Rainbow*, for a while called 'The Wedding Ring', was apparently completed in March 1915. The last page of the manuscript has a note: 'End of Volume I'. *The Rainbow* came out in September 1915; in November the authorities ordered it withdrawn. During most of 1916 Lawrence wrote *Women in Love*, completing it before the year was out. Embittered by the suppression of *The Rainbow* and shaken by the continuance of the war, Lawrence almost totally recast the remaining material of 'The Sisters'. He put some of his recent experiences into the new book, fictionally disguised, and some of his recent friends, recognizably caricatured. The novel was not printed until 1920, in America, where it was issued in a limited edition; it was published in the regular way in England the following year.[1]

[The following excerpts from Lawrence's letters give something of this history in his own words, and also a little of that inner history which can only ever be slightly known and which their composition presupposes. We learn too what Lawrence himself conceived the thematic relation of the two novels to be.]

To Edward Garnett, from Irschenhausen, Germany [late May or early June 1913]

. . . I was glad of your letter about 'The Sisters'. Don't *schimpf*, I shall make it all right when I rewrite it. I shall put it in the third person. All along I knew what ailed the book. But it did me good to theorise myself out, and to depict Frieda's God Almightiness in all its glory. That was the first crude fermenting of the book. I'll make it into art now. I've done 256 pages, but still can't see the end very clear. But it's coming.

To Edward Garnett, from Lerici, Italy, 29 January 1914

I am not very much surprised, nor even very much hurt by your letter – and I agree with you. I agree with you about the Templeman episode.* In the scheme of the novel, however, I *must* have Ella get some experience before she meets her Mr Birkin. . . . I have no longer the joy in creating vivid scenes, that I had in *Sons and Lovers*. I don't care much more about accumulating objects in the powerful light of emotion, and making a scene of them. I have to write differently. I am most anxious about your criticism of this, the second half of the novel, a hundred and fifty pages of which I send you tomorrow. Tell me *very* frankly what you think of it: and if it pleases you, tell me whether you think Ella would be possible, as she now stands, unless she had some experience of love and of men. I think, impossible. Then she must have a love episode, a significant one. But it must not be a Templeman episode.

I shall go on now to the end of the book. It will not take me long. Then I will go over it all again, and I shall be very glad to hear *all* you have to say. But if this, the second half, also disappoints you, I will, when I come to the end, leave this book altogether. Then I should propose to write a story with a plot, and to abandon the exhaustive method entirely – write pure object and story. . . . I feel that this second half of 'The Sisters' is very beautiful, but it may not be sufficiently incorporated to please you. I do not try to incorporate it very much – I prefer the permeating beauty. It is my transition stage.

* Ella Templeman was the precursor of Ursula Brangwen.

To Edward Garnett, from Lerici, 22 April 1914

I send you by this post as much of 'The Wedding Ring' as the consul has as yet typed. I have only some 80 pages more to write. In a fortnight it should be done. You will perhaps get it in three weeks' time, the whole.

From this part that I have sent you, follows on the original 'Sisters' – the School Inspector, and so on.

I am sure of this now, this novel. It is a big and beautiful work. Before, I could not get my soul into it. That was because of the struggle and the resistance between Frieda and me. Now you will find her and me in the novel, I think, and the work is of both of us. . . . You know how willing I am to hear what you have to say, and to take your advice and to act on it when I have taken it. But it is no good unless you will have patience and understand what I *want* to do. I am not after all a child working erratically. All the time, underneath, there is something deep evolving itself out in me. And it is *hard* to express a new thing, in sincerity. And you should understand, and help me to the new thing, not get angry and say it is *common*, and send me back to the tone of the old 'Sisters'. In the 'Sisters' was the germ of this novel: woman becoming individual, self-responsible, taking her own initiative. But the first 'Sisters' was flippant and often vulgar and jeering. I had to get out of that attitude, and make my subject really worthy. You see – you tell me I am half a Frenchman and one-eighth a Cockney. But that isn't it. I have very often the vulgarity and disagreeableness of the common people, as you say Cockney, and I may be a Frenchman. But primarily I am a passionately religious man, and my novels must be written from the depth of my religious experience. That I must keep to, because I can only work like that. And my Cockneyism and commonness are only when the deep feeling doesn't find its way out, and a sort of jeer comes instead, and sentimentality, and purplism. But you should see the religious, earnest, suffering man in me first, and then the flippant or common things after.

To Edward Garnett, from Lerici, 5 June 1914

... I don't agree with you about 'The Wedding Ring'. You will
find that in a while you will like the book as a whole. I don't
think the psychology is wrong: it is only that I have a different
attitude to my characters, and that necessitates a different attitude
in you, which you are not prepared to give. As for its being my
cleverness which would pull the thing through – that sounds odd
to me, for I don't think I am so very clever, in that way. I think
the book is a bit futuristic – quite unconsciously so. But when I
read Marinetti – 'the profound intuitions of life added one to the
other, word by word, according to their illogical conception, will
give us the general lines of an intuitive physiology of matter' –
I see something of what I am after. I translate him clumsily, and
his Italian is obfuscated – and I don't care about physiology of
matter – but somehow – that which is physic – non-human, in
humanity, is more interesting to me than the old-fashioned
human element – which causes one to conceive a character in a
certain moral scheme and make him consistent. The certain moral
scheme is what I object to. In Turgenev, and in Tolstoi, and in
Dostoievsky, the moral scheme into which all the characters fit –
and it is nearly the same scheme – is, whatever the extraordinari-
ness of the characters themselves, dull, old, dead. When Marinetti
writes: 'It is the solidity of a blade of steel that is interesting
by itself, that is, the incomprehending and inhuman alliance of
its molecules in resistance to, let us say, a bullet. The heat of a
piece of wood or iron is in fact more passionate, for us, than the
laughter or tears of a woman' – then I know what he means. He
is stupid, as an artist, for contrasting the heat of the iron and the
laugh of the woman. Because what is interesting in the laugh of
the woman is the same as the binding of the molecules of steel
or their action in heat; it is the inhuman will, call it physiology,
or like Marinetti – physiology of matter, that fascinates me. I
don't so much care about what the woman *feels* – in the ordinary
usage of the word. That presumes an *ego* to feel with. I only care
about what the woman *is* – what she IS – inhumanly, physiologically, materially – according to the use of the word: but for

me, what she *is* as a phenomenon (or as representing some greater, inhuman will), instead of what she feels according to the human conception. That is where the futurists are stupid. Instead of looking for the new human phenomenon, they will only look for the phenomena of the science of physics to be found in human beings. They are crassly stupid. But if anyone would give them eyes, they would pull the right apples off the tree, for their stomachs are true in appetite. You mustn't look in my novel for the old stable *ego* – of the character. There is another *ego*, according to whose action the individual is unrecognisable, and passes through, as it were, allotropic states which it needs a deeper sense than any we've been used to exercise, to discover are states of the same single radically unchanged element. (Like as diamond and coal are the same pure single element of carbon. The ordinary novel would trace the history of the diamond – but I say, 'Diamond, what! This is carbon.' And my diamond might be coal or soot, and my theme is carbon.) You must not say my novel is shaky – it is not perfect, because I am not expert in what I want to do. But it is the real thing, say what you like. And I shall get my reception, if not now, then before long. Again I say, don't look for the development of the novel to follow the lines of certain characters: the characters fall into the form of some other rhythmic form, as when one draws a fiddle-bow across a fine tray delicately sanded, the sand takes lines unknown.

To J. B. Pinker, from Chesham, Bucks, 7 January 1915

Here is another hundred pages of the novel. I am going to split the book into two volumes: it was so unwieldy. It needs to be in two volumes. . . .

To Waldo Frank, from Higher Tregerthen, Cornwall, 27 July 1917

. . . About *The Rainbow*: it was all written before the war, though revised during Sept. and Oct. of 1914. I don't think the war had much to do with it – I don't think the war altered it, from its pre-war statement. I only clarified a little, in revision. I knew I was writing a destructive work, otherwise I couldn't have called it *The Rainbow* – in reference to the Flood. And the book was written and named in Italy, by the Mediterranean, before there was any thought of war. And I knew, as I revised the book, that it was a kind of working up to the dark sensual or Dionysic or Aphrodisic ecstasy, which does actually burst the world, burst the world-consciousness in every individual. What I did through individuals, the world has done through the war. But alas, in the world of Europe I see no Rainbow. I believe the deluge of iron rain will destroy the world here, utterly: no Ararat will rise above the subsiding iron waters. There is a great *consummation* in death, or sensual ecstasy, as in the Rainbow. But there is also death which is the rushing of the Gadarene swine down the slope of extinction. And this is the war in Europe. We have chosen our extinction in death, rather than our Consummation. So be it: it is not my fault.

There is another novel, sequel to *The Rainbow*, called *Women in Love*. I don't know if Huebsch has got the MS. yet. I don't think anybody will publish this, either. This actually does contain the results in one's soul of the war: it is purely destructive, not like *The Rainbow*, destructive-consummating. It is very wonderful and terrifying, even to me who have written it. I have hardly read it again. I suppose, however, it will be a long time without being printed – if ever it is printed.

To Martin Secker, from Capri, Italy, 27 December 1919

. . . Mackenzie said you thought of printing *The Rainbow*. Do that, and you have my eternal allegiance. He suggests it be called *Women in Love*, Vol. I, with a foreword by himself. I think *Women in Love*, Vol. I and Vol. II, is a very good idea. I am anxious to hear from you. If you do this, *The Rainbow* as a Vol. I of *Women in Love*, then I must make a sort of permanent agreement with you. . . .

To Martin Secker, from Capri, 16 January 1920

... Then, honestly, I think you are wrong about the title *Women in Love*. Everybody jumps at it, as an excellent title. *The Rainbow* and *Women in Love* are really an organic artistic whole. ...

SOURCE: *The Collected Letters of D. H. Lawrence*, ed. Harry T. Moore (1962).

NOTE

1. This passage comes from Harry T. Moore's essay on 'The Rainbow' in *The Achievement of D. H. Lawrence*, ed. F. J. Hoffman and Harry T. Moore (Norman, Okla, 1953). For a thorough account of the genesis of the two novels, see the essay by Mark Kinkead-Weekes referred to on page 19 above.

PART TWO

Documents relating to
Women in Love

George H. Ford

INTRODUCTORY NOTE TO
D. H. LAWRENCE'S PROLOGUE TO
WOMEN IN LOVE (1963)

IN 1914, when D. H. Lawrence was tussling with revising his massive novel that was later to appear as *The Rainbow* and *Women in Love*, he spoke of having written a thousand pages which no longer quite satisfied him, pages which he now proposed to burn. Despite his good resolutions, however, some of the thousands of pages from the various rejected versions of this novel were spared from his proposed bonfire. Several fragmentary sections have survived, including, most fortunately, fifty-five pages of manuscript making up two complete introductory chapters from *Women in Love*. These two rejected chapters are of extraordinary interest as a key to understanding one of the basic conflicts in Lawrence's own character and even more in what they tell us of his over-all objectives in writing *Women in Love*, his own favorite among his novels, and generally regarded, by most critical readers, as his masterpiece.

One reason for Lawrence's saying that he liked *Women in Love* 'best of all my works' may have been that of all his novels it was the most laboriously composed. *The White Peacock*, his first novel, had been considerably revised before publication, and *The Plumed Serpent* was later to exhaust his energies, but neither work called for the kind of prodigious effort expended in the creation of *Women in Love*. Seven years passed between the time he began writing it in March 1913, and its publication in New York in 1920. Off and on, during those seven years, Lawrence persisted in rewriting and revising the book. A detailed history of these revisions cannot be given here, but one aspect of these various revisions does call for comment. It is significant how often it was his opening chapters that dissatisfied him. 'I began my novel for about the eleventh time', he complains typically in a letter of March 1914. Students of Lawrence will be aware of his almost obsessive concern with how his novels and stories should end. Often he tried out alternative endings on his friends, asking for their advice. What has been less evident is his almost equally obsessive concern for his opening chapters. The first chapter of *Women in Love*, for example, *seems*, in its published version, to be a casually written talk between two sisters who air, in rather commonplace dialogue, their views of men and marriage. This chapter has fortunately been analyzed by F. R. Leavis, who demonstrates, with his usual generous quantity of quotations, that the casual talk of the sisters is loaded with significance, and that Lawrence has contrived here to launch his novel 'decisively'.

A study of Lawrence's manuscripts and typescripts for *Women in Love* will reinforce Dr Leavis's impression that the scene has been contrived with remarkable attention to detail. The first typescript version (July–October 1916) shows in its pages of interlinear corrections how rigorously Lawrence worked over the scene, and the second typescript (December 1916–January 1917) shows a further reworking. But more telling than these extensive revisions is his having decided, at one point, to begin with a different opening chapter altogether. On this occasion he decided to make the scene between the sisters, Ursula and Gudrun, into his second chapter instead of his first, and to make the opening Prologue chapter focus instead upon the two men, Birkin and Gerald, and to sketch in for us the history of their friendship up to the time of the marriage of Gerald's sister.

The first of these two rejected chapters, entitled 'Prologue', is here published for the first time. Since it involves Birkin and Gerald, it will be of more immediate interest than the second, involving Ursula and Gudrun, which is essentially another version of the presently published opening chapter of the novel. But the first, 'Prologue', is altogether fresh. The topic explored in his Prologue chapter is the nature of friendship between men. The topic is a recurrent one in Lawrence's fiction, from the idyllic picture of the male friendship between George Saxton and Cyril Beardsall in *The White Peacock*, through *Aaron's Rod* and

Kangaroo, to the exotic relationship between Don Cipriano and Don Ramón in *The Plumed Serpent*. And a recently published letter to Henry Savage indicates that as early as 2 December 1913, Lawrence could analyze the physical attraction towards men that he had himself experienced. At the time he was working over *Women in Love*, however, the subject was probably more in the foreground for him than at any other stage of his life. As Birkin says to his wife on the last page of the novel: 'You are all women to me. But I wanted a man friend as eternal as you and I are eternal.' In Middleton Murry, whom he first met in June 1913, Lawrence himself desperately hoped he had found such an eternal friend, but the *Blutbrüderschaft* he kept proposing led, instead, to a gradual dissolution of the relationship. By June 1916, Murry fled in alarm from an incomprehensible and undefined intimacy of which, as he said, he was 'a little scared'. Even after a considerable cooling-off period Lawrence raised the subject again in a letter to Katherine Mansfield in 1918: 'I believe tremendously in friendship between man and man, a pledging of men to each other inviolably. But I have never met or formed such a friendship. . . . Please give the letter to Jack. I say it to him particularly.'

The preoccupation with male friendship as a possible cure for man's loneliness is, of course, a well-known and well-documented aspect of Lawrence as man and writer. What has not been so clearly evident before, however, is made explicit in this rejected Prologue chapter from *Women in Love*, for here the hero bravely confronts his feelings about some of the physical phases of such a relationship. Birkin's realization that he prefers the physiques of the simple soldier or of the Cornishman (the latter attraction is referred to again in the Nightmare chapter of *Kangaroo*) to those of the women he has known may help to explain one of Lawrence's idiosyncrasies, in Thomas Hardy's sense of the term, as a writer. Rarely does he bring his women characters before us as physical presences, whereas his male characters are distinguished by descriptions of their bodies. Often these descriptions focus attention on male loins or thighs. This Laurentian trademark is exemplified in his references to the

'amazing riding-muscles' of the Prussian officer's 'loins', or the
'commonness which revealed itself' in the 'fat thighs and loins' of
Ursula's uncle in *The Rainbow*, or in the vivid picture of the
bridegroom in the very opening chapter of *Women in Love* (as
published):

Like a hound the young man was after her, leaping the steps . . .
his supple haunches working like those of a hound that bears
down on his quarry. . . . In another instant the bridegroom . . .
had swung himself out of sight, his supple, strong loins vanishing
in pursuit.

In *The Common Pursuit* F. R. Leavis describes Lawrence's
art as 'largely a technique of exploration – exploration calling for
critical capacity as well as courage'. Leavis' description applies
nicely to this rejected Prologue chapter; the courage and honesty
with which Lawrence makes a pioneer exploration of a subject
then prohibited are here evident. Why then did he reject the
chapter? Did his courage fail him when confronted with the
dangers of publishing it?

Before this speculation is followed further, some guesses should
be made about when the Prologue chapter might have been written. The week in the Austrian mountains enjoyed by Birkin,
Gerald, and Hosken, which is described in the first part of the
Prologue, probably derives from Lawrence's recollections of a
similar expedition in the Austrian mountains he himself had made
in the summer of 1912 in the company of David Garnett and
Harold Hobson (the latter's name is scarcely disguised). This
incident does not, however, help much in establishing the date.
References in his letters of 1913 to the 'false starts' he had made in
writing 'The Sisters' (an early version of *Women in Love*) are
likewise of little help, for the Prologue could not have been written until after his first meeting, in January 1915, with Lady
Ottoline Morrell, who provided a model for some distinctive
phases of the character of Hermione Roddice. In April 1916,
when he once again began rewriting 'The Sisters', it is probable
that this Prologue chapter was written. It is also probable that

the discarding of this chapter occurred three months later, in July 1916, when he himself began typing out a copy of the novel to send to his publishers.

This sequence of events would seem the most likely one, although we cannot altogether rule out the possibility of its having been written between January 1917, when he completed the version of *Women in Love* we now have, and 1920, the year of publication, as a final attempt to emphasize that his novel is an exploration not only of love between men and women, but also of male relationships. The possibility is, however, remote, and the evidence against it is of interest in its own right.

This evidence derives from some of the corrections Lawrence made in his typewritten drafts of the novel. Several passages which describe the attraction shared for each other by Birkin and Gerald are struck out. For example, in the breakfast scene at Halliday's apartment (ch. VII) Gerald was originally represented as contrasting the African statue with the naked figure of Birkin. The latter, says Lawrence, inspired Gerald 'almost to rhapsody. He stood near the naked man, and the naked carven piece of wood was like dirt beside a jet of pure beauty in his soul.' And again, in another cancelled passage, of Gerald we learn: 'He wanted the other man [Birkin] to put his arms round him, and hold him ... close in peace and love. Yet it was impossible.' In view of Lawrence's decision to cancel several such passages before publication, it seems highly unlikely that he would have written the rejected chapter, with its more specific account of the relationship, after he had decided to make the whole novel less specific in this respect. The date of composing the Prologue chapter seems then to be the spring of 1916.

Why did Lawrence later abandon the chapter and why did he elect to tone down other parts of the novel in which the attraction felt by the two men was commented upon? The obvious answer would be fear of censorship. After the suppression of *The Rainbow* in 1915, he could ill afford another disastrous suppression. Donald Carswell, who read one copy of the typescript of *Women in Love* and annotated it (in December 1916) may have warned him of the risks involved; and the subsequent attacks on the novel, even in its toned-down version as published, are indicative that such advice had to be heeded. 'The chapter headed "Gladiatorial" ', said the reviewer in *John Bull*, 'is sheer filth from beginning to end. . . . This is the sort of book which in the hands of a boy in his teens might pave the way to unspeakable moral disaster.' This explanation may be adequate enough, and one could hardly condemn Lawrence for a prudent loss of nerve. But there may have been an additional reason of more critical significance to our understanding of the action of the novel. One of the passages which Lawrence struck out from his final typescript is in the 'Man to Man' chapter. Birkin has been thinking of Hermione and Ursula, and his reflections then switch to the person of Gerald:

Gerald and he had a curious love for each other. It was a love that was ultimately death, a love which was complemented by the hatred for woman. . . . It tore man from woman, and woman from man. The two halves divided and separated, each drawing away to itself. And the great chasm that came between the two sundered halves was death, universal death.

This remarkable paragraph, which shows that there were at least times when Lawrence had considered the friendship between Birkin and Gerald as something corrupt, may provide a clue to his decision to reject the Prologue chapter. Implicit is the author's own honest bafflement, his painful awareness of attraction and repulsion in such relationships, an ambiguous sense that might have led to a blurred picture of the friendship between the two men. In *The Rainbow* Lawrence had portrayed an incipiently Lesbian relationship between Ursula Brangwen and Winifred Inger, and he had finally exposed what he calls the 'marshy, bitter-sweet corruption' of the older woman. But Winifred Inger is a minor character in *The Rainbow*, and the commentator's stern repudiation of her does not affect the over-all impression the novel makes. With Gerald and Birkin, however, castigation of their friendship on these grounds would have raised insoluble complications in what is already Lawrence's most complex book. The final chapter as we now have it (the 'Epilogue' as he originally called it to balance his 'Prologue'), with Birkin's sad speech over the body of his dead friend, would have had to have been in a vein altogether different. In *Women in Love* as finally published what Lawrence wanted to explore was the *possibility* of two ideal relationships, that between Birkin and Ursula, with its redemptive effects on the hero, and that between Birkin and Gerald. If the male relationship had been represented throughout the novel as simply corrupting, and as an alternative rather than as a coordinate relationship, then Gerald would appear not as a possible friend but as a purely destructive agent, like Winifred Inger – one who would destroy the hero's hard-won victory, his awareness, through love, that life is worth living. 'This marriage with her was his resurrection and his life.' In the published novel, the friendship with Gerald is not usually represented as rivalling this affirmative love for woman but as a possible complement, a possibility not realized but wistfully longed for by the hero. 'You can't have two kinds of love,' Ursula exclaims in the Epilogue. 'It's false, impossible.'* Birkin does have the last word, a quiet one ('I don't believe that,' he says), but the possibility is left, as in the best of Lawrence's writings, dangling.

Women in Love as published has thus its own kind of drama. If the rejected chapter and other passages had been retained, there would have been a different kind of drama and an even more highly complex novel than we now have. It seems likely that fear of censorship was not the only reason that led Lawrence to abandon his Prologue chapter.

A further comment needs to be made about the possible gains or losses that would occur if this rejected chapter were to be re-inserted into the book. Angus Wilson and others have likened the structure of *Women in Love* to a quartet. The rejected opening in which the men players are heard before the women begin to play their parts does have one advantage. It establishes a fact,

---

* Cf. Frieda Lawrence's remarking in 1951: 'I also know he [Lawrence] wanted a real man friend. He never found him. I doubt whether I could have stood it. I would have fought. . . .' *Frieda Lawrence: Memoirs and Correspondence* (1961).

obscured by the title, that the novel is a real quartet, not two duets, and that the testing of some phases of the relationship between men is as dominant in its subtle counterpointing as the testing of relationships between men and women. It reinforces unity by tying together the final scenes of Birkin's confronting Gerald's frozen body with the opening scenes in the mountains when their friendship was first established.

The Prologue chapter also provides fresh information about the earlier stages of the relationship between Hermione and Birkin. Many readers of *Women in Love* have been baffled by the scene of Hermione's murderous attack on Birkin when she tries to smash his skull with a stone. Readers are also baffled by Birkin's strange behavior afterwards when he rolls naked among the flowers. The unpublished preliminary chapter, with its full account of the earlier stages of this frustrating affair, prepares us for the violence of Hermione's attack and even for its incongruous aftermath. We can more readily understand the bitterness of the tormented and rejected woman, and also Birkin's sick sense of guilt. Realizing that he had himself provoked Hermione's attack by his long drawn out spiritual debauch, he seeks in the contact of flowers a washing away, or more exactly, a rubbing away, of his own guilt.

On the other hand, Lawrence may have detected another kind of flaw in his Prologue chapter, an artistic flaw: its occasionally excessive weight of exposition. Like many novelists and dramatists in their opening scenes, Lawrence sometimes succumbs in his Prologue to the temptation of directly unloading information instead of representing characters in action. The published version may be, on these grounds, superior. The hitherto unpublished chapter can nevertheless be enjoyed as a statement of the author's original intentions (if the old New Critics will allow us to revive a useful term). It is a kind of preface, in effect, that helps to explain some of the puzzling aspects of an intricately contrived and difficult book.

SOURCE: *Texas Quarterly*, VI (Spring 1963).

D. H. Lawrence

PROLOGUE TO
WOMEN IN LOVE

THE acquaintance between the two men was slight and insignificant. Yet there was a subtle bond that connected them.

They had met four years ago, brought together by a common friend, Hosken, a naval man. The three, Rupert Birkin, William Hosken, and Gerald Crich had then spent a week in the Tyrol together, mountain-climbing.

Birkin and Gerald Crich felt take place between them, the moment they saw each other, that sudden connection which sometimes springs up between men who are very different in temper. There had been a subterranean kindling in each man. Each looked towards the other, and knew the trembling nearness.

Yet they had maintained complete reserve, their relations had been, to all knowledge, entirely casual and trivial. Because of the inward kindled connection, they were even more distant and slight than men usually are, one towards the other.

There was, however, a certain tenderness in their politeness, an almost uncomfortable understanding lurked under their formal, reserved behaviour. They were vividly aware of each other's presence, and each was just as vividly aware of himself, in presence of the other.

The week of mountain-climbing passed like an intense brief life-time. The three men were very close together, and lifted into an abstract isolation, among the upper rocks and the snow. The world that lay below, the whole field of human activity, was sunk and subordinated, they had trespassed into the upper silence and loneliness. The three of them had reached another state of being, they were enkindled in the upper silences into a rare, unspoken intimacy, an intimacy that took no expression, but which was between them like a transfiguration. As if thrown into the strange fire of abstraction, up in the mountains, they knew and were known to each other. It was another world, another life, transfigured, and yet most vividly corporeal, the senses all raised till each felt his own body, and the presence of his companions, like an essential flame, they radiated to one enkindled, transcendent fire, in the upper world.

Then had come the sudden falling down to earth, the sudden extinction. At Innsbruck they had parted, Birkin to go to Munich, Gerald Crich and Hosken to take the train for Paris and London. On the station they shook hands, and went asunder, having spoken no word and given no sign of the transcendent intimacy which had roused them beyond the everyday life. They shook hands and took leave casually, as mere acquaintances going their separate ways. Yet there remained always, for Birkin and for Gerald Crich, the absolute recognition that had passed between them then, the knowledge that was in their eyes as they met at the moment of parting. They knew they loved each other, that each would die for the other.

Yet all this knowledge was kept submerged in the soul of the two men. Outwardly they would have none of it. Outwardly they only stiffened themselves away from it. They took leave from each other even more coldly and casually than is usual.

And for a year they had seen nothing of each other, neither had they exchanged any word. They passed away from each other, and, superficially, forgot.

But when they met again, in a country house in Derbyshire, the enkindled sensitiveness sprang up again like a strange, embarrassing fire. They scarcely knew each other, yet here was this strange, unacknowledged, inflammable intimacy between them. It made them uneasy.

Rupert Birkin, however, strongly centred in himself, never gave way in his soul, to anyone. He remained in the last issue detached, self-responsible, having no communion with any other soul. Therefore Gerald Crich remained intact in his own form.

The two men were very different. Gerald Crich was the fair, keen-eyed Englishman of medium stature, hard in his muscles and full of energy as a machine. He was a hunter, a traveller, a soldier, always active, always moving vigorously, and giving orders to some subordinate.

Birkin on the other hand was quiet and unobtrusive. In stature he was long and very thin, and yet not bony, close-knit, flexible, and full of repose, like a steel wire. His energy was not evident, he seemed almost weak, passive, insignificant. He was delicate in health. His face was pale and rather ugly, his hair dun-coloured, his eyes were of a yellowish-grey, full of life and warmth. They were the only noticeable thing about him, to the ordinary observer, being very warm and sudden and attractive, alive like fires. But this chief attraction of Birkin's was a false one. Those that knew him best knew that his lovable eyes were, in the last issue, estranged and unsoftening like the eyes of a wolf. In the last issue he was callous, and without feeling, confident, just as Gerald Crich in the last issue was wavering and lost.

The two men were staying in the house of Sir Charles Roddice, Gerald Crich as friend of the host, Rupert Birkin as friend of his host's daughter, Hermione* Roddice. Sir Charles would have been glad for Gerald Crich to marry the daughter of the house, because this young man was a well-set young Englishman of strong conservative temperament, and heir to considerable wealth. But Gerald Crich did not care for Hermione Roddice, and Hermione Roddice disliked Gerald Crich.

She was a rather beautiful woman of twenty-five, fair, tall, slender, graceful, and of some learning. She had known Rupert Birkin in Oxford. He was a year her senior. He was a fellow of Magdalen College, and had been, at twenty-one, one of the young lights of the place, a coming somebody. His essays on Education were brilliant, and he became an inspector of schools.

Hermione Roddice loved him. When she had listened to his passionate declamations, in his rooms in the Blackhorse Road, and when she had heard the respect with which he was spoken of, five years ago, she being a girl of twenty, reading political

* Lawrence substituted the name *Hermione* in place of the name *Ethel.*

economy, and he a youth of twenty-one, holding forth against Nietzsche, then she devoted herself to his name and fame. She added herself to his mental and spiritual flame.

Sir Charles thought they would marry. He considered that Birkin, hanging on year after year, was spoiling all his daughter's chances, and without pledging himself in the least. It irked the soldierly knight considerably. But he was somewhat afraid of the quiet, always-civil Birkin. And Hermione, when Sir Charles mentioned that he thought of speaking to the young man, in order to know his intentions, fell into such a white and overweening, contemptuous passion, that her father was non-plussed and reduced to irritated silence.

'How vulgar you are!' cried the young woman. 'You are not to dare to say a word to him. It is a friendship, and it is not to be broken-in upon in this fashion. Why should you want to rush me into marriage? I am more than happy as I am.'

Her liquid grey eyes swam dark with fury and pain and resentment, her beautiful face was convulsed. She seemed like a prophetess violated. Her father withdrew, cold and huffed.

So the relationship between the young woman and Birkin continued. He was an inspector of schools, she studied Education. He wrote also harsh, jarring poetry, very real and painful, under which she suffered; and sometimes, shallower, gentle lyrics, which she treasured as drops of manna. Like a priestess she kept his records and his oracles, he was like a god who would be nothing if his worship were neglected.

Hermione could not understand the affection between the two men. They would sit together in the hall, at evening, and talk without any depth. What did Rupert find to take him up, in Gerald Crich's conversation? She, Hermione, was only rather bored, and puzzled. Yet the two men seemed happy, holding their commonplace discussion. Hermione was impatient. She knew that Birkin was, as usual, belittling his own mind and talent, for the sake of something that she felt unworthy. Some common correspondence which she knew demeaned and belied him. Why would he always come down so eagerly to the level of common people, why was he always so anxious to vulgarise and betray

himself? She bit her lip in torment. It was as if he were anxious
to deny all that was fine and rare in himself.

Birkin knew what she was feeling and thinking. Yet he continued almost spitefully against her. He *did* want to betray the
heights and depths of nearly religious intercourse which he had
with her. He, the God, turned round upon his priestess, and
became the common vulgar man who turned her to scorn. He
performed some strange metamorphosis of soul, and from being
a pure, incandescent spirit burning intense with the presence of
God, he became a lustful, shallow, insignificant fellow running in
all the common ruts. Even there was some vindictiveness in him
now, something jeering and spiteful and low, unendurable. It
drove her mad. She had given him all her trembling, naked soul,
and now he turned mongrel, and triumphed in his own degeneration. It was his deep desire, to be common, vulgar, a little
gross. She could not bear the look of almost sordid jeering with
which he turned on her, when she reached out her hand, im-
ploring. It was as if some rat bit her, she felt she was going insane.
And he jeered at her, at the spiritual woman who waited at the
tomb, in her sandals and her mourning robes. He jeered at her
horribly, knowing her secrets. And she was insane, she knew she
was going mad.

But he plunged on triumphant into intimacy with Gerald
Crich excluding the woman, tormenting her. He knew how to
pitch himself into tune with another person. He could adjust his
mind, his consciousness, almost perfectly to that of Gerald Crich,
lighting up the edge of the other man's limitation with a glimmering light that was the essence of exquisite adventure and
liberation to the confined intelligence. The two men talked
together for hours, Birkin watching the hard limbs and the rather
stiff face of the traveller in unknown countries, Gerald Crich
catching the pale, luminous face opposite him, lit up over the
edge of the unknown regions of the soul, trembling into new
being, quivering with new intelligence.

To Hermione, it was insupportable degradation that Rupert
Birkin should maintain this correspondence, prostituting his
mind and his understanding to the coarser stupidity of the other

man. She felt confusion gathering upon her, she was unanchored on the edge of madness. Why did he do it? Why was he, whom she knew as her leader, starlike and pure, why was he the lowest betrayer and the ugliest of blasphemers? She held her temples, feeling herself reel towards the bottomless pit.

For Birkin did get a greater satisfaction, at least for the time being, from his intercourse with the other man, than from his spiritual relation with her. It satisfied him to have to do with Gerald Crich, it fulfilled him to have this other man, this hard-limbed traveller and sportsman, following implicitly, held as it were consummated within the spell of a more powerful understanding. Birkin felt a passion of desire for Gerald Crich, for the clumsier, cruder intelligence and the limited soul, and for the striving, unlightened body of his friend. And Gerald Crich, not understanding, was transfused with pleasure. He did not even know he loved Birkin. He thought him marvellous in understanding, almost unnatural, and on the other hand pitiful and delicate in body. He felt a great tenderness towards him, of superior physical strength, and at the same time some reverence for his delicacy and fineness of being.

All the same, there was no profession of friendship, no open mark of intimacy. They remained to all intents and purposes distant, mere acquaintances. It was in the other world of the subconsciousness that the interplay took place, the interchange of spiritual and physical richness, the relieving of physical and spiritual poverty, without any intrinsic change of state in either man.

Hermione could not understand it at all. She was mortified and in despair. In his lapses, she despised and revolted from Birkin. Her mistrust of him pierced to the quick of her soul. If his intense and pure flame of spirituality only sank to this guttering prostration, a low, degraded heat, servile to a clumsy Gerald Crich, fawning on a coarse, unsusceptible being, such as was Gerald Crich and all the multitudes of Gerald Criches of this world, then nothing was anything. The transcendent star of one evening was the putrescent phosphorescence of the next, and glory and corruptibility were interchangeable. Her soul was convulsed with cynicism. She despised her God and her angel. Yet she could not do without him. She believed in herself as a priestess, and that was all. Though there were no God to serve, still she was a priestess. Yet having no altar to kindle, no sacrifice to burn, she would be barren and useless. So she adhered to her God in him, which she claimed almost violently, whilst her soul turned in bitter cynicism from the prostitute man in him. She did not believe in him, she only believed in that which she could gather from him, as one gathers silk from the corrupt worm. She was the maker of gods.

So, after a few days, Gerald Crich went away and Birkin was left to Hermione Roddice. It is true, Crich said to Birkin: 'Come and see us, if ever you are near enough, will you?', and Birkin had said yes. But for some reason, it was concluded beforehand that this visit would never be made, deliberately.

Sick, helpless, Birkin swung back to Hermione. In the garden, at evening, looking over the silvery hills, he sat near to her, or lay with his head on her bosom, while the moonlight came gently upon the trees, and they talked, quietly, gently as dew distilling, their two disembodied voices distilled in the silvery air, two voices moving and ceasing like ghosts, like spirits. And they talked of life, and of death, but chiefly of death, his words turning strange and phosphorescent, like dark water suddenly shaken alight, whilst she held his head against her breast, infinitely satisfied and completed by its weight upon her, and her hand travelled gently, finely, oh, with such exquisite quivering adjustment, over his hair. The pain of tenderness he felt for her was almost unendurable, as her hand fluttered and came near, scarcely touching him, so light and sensitive it was, as it passed over his hair, rhythmically. And still his voice moved and thrilled through her like the keenest pangs of embrace, she remained possessed by him, possessed by the spirit. And the sense of beauty and perfect, blade-keen ecstasy was balanced to perfection, she passed away, was transported.

After these nights of superfine ecstasy of beauty, after all was consumed in the silver fire of moonlight, all the soul caught up in the universal chill-blazing bonfire of the moonlit night, there came the morning, and the ash, when his body was grey and consumed, and his soul ill. Why should the sun shine, and hot gay flowers come out, when the kingdom of reality was the silver-cold night of death, lovely and perfect.

She, like a priestess, was fulfilled and rich. But he became more hollow and ghastly to look at. There was no escape, they penetrated further and further into the regions of death, and soon the connection with life would be broken.

Then came his revulsion against her. After he loved her with a tenderness that was anguish, a love that was all pain, or else transcendent white ecstasy, he turned upon her savagely, like a maddened dog. And like a priestess who is rended for sacrifice, she submitted and endured. She would serve the God she possessed, even though he should turn periodically into a fierce dog, to rend her.

So he went away, to his duties, and his work. He had made a passionate study of education, only to come, gradually, to the knowledge that education is nothing but the process of building up, gradually, a complete unit of consciousness. And each unit of consciousness is the living unit of that great social, religious, philosophic idea towards which mankind, like an organism seeking its final form, is laboriously growing. But if there *be* no great philosophic idea, if, for the time being, mankind, instead of going through a period of growth, is going through a corresponding process of decay and decomposition from some old, fulfilled, obsolete idea, then what is the good of educating? Decay and decomposition will take their own way. It is impossible to educate for this end, impossible to teach the world how to die away from its achieved, nullified form. The autumn must take place in every individual soul, as well as in all the people, all must die, individually and socially. But education is a process of striving to a new, unanimous being, a whole organic form. But when winter has set in, when the frosts are strangling the leaves off the trees and the birds are silent knots of darkness, how can there be a unanimous movement towards a whole summer of florescence? There can be none of this, only submission to the death of this nature, in the winter that has come upon mankind, and a cherishing of the unknown that is unknown for many a day yet, buds that may not open till a far off season comes, when the season of death has passed away.

And Birkin was just coming to a knowledge of the essential futility of all attempt at social unanimity in constructiveness. In the winter, there can only be unanimity of disintegration, the leaves fall unanimously, the plants die down, each creature is a soft-slumbering grave, as the adder and the dormouse in winter are the soft tombs of the adder and the dormouse, which slip about like rays of brindled darkness, in summer.

How to get away from this process of reduction, how escape this phosphorescent passage into the tomb, which was universal though unacknowledged, this was the unconscious problem which tortured Birkin day and night. He came to Hermione, and found with her the pure, translucent regions of death itself, of ecstasy. In the world the autumn was setting in. What should a man add himself on to? – to science, to social reform, to aestheticism, to sensationalism? The whole world's constructive activity was a fiction, a lie, to hide the great process of decomposition, which had set in. What then to adhere to?

He ran about from death to death. Work was terrible, horrible because he did not believe in it. It was almost a horror to him, to think of going from school to school, making reports and giving suggestions, when the whole process to his soul was pure futility, a process of mechanical activity entirely purposeless, sham growth which was entirely rootless. Nowhere more than in education did a man feel the horror of false, rootless, spasmodic activity more acutely. The whole business was like dementia. It created in him a feeling of nausea and horror. He recoiled from it. And yet, where should a man repair, what should he do?

In his private life the same horror of futility and wrongness dogged him. Leaving alone all ideas, religious or philosophic, all of which are mere sounds, old repetitions, or else novel, dexterous, sham permutations and combinations of old repetitions, leaving alone all the things of the mind and the consciousness, what remained in a man's life? There is his emotional and his sensuous activity, is not this enough?

Birkin started with madness from this question, for it touched the quick of torture. There was his love for Hermione, a love based entirely on ecstasy and on pain, and ultimate death. He *knew* he did not love her with any living, creative love. He did not even desire her: he had no passion for her, there was no hot impulse of growth between them, only this terrible reducing activity of phosphorescent consciousness, the consciousness ever liberated more and more into the void, at the expense of the flesh, which was burnt down like dead grey ash.

He did not call this love. Yet he was bound to her, and it was agony to leave her. And he did not love anyone else. He did not love any woman. He *wanted* to love. But between wanting to love, and loving, is the whole difference between life and death.

The incapacity to love, the incapacity to desire any woman, positively, with body and soul, this was a real torture, a deep torture indeed. Never to be able to love spontaneously, never to be moved by a power greater than oneself, but always to be within one's own control, deliberate, having the choice, this was horrifying, more deadly than death. Yet how was one to escape. How could a man escape from being deliberate and unloving, except a greater power, an impersonal, imperative love should take hold of him? And if the greater power should not take hold of him, what could he do but continue in his deliberateness, without any fundamental spontaneity?

He did not love Hermione, he did not desire her. But he wanted to force himself to love her and to desire her. He was consumed by sexual desire, and he wanted to be fulfilled. Yet he did not desire Hermione. She repelled him rather. Yet he *would* have this physical fulfilment, he would have the sexual activity. So he forced himself towards her.

She was hopeless from the start. Yet she resigned herself to him. In her soul, she knew this was not the way. And yet even she was ashamed, as of some physical deficiency. She did not want him either. But with all her soul, she *wanted* to want him. She would do anything to give him what he wanted, that which he was raging for, this physical fulfilment he insisted on. She was wise; she thought for the best. She prepared herself like a perfect sacrifice to him. She offered herself gladly to him, gave herself into his will.

And oh, it was all such a cruel failure, just a failure. This last act of love which he had demanded of her was the keenest grief of all, it was so insignificant, so null. He had no pleasure of her, only some mortification. And her heart almost broke with grief.

She wanted him to take her. She wanted him to take her, to break her with his passion, to destroy her with his desire, so long as he got satisfaction. She looked forward, tremulous, to a kind of death at his hands, she gave herself up. She would be broken and dying, destroyed, if only he would rise fulfilled.

But he was not capable of it, he failed. He could not take her and destroy her. He could not forget her. They had too rare a spiritual intimacy, he could not now tear himself away from all this, and come like a brute to take its satisfaction. He was too much aware of her, and of her fear, and of her writhing torment, as she lay in sacrifice. He had too much deference for her feeling. He could not, as she madly wanted, destroy her, trample her, and crush a satisfaction from her. He was not experienced enough, not hardened enough. He was always aware of *her* feelings, so that he had none of his own. Which made this last love-making between them an ignominious failure, very, very cruel to bear.

And it was this failure which broke the love between them. He hated her, for her incapacity in love, for her lack of desire for him, her complete and almost perfect lack of any physical desire towards him. Her desire was all spiritual, all in the consciousness. She wanted him all, all through the consciousness, never through the senses.

And she hated him, and despised him, for his incapacity to wreak his desire upon her, his lack of strength to crush his satisfaction from her. If only he could have taken her, destroyed her, used her all up, and been satisfied, she would be at last free. She might be killed, but it would be the death which gave her consummation.

It was a failure, a bitter, final failure. He could not take from her what he wanted, because he could not, bare-handed, destroy her. And she despised him that he could not destroy her.

Still, though they had failed, finally, they did not go apart. Their relation was too deep-established. He was by this time twenty-eight years old, and she twenty-seven. Still, for his spiritual delight, for a companion in his conscious life, for some-one to share and heighten his joy in thinking, or in reading, or in feeling beautiful things, or in knowing landscape intimately and poignantly, he turned to her. For all these things, she was still with him, she made up the greater part of his life. And he, she knew to her anguish and mortification, he was still the master-key to almost all life, for her. She wanted it not to be so, she wanted to be free of him, of the strange, terrible bondage of his domination. But as yet, she could not free herself from him.

He went to other women, to women of purely sensual, sen-sational attraction, he prostituted his spirit with them. And he got *some* satisfaction. She watched him go, sadly, and yet not without a measure of relief. For he would torment her less, now.

She knew he would come back to her. She knew, inevitably as the dawn would rise, he would come back to her, half exultant and triumphant over her, half bitter against her for letting him go, and wanting her now, wanting the communion with her. It was as if he went to the other, the dark, sensual, almost bestial woman thoroughly and fully to degrade himself. He despised himself, essentially, in his attempts at sensuality, she knew that. So she let him be. It was only his rather vulgar arrogance of a sinner that she found hard to bear. For before her, he wore his sins with braggadocio, flaunted them a little in front of her. And this alone drove her to exasperation, to the point of uttering her contempt for his childishness and his instability.

But as yet, she forbore, because of the deference he still felt towards her. Intrinsically, in his spirit, he still served her. And this service she cherished.

But he was becoming gnawed and bitter, a little mad. His whole system was inflamed to a pitch of mad irritability, he became blind, unconscious to the greater half of life, only a few things he saw with feverish acuteness. And she, she kept the key to him, all the while.

The only thing she dreaded was his making up his mind. She dreaded his way of seeing some particular things vividly and feverishly, and of his acting upon this special sight. For once he decided a thing, it became a reigning universal truth to him, and he was completely inhuman.

He was, in his own way, quite honest with himself. But every man has his own truths, and is honest with himself according to them. The terrible thing about Birkin, for Hermione was that when once he decided upon a truth, he acted upon it, cost what it might. If he decided that his eye did really offend him, he would in truth pluck it out. And this seemed to her so inhuman, so abstract, that it chilled her to the depths of her soul, and made him seem to her inhuman, something between a monster and a complete fool. For might not she herself easily be found to be this eye which must needs be plucked out?

He had stuck fast over this question of love and of physical fulfilment in love, till it had become like a monomania. All his thought turned upon it. For he wanted to keep his integrity of being, he would not consent to sacrifice one half of himself to the other. He would not sacrifice the sensual to the spiritual half of himself, and he could not sacrifice the spiritual to the sensual half. Neither could he obtain fulfilment in both, the two halves always reacted from each other. To be spiritual, he must have a Hermione, completely without desire: to be sensual, he must have a slightly bestial woman, the very scent of whose skin soon disgusted him, whose manners nauseated him beyond bearing, so that Hermione, always chaste and always stretching out her hands for beauty, seemed to him the purest and most desirable thing on earth.

He knew he obtained no real fulfilment in sensuality, he became disgusted and despised the whole process as if it were dirty. And he knew that he had no real fulfilment in his spiritual and aesthetic intercourse with Hermione. That process he also despised, with considerable cynicism.

And he recognized that he was on the point either of breaking, becoming a thing, losing his integral being, or else of becoming insane. He was now nothing but a series of reactions from dark to light, from light to dark, almost mechanical, without unity or meaning.

This was the most insufferable bondage, the most tormenting affliction, that he could not save himself from these extreme reactions, the vibration between two poles, one of which was Hermione, the centre of social virtue, the other of which was a prostitute, anti-social, almost criminal. He knew that in the end, subject to this extreme vibration, he would be shattered, would die, or else, worse still, would become a mere disordered set of processes, without purpose or integral being. He knew this, and dreaded it. Yet he could not save himself.

To save himself, he must unite the two halves of himself, spiritual and sensual. And this is what no man can do at once, deliberately. It must happen to him. Birkin willed to be sensual, as well as spiritual, with Hermione. He might will it, he might act according to his will, but he did not bring to pass that which he willed. A man cannot create desire in himself, nor cease at will from desiring. Desire, in any shape or form, is primal, whereas the will is secondary, derived. The will can destroy, but it cannot create.

So the more he tried with his will, to force his senses towards Hermione, the greater misery he produced. On the other hand his pride never ceased to contemn his profligate intercourse elsewhere. After all, it was *not* that which he wanted. He did not want libertine pleasures, not fundamentally. His fundamental desire was, to be able to love completely, in one and the same act: both body and soul at once, struck into a complete oneness in contact with a complete woman.

And he failed in this desire. It was always a case of one or the other, of spirit or of senses, and each, alone, was deadly. All history, almost all art, seemed the story of this deadly half-love: either passion, like Cleopatra, or else spirit, like Mary of Bethany or Vittoria Colonna.

He pondered on the subject endlessly, and knew himself in his reactions. But self-knowledge is not everything. No man, by taking thought, can add one cubit to his stature. He can but know his own height and limitation.

He knew that he loved no woman, that in nothing was he really complete, really himself. In his most passionate moments of spiritual enlightenment, when like a saviour of mankind he would pour out his soul for the world, there was in him a capacity to jeer at all his own righteousness and spirituality, justly and sincerely to make a mock of it all. And the mockery was so true, it bit to the very core of his righteousness, and showed it rotten, shining with phosphorescence. But at the same time, whilst quivering in the climax-thrill of sensual pangs, some cold voice could say in him: 'You are not really moved; you could rise up and go away from this pleasure quite coldly and calmly; it is not radical, your enjoyment.'

He knew he had not loved, could not love. The only thing then was to make the best of it, have the two things separate, and over them all, a calm detached mind. But to this he would not acquiesce. 'I should be like a Neckan,' he said to himself, 'like a sea-water being, I should have no soul.' And he pondered the stories of the wistful, limpid creatures who watched ceaselessly, hoping to gain a soul.

So the trouble went on, he became more hollow and deathly, more like a spectre with hollow bones. He knew that he was not very far from dissolution.

All the time, he recognized that, although he was always drawn to women, feeling more at home with a woman than with a man, yet it was for men that he felt the hot, flushing, roused attraction which a man is supposed to feel for the other sex. Although nearly all his living interchange went on with one woman or another, although he was always terribly intimate with at least one woman, and practically never intimate with a man, yet the male physique had a fascination for him, and for the female physique he felt only a fondness, a sort of sacred love, as for a sister.

In the street, it was the men who roused him by their flesh and their manly, vigorous movement, quite apart from all individual character, whilst he studied the women as sisters, knowing their

meaning and their intents. It was the men's physique which
held the passion and the mystery to him. The women he seemed
to be kin to, he looked for the soul in them. The soul of a woman
and the physique of a man, these were the two things he watched
for, in the street.

And this was a new torture to him. Why did not the face of a
woman move him in the same manner, with the same sense of
handsome desirability, as the face of a man? Why was a man's
beauty, the *beauté mâle*, so vivid and intoxicating a thing to him,
whilst female beauty was something quite unsubstantial, con-
sisting all of look and gesture and revelation of intuitive intelligence? He thought women beautiful purely because of their
expression. But it was plastic form that fascinated him in men,
the contour and movement of the flesh itself.

He wanted all the time to love women. He wanted all the while
to feel this kindled, loving attraction towards a beautiful woman,
that he would often feel towards a handsome man. But he could
not. Whenever it was a case of a woman, there entered in too
much spiritual, sisterly love; or else, in reaction, there was only
a brutal, callous sort of lust.

This was an entanglement from which there seemed no escape.
How can a man *create* his own feelings? He cannot. It is only in
his power to suppress them, to bind them in the chain of the will.
And what is suppression but a mere negation of life, and of living.

He had several friendships wherein this passion entered, friendships with men of no very great intelligence, but of pleasant
appearance: ruddy, well-nourished fellows, good-natured and
easy, who protected him in his delicate health more gently than
a woman would protect him. He loved his friend, the beauty of
whose manly limbs made him tremble with pleasure. He wanted
to caress him.

But reserve, which was as strong as a chain of iron in him, kept
him from any demonstration. And if he were away for any length
of time from the man he loved so hotly, then he forgot him, the
flame which invested the beloved like a transfiguration passed
away, and Birkin remembered his friend as tedious. He could
not go back to him, to talk as tediously as he would have to talk,

to take such a level of intelligence as he would have to take. He forgot his men friends completely, as one forgets the candle one has blown out. They remained as quite extraneous and uninteresting persons living their life in their own sphere, and having not the slightest relation to himself, even though they themselves maintained a real warmth of affection, almost of love for him. He paid not the slightest heed to this love which was constant to him, he felt it sincerely to be just nothing, valueless.

So he left his old friends completely, even those to whom he had been attached passionately, like David to Jonathan. Men whose presence he had waited for cravingly, the touch of whose shoulder suffused him with a vibration of physical love, became to him mere figures, as nonexistent as is the waiter who sets the table in a restaurant.

He wondered very slightly at this, but dismissed it with hardly a thought. Yet, every now and again, would come over him the same passionate desire to have near him some man he saw, to exchange intimacy, to unburden himself of love to this new beloved.

It might be any man, a policeman who suddenly looked up at him, as he inquired the way, or a soldier who sat next to him in a railway carriage. How vividly, months afterwards, he would recall the soldier who had sat pressed up close to him on a journey from Charing Cross to Westerham; the shapely, motionless body, the large, dumb, coarsely-beautiful hands that rested helpless upon the strong knees, the dark brown eyes, vulnerable in the erect body. Or a young man in flannels on the sands at Margate, flaxen and ruddy, like a Viking of twenty-three, with clean, rounded contours, pure as the contours of snow, playing with some young children, building a castle in sand, intent and abstract, like a seagull or a keen white bear.

In his mind was a small gallery of such men: men whom he had never spoken to, but who had flashed themselves upon his senses unforgettably, men whom he apprehended intoxicatingly in his blood. They divided themselves roughly into two classes: these white-skinned, keen limbed men with eyes like blue-flashing ice and hair like crystals of winter sunshine, the northmen, inhuman as sharp-crying gulls, distinct like splinters of ice, like crystals, isolated, individual; and then the men with dark eyes that one can enter and plunge into, bathe in, as in a liquid darkness, dark-skinned, supple, night-smelling men, who are the living substance of the viscous, universal heavy darkness.

His senses surged towards these men, towards the perfect and beautiful representatives of these two halves. And he knew them, by seeing them and by apprehending them sensuously, he knew their very blood, its weight and savour; the blood of the northmen sharp and red and light, tending to be keenly acrid, like cranberries, the blood of the dark-limbed men heavy and luscious and in the end nauseating, revolting.

He asked himself, often, as he grew older, and more unearthly, when he was twenty-eight and twenty-nine years old, would he ever be appeased, would he ever cease to desire these two sorts of men. And a wan kind of hopelessness would come over him, as if he would never escape from this attraction, which was a bondage.

For he would never acquiesce to it. He could never acquiesce to his own feelings, to his own passion. He could never grant that it should be so, that it was well for him to feel this keen desire to have and to possess the bodies of such men, the passion to bathe in the very substance of such men, the substance of living, eternal light, like eternal snow, and the flux of heavy, rank-smelling darkness.

He wanted to cast out these desires, he wanted not to know them. Yet a man can no more slay a living desire in him, than he can prevent his body from feeling heat and cold. He can put himself into bondage, to prevent the fulfilment of the desire, that is all. But the desire is there, as the travelling of the blood itself is there, until it is fulfilled or until the body is dead.

So he went on, month after month, year after year, divided against himself, striving for the day when the beauty of men should not be so acutely attractive to him, when the beauty of woman should move him instead.

But that day came no nearer, rather it went further away. His deep dread was that it would always be so, that he would never be free. His life would have been one long torture of struggle against his own innate desire, his own innate being. But to be so divided against oneself, this is terrible, a nullification of all being.

He went into violent excess with a mistress whom, in a rather anti-social, ashamed spirit, he loved. And so for a long time he forgot about this attraction that men had for him. He forgot about it entirely. And then he grew stronger, surer.

But then, inevitably, it would recur again. There would come into a restaurant a strange Cornish type of man, with dark eyes like holes in his head, or like the eyes of a rat, and with dark, fine, rather stiff hair, and full, heavy, softly-strong limbs. Then again Birkin would feel the desire spring up in him, the desire to know this man, to have him, as it were to eat him, to take the very substance of him. And watching the strange, rather furtive, rabbit-like way in which the strong, softly-built man ate, Birkin would feel the rousedness burning in his own breast, as if this were what he wanted, as if the satisfaction of his desire lay in the body of the young, strong man opposite.

And then in his soul would succeed a sort of despair, because this passion for a man had recurred in him. It was a deep misery to him. And it would seem as if he had always loved men, always and only loved men. And this was the greatest suffering to him.

But it was not so, that he always loved men. For weeks it would be all gone from him, this passionate admiration of the rich body of a man. For weeks he was free, active, and living. But he had such a dread of his own feelings and desires, that when they recurred again, the interval vanished, and it seemed the bondage and the torment had been continuous.

This was the one and only secret he kept to himself, this secret of his passionate and sudden, spasmodic affinity for men he saw. He kept this secret even from himself. He knew what he felt, but he always kept the knowledge at bay. His *a priori* were: 'I *should not* feel like this', and 'It is the ultimate mark of my own deficiency, that I feel like this.' Therefore, though he admitted everything, he never really faced the question. He never accepted the desire, and received it as part of himself. He always tried to keep it expelled from him.*

Gerald Crich was the one towards whom Birkin felt most strongly that immediate, roused attraction which transfigured the person of the attracter with such a glow and such a desirable beauty. The two men had met once or twice, and then Gerald Crich went abroad, to South America. Birkin forgot him, all connection died down. But it was not finally dead. In both men were the seeds of a strong, inflammable affinity.

Therefore, when Birkin found himself pledged to act as best man at the wedding of Hosken, the friend of the mountain-climbing holiday, and of Laura Crich, sister of Gerald, the old affection sprang awake in a moment. He wondered what Gerald would be like now.

Hermione, knowing of Hosken's request to Birkin, at once secured for herself the position of bridesmaid to Laura Crich. It was inevitable. She and Rupert Birkin were running to the end of their friendship. He was now thirty years of age, and she twenty-nine. His feeling of hostility towards Hermione had grown now to an almost constant dislike. Still she held him in her power. But the hold became weaker and weaker. 'If he breaks loose,' she said, 'he will fall into the abyss.'

Nevertheless he was bound to break loose, because his reaction against Hermione was the strongest movement in his life, now. He was thrusting her off, fighting her off all the while, thrusting himself clear, although he had no other foothold, although he was breaking away from her, his one rock, to fall into a bottom-less sea.

SOURCE: *Texas Quarterly*, VI (Spring 1963).

* At one time the Prologue chapter ended here, for the next page of the manuscript is headed 'Chapter II The Wedding'. This heading is cancelled and the direction 'Run on' is twice inserted.

D. H. Lawrence

FOREWORD TO
WOMEN IN LOVE (1920)

THIS novel was written in its first form in the Tyrol, in 1913. It was altogether rewritten and finished in Cornwall in 1917. So that it is a novel which took its final shape in the midst of the period of war, though it does not concern the war itself. I should wish the time to remain unfixed, so that the bitterness of the war may·be taken for granted in the characters.

The book has been offered to various London publishers. Their almost inevitable reply has been: 'We should like very much to publish, but feel we cannot risk a prosecution.' They remember the fate of *The Rainbow*, and are cautious. This book is a potential sequel to *The Rainbow*.

In England, I would never try to justify myself against any accusation. But to the Americans, perhaps I may speak for myself. I am accused, in England, of uncleanness and pornography. I deny the charge, and take no further notice.

In America the chief accusation seems to be one of 'Eroticism'. This is odd, rather puzzling to my mind. Which Eros? Eros of the jaunty 'amours', or Eros of the sacred mysteries? And if the latter, why accuse, why not respect, even venerate?

Let us hesitate no longer to announce that the sensual passions and mysteries are equally sacred with the spiritual mysteries and passions. Who would deny it any more? The only thing unbearable is the degradation, the prostitution of the living mysteries in us. Let man only approach his own self with a deep respect, even reverence for all that the creative soul, the God-mystery within us, puts forth. Then we shall all be sound and free. Lewdness is hateful because it impairs our integrity and our proud being.

The creative, spontaneous soul sends forth its promptings of desire and aspiration in us. These promptings are our true fate, which is our business to fulfil. A fate dictated from outside, from theory or from circumstance, is a false fate.

This novel pretends only to be a record of the writer's own desires, aspirations, struggles; in a word, a record of the profoundest experiences in the self. Nothing that comes from the deep, passional soul is bad, or can be bad. So there is no apology to tender, unless to the soul itself, if it should have been belied.

Man struggles with his unborn needs and fulfilment. New unfoldings struggle up in torment in him, as buds struggle forth from the midst of a plant. Any man of real individuality tries to know and to understand what is happening, even in himself, as he goes along. This struggle for verbal consciousness should not be left out in art. It is a very great part of life. It is not superimposition of a theory. It is the passionate struggle into conscious being.

We are now in a period of crisis. Every man who is acutely alive is acutely wrestling with his own soul. The people that can bring forth the new passion, the new idea, this people will endure. Those others, that fix themselves in the old idea, will perish with the new life strangled unborn within them. Men must speak out to one another.

In point of style, fault is often found with the continual, slightly modified repetition. The only answer is that it is natural to the author; and that every natural crisis in emotion or passion or understanding comes from this pulsing, frictional to-and-fro which works up to culmination.

PART THREE

Critical Studies

John Middleton Murry

(i) A REVIEW OF
WOMEN IN LOVE (1921)

MR LAWRENCE is set apart from the novelists who are his
contemporaries by the vehemence of his passion. In the time
before the war we should have distinguished him by other
qualities – a sensitive and impassioned apprehension of natural
beauty, for example, or an understanding of the strange blood
bonds that unite human beings, or an exquisite discrimination
in the use of language, based on a power of natural vision. All
these things Mr Lawrence once had, in the time when he thrilled
us with the expectation of genius: now they are dissolved in the
acid of a burning and vehement passion. These qualities are
individual no longer; they no longer delight us; they have been
pressed into the service of another power, they walk in bondage
and in livery.

It is useless for us to lament their servitude; with Mr Lawrence
– and the feeling is our involuntary acknowledgment of his
power and uniqueness – we feel we must

> let determined things to destiny
> Hold unbewailed their way.

Mr Lawrence is what he is: a natural force over which we have
no power of command or persuasion. He has no power of command or persuasion over himself. It was not his deliberate choice
that he sacrificed his gifts, his vision, his delicacy, and his elo-
quence. If ever a writer was driven, it is he.

Not that we absolve him from responsibility for his own
disaster. It is part of our creed that he must be responsible; but
it is part of his creed that he is not. We stand by the consciousness
and the civilisation of which the literature we know is the finest

flower; Mr Lawrence is in rebellion against both. If we try him
before our court, he contemptuously rejects the jurisdiction. The
things we prize are the things he would destroy; what is triumph
to him is catastrophe to us. He is the outlaw of modern English
literature; and he is the most interesting figure in it. But he must
be shown no mercy.

Women in Love is five hundred pages of passionate vehemence,
wave after wave of turgid, exasperated writing impelled towards
some distant and invisible end; the persistent underground beating of some dark and inaccessible sea in an underworld whose
inhabitants are known by this alone, that they writhe continually,
like the damned, in a frenzy of sexual awareness of one another.
Their creator believes that he can distinguish the writhing of one
from the writhing of another; he spends pages and pages in
describing the contortions of the first, the second, the third, and
the fourth. To him they are utterly and profoundly different; to
us they are all the same. And yet Mr Lawrence has invented a
language, as we are forced to believe he has discovered a perception for them. The eyes of these creatures are 'absolved'; their
bodies (or their souls: there is no difference in this world) are
'suspended'; they are 'polarised'; they 'lapse out'; they have, all
of them, 'inchoate' eyes. In this language their unending contortions are described; they struggle and writhe in these terms;
they emerge from dark hatred to darker beatitudes; they grope
in their own slime to some final consummation, in which they
are utterly 'negated' or utterly 'fulfilled'. We remain utterly indifferent to their destinies, we are weary to death of them.

At the end we know one thing and one thing alone: that Mr
Lawrence believes, with all his heart and soul, that he is revealing
to us the profound and naked reality of life, that it is a matter of
life and death to him that he should persuade us that it is a matter
of life and death to ourselves to know that these things are so.
These writhings are the only real, and these convulsive raptures,
these oozy beatitudes the only end in human life. He would, if
he could, put us all on the rack to make us confess his protozoic
god; he is deliberately, incessantly, and passionately obscene in
the exact sense of the word. He will uncover our nakedness. It is

of no avail for us to protest that the things he finds are not there; a fanatical shriek arises from his pages that they are there, but we deny them.

If they are there, then it is all-important that we should not deny them. Whether we ought to expose them is another matter. The fact that European civilisation has up to the advent of Mr Lawrence ignored them can prove nothing, though it may indicate many things. It may indicate that they do not exist at all; or it may indicate that they do exist, but that it is bound up with the very nature of civilisation that they should not be exposed. Mr Lawrence vehemently believes the latter. It is the real basis of his fury against the consciousness of European civilisation which he lately expounded in these pages in a paper on Whitman. He claims that his characters attain whatever they do attain by their power of going back and re-living the vital process of pre-European civilisation. His hero, Rupert Birkin, after reaching the beginning of 'consummation' with his heroine, Ursula Brangwen, is thus presented:

He sat still like an Egyptian Pharaoh, driving the car. He felt as if he were seated in immemorial potency, like the great carven statues of real Egypt, as real and as fulfilled with subtle strength, as these are, with a vague, inscrutable smile on the lips. He knew what it was to have the strange and magical current of force in his back and loins, and down his legs, force so perfect that it stayed him immobile and left his face subtly, mindlessly smiling. He knew what it was to be awakened and potent in that other basic mind, the deepest physical mind. And from this source he had a pure and magic control, magical, mystical, a force in darkness, like electricity.

Through such strange avatars his characters pass, 'awakened and potent in his deepest physical mind'. European civilisation has ignored them. Was it from interested motives, or do they indeed exist?

Is Mr Lawrence a fanatic or a prophet? That he is an artist no longer is certain, as certain as it is that he has no desire to be one; for whatever may be this 'deep physical mind' that expresses its satisfaction in 'a subtle mindless smile', whether it have a real existence or not, it is perfectly clear that it does not admit of individuality as we understand it. No doubt Mr Lawrence intends to bring us to a new conception of individuality also; but in the interim we must use the conceptions and the senses that we have. Having these only, having, like Sam Weller in the divorce court, 'only a hordinary pair of eyes', we can discern no individuality whatever in the denizens of Mr Lawrence's world. We should have thought that we should be able to distinguish between male and female, at least. But no! Remove the names, remove the sedulous catalogues of unnecessary clothing – a new element and a significant one, this, in our author's work – and man and woman are indistinguishable as octopods in an aquarium tank.

The essential crisis of the book occurs in a chapter called, mystically enough, 'Excurse'. In that chapter Rupert and Ursula, who are said to reach salvation at the end of the history, have a critical and indescribable experience. It is not a matter of sexual experience, though that is, of course, incidentally thrown in; but there is a very great deal to do with 'loins'. They are loins of a curious kind, and they belong to Rupert. Mr Lawrence calls them 'his suave loins of darkness'. These Ursula 'comes to know'. It is, fortunately or unfortunately, impossible to quote these crucial pages. We cannot attempt to paraphrase them; for to us they are completely and utterly unintelligible if we assume (as we must assume if we have regard to the vehemence of Mr Lawrence's passion) that they are not the crudest sexuality. Rupert and Ursula achieve their esoteric beatitude in a tearoom; they discover by means of 'the suave loins of darkness' the mysteries of 'the deepest physical mind'. They die, and live again. After this experience (which we must call x):

They were glad, and they could forget perfectly. They laughed and went to the meal provided. There was a venison pasty, of all things, a large broad-faced cut ham, eggs and cresses and red beetroot, and medlars and apple-tart and tea.

We could not resist quoting the final paragraph if only as

evidence that 'the deepest physical mind' has no sense of humour. Why, in the name of darkness, 'a venison pasty, *of all things*'? Is a venison pasty more incongruous with this beatitude than a large ham? Does the 'deepest physical mind' take pleasure in a tart when it is filled with apples and none when it is filled with meat?

We have given, in spite of our repulsion and our weariness, our undivided attention to Mr Lawrence's book for the space of three days; we have striven with all our power to understand what he means by the experience x; we have compared it with the experience y, which takes place between the other pair of lovers, Gudrun and Gerald; we can see no difference between them, and we are precluded from inviting our readers to pronounce. We are sure that not one person in a thousand would decide that they were anything but the crudest kind of sexuality, wrapped up in what Mr S. K. Ratcliffe has aptly called the language of Higher Thought. We feel that the solitary person may be right; but even he, we are convinced, would be quite unable to distinguish between experience x and experience y. Yet x leads one pair to undreamed-of happiness, and y conducts the other to attempted murder and suicide.

This x and y are separate, if they are separate, on a plane of consciousness other than ours. To our consciousness they are indistinguishable; either they belong to the nothingness of unconscious sexuality, or are utterly meaningless. For Mr Lawrence they are the supreme realities, positive and negative, of a plane of consciousness the white race has yet to reach. Rupert Birkin has a negroid, as well as an Egyptian avatar; he sees one of those masterpieces of negro sculpture to which we have lately become accustomed. It is not the plastic idea which he admires:

There is a long way we can travel after the death-break; after that point when the soul in intense suffering breaks, breaks away from its organic hold like a leaf that falls. We fall from the connection with life and hope, we lapse from pure integral being, from creation and liberty, and we fall into the long African process of purely sensuous understanding, knowledge in the mystery of dissolution.

He realised now that this is a long process – thousands of years it takes, after the death of the creative spirit. He realised that there were great mysteries to be unsealed, sensual, mindless mysteries, far beyond the phallic cult. How far, in their inverted culture, had these West Africans gone beyond phallic knowledge? Very, very far. Birkin recalled again the female figure: the elongated, long, long body . . . the long imprisoned neck, the face with tiny features like a beetle's. This was far beyond the phallic knowledge, sensual, subtle realities far beyond the scope of phallic investigation.

There remained this way, this awful African process to be fulfilled. It would be done differently by the white races.

We believe Mr Lawrence's book is an attempt to take us through the process. Unless we pass through this we shall never see the light. If the experiences which he presents to us as a part of this process mean nothing, the book means nothing; if they mean something, the book means something; and the value of the book is precisely the value of those experiences. Whatever they are, they are of ultimate and fundamental importance to Mr Lawrence. He has sacrificed everything to achieve them; he has murdered his gifts for an acceptable offering to them. Those gifts were great; they were valuable to the civilisation which he believes he has transcended. It may be that we are benighted in the old world, and that he belongs to the new; it may be that he is, like his Rupert, a 'son of God'; we certainly are the sons of men, and we must be loyal to the light we have. By that light Mr Lawrence's consummation is a degradation, his passing beyond a passing beneath, his triumph a catastrophe. It may be superhuman, we do not know; by the knowledge that we have we can only pronounce it sub-human and bestial, a thing that our forefathers had rejected when they began to rise from the slime.

(ii) *THE RAINBOW* (1931)

GRADUALLY, Anton breaks down. Ursula says she does not want to marry him, and he collapses upon himself. Yet although she is afraid of the fearful compulsion of his utter dependence upon her, tacitly she seems to have given in to marrying him. They go away together to a house by the sea as an engaged couple. The physical contact goes on, but she is indifferent. One night, once more in the presence of a great burning moon, beneath which once more Anton 'felt himself fusing down into nothingness, like a bead that rapidly disappears in an incandescent flame', they reach their terrible consummation.

Then there in the great flare of light, she clinched hold of him, hard, as if suddenly she had the strength of destruction, she fastened her arms round him and tightened him in her grip, whilst her mouth sought his in a hard, rending, ever-increasing kiss, till his body was powerless in her grip, his heart melted in fear from the fierce, beaked, harpy's kiss. The water washed again over their feet, but she took no notice. She seemed unaware, she seemed to be pressing in her beaked mouth till she had the heart of him. Then, at last, she drew away and looked at him – looked at him. He knew what she wanted. He took her by the hand and led her across the foreshore back to the sand-hills. She went silently. He felt as if the ordeal of proof was upon him, for life or death. He led her to a dark hollow.
'No, here,' she said, going out to the slope full under the moonshine. She lay motionless, with wide-open eyes looking at the moon. He came direct to her, without preliminaries. She held him pinned down at the chest, awful. The fight, the struggle for consummation was terrible. It lasted till it was agony to his soul, till he succumbed, till he gave way as if dead, and lay with his face buried, partly in her hair, partly in the sand, motionless, as if he would be motionless now for ever, hidden away in the dark, buried, only buried, he only wanted to be buried in the goodly darkness, only that, and no more.

This is the end. Anton has failed at the proof. Ursula lies in a cold agony of un-satisfaction, and he creeps away a broken man.

To discover all that underlies this fearful encounter, we should have to go to *Lady Chatterley's Lover*, to Mellors' account of his sexual experience with Bertha Coutts. That is, in the present state of affairs, unquotable. But in that page and a half the curious will find not only the naked physical foundation – 'the blind beakishness' – of this experience of Ursula and Anton, but also Lawrence's final account of the sexual experience from which both the sexual experience of Will and Anna, and of Anton and Ursula is derived. *The Rainbow* is, radically, the history of Lawrence's final sexual failure.

It is much beside that; but that it is. And unless we grasp the fact, the inward meaning of *The Rainbow* and its sequel, *Women in Love*, must be concealed from us. One shrinks from the necessity of thus laying bare the physical secrets of a dead man; but in the case of Lawrence we have no choice. To the last he conceived it as his mission to teach us the way to sexual regeneration, and he claimed to give the world the ultimate truth about sex. If we take him seriously, we must take his message seriously. Continually in his work we are confronted with sexual experience of a peculiar kind; it is quite impossible to ignore it. The work of a great man, as Lawrence was, is always an organic whole. If we shrink from following the vital thread of experience from which it all derives, then we shrink from him altogether. It is all or nothing, with such a man as Lawrence; and, since it must not be nothing, it must be all.

The Rainbow is the story of Lawrence's sexual failure. The two men, who have succumbed to the woman, are one man – himself. The rainbow, in the symbolic sense of a harmony between spirit and flesh, is as far away as ever at the end of the book. It shines over the first generation, where man is really man, and does not need to arrogate authority over woman, it begins to be remote in the second, where the woman begins to establish the mastery; in the third, where woman is not only *victrix* but *triumphans*, it fades into the dim future. Ursula, the woman, becomes the protagonist; the man is secondary, an attribute of the woman. Nevertheless, Ursula is an unconvincing character in *The Rainbow*. She is a composite figure, made of the hated sexual woman, and of some of Lawrence's own manly experiences. Thus she is made to carry much of his experience as a schoolmaster, and of his own disappointment with the university; and more important, she is made to undergo a sort of physical-mystical experience, an annihilation of the personality. When in the last chapter the horses stampede upon her, she dies, and rises again in a new world: she becomes the mouthpiece of Lawrence's own visions.

The chief vision of which she is the vehicle is the vision of the darkness with which the conscious, personal, deliberate social life of mankind is surrounded.

This inner circle of light in which she lived and moved . . . suddenly seemed like the area under an arc-lamp, wherein the moths and the children played in the security of blinding light, not even knowing there was any darkness, because they stayed in the light. . . .
Nevertheless the darkness wheeled round about, with grey shadow-shapes of wild beasts, and also with dark shadow-shapes of the angels, whom the light fenced out, as it fenced out the more familiar beasts of darkness. And some, having for a moment seen the darkness, saw it bristling with the tufts of the hyæna and the wolf; and some, having given up their vanity of the light, having died in their own conceit, saw the gleam in the eyes of the wolf and the hyæna, that it was the flash of the sword of angels, flashing at the door to come in, that the angels in the darkness were lordly and terrible and not to be denied, like the flash of fangs.

It is not easy to be sure what Lawrence means by this. Is the surrounding darkness the darkness of 'the sensual sub-consciousness' which Ursula and Anton inhabited like wild animals? Or is it that darkness whose 'unclean dogs' Will Brangwen feared would devour him if Anna left him? Or are both these darknesses the same darkness? Is this darkness beneficent, or is it horrible? – creative, or destroying?

It would be hard to say. For this conception of the surrounding 'darkness', which will return in many forms in Lawrence's work, is an intensely personal conception. It derives, once more, from his peculiar experience. It is the darkness of pure animality as conceived and experienced by an intensely spiritual man. It is, therefore, essentially a horrible darkness of sin and evil, the enemy and destroyer of the light. To explore it, to surrender to it, is for Lawrence a self-violation, a perversity. Of this deliberate and willed surrender to the horror of darkness, the woman really knows nothing; because the woman is not spiritual. To her, what darkness she knows is warm and natural. Her darkness is not the same as his, because she is not divided. In the religious phrase, she has no sense of sin.

Therefore, to represent her in Ursula as realising the horror and majesty of the darkness is false. Neither the conception nor the experience belong to her at all. All that she knows of this darkness comes to her from and through the man. She represents that darkness to him; indeed she *is* that darkness to him: but she is completely unconscious of it. That the man should regard her as the creature and embodiment of *his* darkness horrifies her. She repudiates it utterly. She does not belong to his darkness at all. She recoils instinctively away. The truth of the whole strange situation is in the momentous poem, 'In the Dark', where she cries:

> I am afraid of you, I am afraid, afraid!
> There is something in you destroys me – !

And it is so. His darkness is necessarily death to her. For she is the real animal, unconscious of evil; but he is a spiritual man, willing himself into animality, into a deadly darkness, which if once she really entered, her innocent integrity would be shattered, and she would be destroyed.

This profound conflict is terrible indeed. The man is trying to compel the woman out of her own innocent darkness into the utterly different darkness of depravity. Neither he nor she know quite what is happening; but he knows far better than she. She is simply conscious of a horror from which she shrinks. And in creating the character of Ursula in *The Rainbow*, Lawrence has begun an effort of imaginative duplicity which will be decisive. For, in creating Ursula, he makes the woman a denizen of his darkness, not of her own; and he makes her in the final pages consciously submit herself and do homage to the darkness in which she would die. Ursula Brangwen of *The Rainbow*, is, in fact, a completely incredible character. She is the woman who accepts the man's vision of herself; accepts it, believes in it, and obeys it. She, therefore, becomes a monster, a chimæra.

Only in *Women in Love* does Ursula Brangwen really come alive; and then she is manifestly her mother, Anna Brangwen, continued from the point at which her imaginary child-bearing began. She becomes the woman who is constant in Lawrence's books – the woman whom Lawrence can never really understand, the innocent sensual woman, whom he can only watch and wonder at, love and hate, and cleave to until the end.

(iii) 'THE FUNDAMENTAL EQUIVOCATION OF *WOMEN IN LOVE*' *(1931)*

I

'THE Nightmare' is the title of a retrospective and autobiographical chapter of his later novel *Kangaroo*, which covers the three years from the beginning of 1916 to the end of 1918: that is, the period of writing *Women in Love* and two years after. In that record, which is of a veritable nightmare, and sometimes seems definitely to cross the border-line of sanity, there are clear traces of an endeavour by Lawrence to satisfy his hunger for a man. The threads of the narrative are mingled, and the one which is apparently dominant is Lawrence's horror of the war, and the effect of that horror upon him. Lawrence's horror of the war was real and profound, so were its effects upon him. Nevertheless, the war was only the secondary cause of his suffering. Even if there had been no war, some such experience as 'The Nightmare' was bound to have befallen him. It lay in his destiny.

Two things existed together in Lawrence: they were, perhaps, in the last analysis, dependent upon each other. One was an extraordinary spiritual sensitiveness, the other a less than normal sexual vitality. So that, instead of being strengthened by his relation with a woman, he was weakened by his own vain struggle to be dominant and lacerated by his sense of guilt; instead of being refreshed and renewed by physical communion, he was only the more enfeebled and divided by it. His sexual life was an added burden to his spirit, instead of a release from burdening. The horror of the war doubled the burden of his spirit, and made more agonised and desperate his attempts to find release in the woman. Defeat became only the more inevitable; and the burden increased till it became intolerable. I knew Lawrence well at the beginning of the period of 'The Nightmare': I lived for some three months in close contact with him in Cornwall. He had made a desperate call to Katherine Mansfield and me to join him and his wife, and live together in unity. And we responded, because we loved him and his wife. He was to us a wonderful and beloved being. And, I think, he was depending upon us. 'There remain only you and Murry in our lives,' he wrote to Katherine, beseeching her to come. 'We look at the others as across a grave. . . . Let us all live together and create a new world.'

The attempt was a painful failure. There were moments of blissful happiness: when were there not moments of simple bliss for any one who lived with Lawrence? But the failure was only the more painful. Katherine and I were bewildered by Lawrence. All the knowledge of him contained in this book was completely hidden from me then; it was, in the main, concealed from me all through his life. When he died, something broke in my heart: but all I knew was that I had loved him, and that, at times at least, he had loved me. I knew that our relation had been a miserable and tragic failure, and I felt that the failure had been inevitable, necessary as fate. And that was all I knew when Lawrence died. Only since his death have I been driven by some inward compulsion to try to understand him. The attempt would have been impossible while he yet lived.

Katherine and I were completely ignorant of the nature of the struggle which was then devouring him like a disease. We saw, and felt on our pulses, only the incredible mingling of love and hatred that was in him. He seemed to us like a man possessed, now by an angel, now by a devil. Both were beyond our comprehension; but to the angel we responded, the devil tortured us beyond endurance. It was pain to see him so transformed and transfigured by the paroxysms of murderous hatred, of his wife, of us, of all mankind, that swept over him. They would leave him white, bowed, spent, silent and shuddering. Such a happening was beyond our experience and beyond our understanding. Gradually, we became oppressed and frightened; it seemed as though we could not breathe, and that our only hope was to get away. We packed up our few possessions and went away to the other side of Cornwall.

We did not understand; but we could have done nothing if we had understood. The horror of the war was not the cause of his strange and terrifying condition. We also felt the horror of the war, but Lawrence's horror was a frenzy. It utters itself as such in 'The Nightmare' chapter of *Kangaroo*, written years later.

And now, if circumstances had roped nearly all men into the horror, and it was a case of adding horror to horror, or dying well, on the other hand, the irremediable circumstance of his own separate soul made inevitable Richard Lovat's standing out. If there is outward, circumstantial unreason and fatality, there is inward unreason and inward fate. He would have to dare to follow his inward fate. He must remain alone, outside of everything, everything, conscious of what was going on, conscious of what he was doing and not doing. Conscious he must be, and consciously he must stick to it. To be forced into nothing.

But there was, and Lawrence knew it, no danger of his being

forced into anything. He was completely unfit for any kind of
military service. The most obtuse doctor had only to put a
stethoscope to his chest for a second to know that as a soldier he
was unthinkable. Moreover, for his own occupation – he had
now, after finishing *Women in Love*, practically given up writing
– he was working hard on the farm below his cottage at Zennor;
he was, though not with that intention, doing 'national service'
of the most necessary kind. All that could happen to him in the
normal course was a periodic summons for medical examination,
of which the conclusion was foregone. But this had become to
him an unspeakable horror: the mere recollection of it, six years
later, when he was writing *Kangaroo*, drove him once more to
insane fury.

Not while life was life, should they lay hold of him. Never
again. Never would he be touched again. And because they had
handled his private parts, and looked into them, their eyes should
burst and their hands should wither and their hearts should rot.

That refers to the last medical examination in 1918. The war
had ended before Lawrence's resolution could be put to the test.

II

Lawrence was, at this time, suffering from a kind of persecution-
mania. He believed he was a marked man, and that 'the authorities' had taken good note of his inward resistance. This was, I
believe, pure delusion; but Lawrence had more excuse for the
delusion than most people who suffer from persecution-mania.
He had as good an excuse as Jean-Jacques Rousseau. He knew
himself to be an extraordinary man; and to suppose that the
vague 'authorities' knew it also was only natural to him. Moreover, *The Rainbow* had been suppressed, and no one had uttered
a word in its defence. It was put aside, annihilated, as unspeakable.
Lawrence had some excuse for believing that the powers that
were, were determined to destroy him. These convictions worked
on him in his isolation in Cornwall. His behaviour became

deliberately intransigent. Among the ignorant and often mali-
cious Cornish peasantry, the fact that his wife was German was
suspicious. The submarine menace was at its height, their cottage looked directly over the Bristol Channel; they had no
visible means of subsistence. Another man, even Lawrence himself at another moment, would simply have removed inland. But
the devil of perversity had now taken hold of him; he willed to
stay and be persecuted by skulking coast-watchers; he wanted to
drink the cup to the dregs and make the potion as bitter as he
could. So he stuck fast in Cornwall, and sang German songs to
the spell-bound ears of the coast-watchers crouching beneath his
cottage-windows. The longer he stayed, the more suspect he
inevitably became. *Why* did he stay there, when any other man
would simply have gone somewhere else? The answer was as
natural as the question to the local jacks-in-office. He was there
for no good.

And, of course, if someone had been there to answer the
question correctly, and to say that he stayed there because he
wanted to be persecuted, because he wanted to suffer, because he
wanted to hate them and mankind for making him suffer, because
he wanted to be able to spew England out of his mouth, the
answer would have seemed pure nonsense. But it would have
been true. Lawrence wanted the darkness and the horror and the
sense of malignancy that he felt in Cornwall.

The Cornish night would gradually come down upon the
dark shaggy moors, that were like the fur of some beast, and upon
the pale-grey granite masses, so ancient and so Druidical, suggesting blood-sacrifice. And as Somers sat there on the sheaves in
the underdark, seeing the light swim above the sea, he felt he
was over the border, in another world. Over the border, in that
twilight awesome world of the previous Celts. The spirit of the
ancient pre-Christian world, which lingers still in the truly Celtic
places, he could feel it invade him in the savage dusk, making him
savage too, and at the same time strangely sensitive and subtle,
understanding the mystery of blood-sacrifice: to sacrifice one's
victim, and let the blood run to the fire, there beyond the gorse on
the old grey granite: and at the same time to understand most

sensitively the dark flicker of animal life about him, even in a bat, even in the writhing of a maggot in a dead rabbit. Writhe then, Life, he seemed to say to the things – and he no longer saw its sickeningness.

Not to see its sickeningness is one thing; Lawrence wanted something different. He wanted to exult in its sickeningness, to let himself lapse into an ecstasy of decay and disintegration. The tendency thus to escape from the burden of the spiritual consciousness was always in him. Even so far back as *The White Peacock* it is with Cyril's fascinated watching of the maggots in a dead rabbit that his friendship with Annable begins. Lawrence was now deliberately seeking that decomposition of the spiritual consciousness which circumstance and place offered him. He consciously sought to lapse from consciousness. 'He could feel himself metamorphosing. He no longer wanted to struggle consciously along, a thought-adventurer. He preferred to drift into a sort of blood-darkness.' Of this deliberate drift out of consciousness, Richard Somers' affair with the young Cornish farmer was an integral part. It was also deliberately directed against his wife: against 'the love and marriage ideal', as embodied in her. The relation with the young farmer was in malignant opposition to her: a consciously willed destruction of his wife's being.

Poor Harriet spent many lonely days in the cottage. Richard was not interested in her now. He was only interested in John Thomas and the farm-people, and he was growing more like a labourer every day. And the farm-people didn't mind how long *she* was left alone, at night too, in that lonely little cottage, and with all the tension of fear upon her. . . . Richard . . . neglected her and hated her. She was driven back on herself like a fury.

It was the deliberate seeking of a death-relation – the farmer and he 'would talk of death, and the powers of death' – a deliberate denial of the life-relation. It was the proving, in bitter life-experience, of the truth of Ursula Brangwen's instinct that

Birkin's wanting 'another kind of love' with a man was an obstinacy, a theory, a perversity. 'Somers seemed to come home (from his farmer-friend) like an enemy, with that look on his face, and that pregnant malevolency of Cornwall investing him.'

Inevitably, Lawrence felt that he was violating himself. This conscious perversion, this wilful degradation, of his spirit could never have the entire man behind it. He was not, and never could be, 'mindless'; the spirit was still there, watching him.

'I declare!' said John Thomas, as Somers appeared in the cornfield, 'you look more like one of us every day.' And he looked with a bright Cornish eye at Somers' careless, belted figure and old jacket. The speech struck Richard: it sounded half triumphant, half mocking. 'He thinks I'm coming down in the world – it is half a rebuke,' thought Somers to himself. But he was half pleased: and half he *was* rebuked.

Even in the simple human way his man-friend failed him. Subtly, it is easy to see from the story, Buryan despised Lawrence. He left Lawrence's passionate letters unanswered, made no response to his appeals, treated him as of no account. Lawrence would have us and himself believe that it was because he was afraid of his association with a marked man. But the explanation does not fit with Buryan's deliberate neglect of him in the episode of the journey to the market town. The cause is plain to see: at bottom Buryan despised Lawrence for his own self-degradation.

Of this strange period, Lawrence said that 'it changed his life for ever'. It may have done; in the sense that it may have confirmed and made inveterate his appetite towards disintegration and death, his mood of loathing and hatred for all mankind. But both were manifest long before, and long before the war. What had happened now was that he had given rein to his devil, and the devil was never afterwards in subjection very long. But whether in fact he had any real power to choose, who shall say? I am no believer in free-will; it seems to me a childish superstition. Humanly speaking, I wish that Lawrence had been an undivided man; but since it seems plain to me that those precious qualities in him which made him wonderful were corollary to that weakness which I would have had him spared, even the human wish seems childish to me.

III

So with *Women in Love*, the novel of this period. I hold it to be built upon a lie, or on many lies; yet I would not have it otherwise. The haunted, tortured, divided, angel-devil of a man is in it. He is not like the Lawrence whom I loved; but (as I learned to my sorrow) the Lawrence whom I loved was only half the Lawrence whom I knew.

Women in Love is an amazing book; amazing for the subtlety of its falsity, amazing for the intricacy of its self-deception. It is the imperishable monument of one of the strangest moments of Lawrence's strange destiny.

The main argument of the book, which is the distinction between the 'love' of Rupert and Ursula on the one hand, and of Gerald and Gudrun on the other, is false. Rupert and Ursula are represented as in the way of salvation, Gerald and Gudrun as in the way of damnation: and this is superficially plausible for the simple reason that Rupert and Ursula are in the main real people, while Gerald and Gudrun are not. But when we consider the principles which these opposed couples really embody, we discover that the difference between them is that Rupert and Ursula are a whole stage further on in the process of damnation, for Gerald and Gudrun simply represent Rupert and Ursula at their previous stage of sensual self-destruction. Lawrence claims that Rupert and Ursula escape from it into the ultra-phallic realm of utter separateness and mindless sensuality. It was untrue. What happened was that Lawrence tried to escape thither, and left Ursula where she was; and some record of what happened in consequence of this escape is written in 'The Nightmare'.

Lawrence, who was a supremely conscious man, was not unaware of the deception he was trying to work upon himself. There is a point in the story where Birkin wonders whether he has done wrong to refuse Ursula's proffered love. 'Perhaps', he thinks, 'he had been wrong to go to her with an idea of what he wanted.' The idea of what he wanted is expressed in fifty different ways in the novel; sometimes very deceptively, but the substance beneath is always the same. The phallic relation is to be superseded by a new sexuality of separateness and touch. Perhaps the 'idea' is most clearly expressed, with much that lay behind it, in this passage:

On the whole he hated sex, it was such a limitation. . . . He wanted sex to revert to the level of the other appetites, to be regarded as a functional process, not as a fulfilment. He believed in sex-marriage. But beyond this he wanted a further conjunction, where man had being and woman had being, two pure beings, each constituting the freedom of the other, balancing each other like two poles of one force, like two angels or two demons.

He wanted so much to be free, not under the compulsion of any need for unification, or tortured by unsatisfied desire. . . . The merging, the clutching, the mingling of love was become madly abhorrent to him. But it seemed to him, woman was always so horrible and clutching, she had such a lust for possession, a greed of self-importance in love. She wanted to have, to own, to control, to be dominant. Everything must be referred back to her, to Woman, the Great Mother of everything, out of whom proceeded everything and to whom everything must be rendered up.

It filled him with almost insane fury, this calm assumption of the Magna Mater. . . . He had a horror of the Magna Mater, she was detestable.

Were it not that we have learned to read this language, it might be plausible. Lawrence seems half to have deceived himself by his phrases. For Birkin, when he wonders whether he was wrong to go to Ursula with this idea of what he wanted, asks himself: 'Was it really only an idea, or was it the interpretation of a profound yearning? If the latter, how was it he was always talking about sensual fulfilment? The two did not agree very well together.' They agreed, in reality, perfectly well together.

Sensual domination, not sexual fulfilment, is his desire. A sexual marriage in which he does not have to satisfy the woman, where the sexuality, being transformed into sensuality, may give him the opportunity of re-asserting the manhood he had lost – this is precisely Lawrence's dream. It is the dream of a man who would give his soul to be free of the woman, but has not the courage to make himself free of her.

Suddenly he found himself face to face with a situation. It was as simple as this: fatally simple. On the one hand, he knew he did not want a further sensual experience – something deeper, darker than ordinary life could give. [He thinks of an African carving of a negro woman, which is for him the expression of the 'deeper, darker' sensual mystery.] Thousands of years ago, that which was imminent in himself must have taken place in these Africans: the goodness, the holiness, the desire for creation and productive happiness must have lapsed, leaving the single impulse for knowledge in one sort, mindless progressive knowledge through the senses, knowledge arrested and ending in the senses, mystic knowledge in disintegration and dissolution. . . .

Birkin shrinks back in horror from the lapse from goodness that is imminent in himself. No, there is another way, he cries in anguish.

There was the paradisal entry into pure, single being, the individual soul taking precedence over love and desire for union, stronger than any pangs of emotion, a lovely state of free proud singleness, which accepted the obligation of the permanent connection with others, and with the other, submits to the yoke and leash of love, but never forfeits its own proud individual singleness, even while it loves and yields. There was the other way, the remaining way. And he must run to follow it. . . .

He goes off to ask Ursula to marry him. Which eventually she does. And then we find, as we have found, that the consummation between them has nothing whatever to do with these brave words of spiritual achievement, this mutual acknowledgment of the proud single soul; on the contrary, it is an attempt, to which Ursula is represented (falsely, as 'The Nightmare' shows) to have been converted, to experience precisely those 'sensual subtle realities far beyond the scope of phallic investigation', those mindless but not unconscious ecstasies of dissolution, which Birkin has ostensibly rejected for 'the paradisal way' of marriage with Ursula.

I believe that Lawrence changed while *Women in Love* was actually being written: that he really did mean to reject the way of sensuality and dissolution, and that he succumbed to it in spite of himself. And Lawrence at the end of his novel is trying to persuade himself that his defeat is a victory; to deceive himself and his reader into the belief that the mutual acknowledgment of the proud single soul (which is spiritual) and the mutual exploration of 'the ultra-phallic otherness' (which is sensual) are the same. Somewhere in his inward soul Lawrence must have known what he was doing; just as Birkin 'knew that his spirituality was concomitant of a process of depravity, a sort of pleasure in self-destruction. There really *was* a certain stimulant in self-destruction, for him – especially when it was translated spiritually. But then he knew it – he knew it, and had done.' That was an easy thing to say; but a man who, like Lawrence, 'is damned and doomed to the old effort at serious living', cannot violate himself with impunity. He has finally broken something, deliberately riven his secret soul in sunder; and no power in earth or heaven can make him whole again.

The fundamental equivocation of *Women in Love* repels me. It is not that I blame Lawrence for yielding to a longing from which in his inward soul he shrank away. Lawrence was Lawrence – a destiny-driven man, if ever there was one. If the realm of mindless sensuality offered or seemed to offer the only way of escape for his tortured spirit, then he was driven to explore it. But I think he is to be condemned for painting his devil as an angel, for the duplicity with which he represents himself as turning away from this mindless sensuality towards a paradisal relation with the woman, yet subtly perverts this very relation (in defiance of all truth, factual or imaginative) into a form of that mindless sensuality from which it was to be an escape. Lawrence, in the essential and vital argument of *Women in Love*, behaves like a cheat. To behave like a cheat in these momentous issues of human destiny is to play the Judas to humanity. The man who betrays himself in such an issue betrays all men.

The failure was momentous. Lawrence, in the outcome, was never to recover from it. He would make the heroic effort – a truly heroic effort – to assert himself against the consequences of his own spiritual suicide. But he was, henceforward, veritably a doomed man. He had made the great refusal, and it was irrevocable.

My mind tells me that this was inevitable, my heart tells me that it was not. When I think, childishly, of what Lawrence might have been, and of what he actually became, my heart is wrung with anguish. The slow recantation of all that was most precious to him, the gradual disintegration which an inexorable justice exacted from him, is fearful to contemplate. To mitigate the tragedy of this retribution, let us remember this, which I believe to be true.

Lawrence was denied the basic strength to bear the burden of the human spirit which lay more heavily on him than any other man of his time. The extreme knowledge of the burden to be borne, the secret inability to bear it – these were, I believe, given together. The excessive sensitiveness to the demands of the spirit, prematurely awakened in him, prevented that true physical maturity which would have enabled him either to maintain himself in physical isolation, or to draw upon the woman's vital strength, to take through her the healing virtue of the unknown which is beyond and below life itself. So he was driven consciously to seek not the unconscious, which he could not fully enter, but the mindless, which he believed he could. But even this he could not do, without his woman. She must submit her instinctive knowledge to his strange necessities; she must believe in his unnatural consummations; she must be convinced that humanity was involved in a destiny of mindless dissolution; she must submit to the idea that sex was a functional process, not a fulfilment; she must acknowledge that they were not man and woman, discovering and re-discovering their own integral being through their perfect union, but polarised demons inhabiting the mindless realm. She submits, believes, is convinced; in the book she obeys. In life she resists; and the victory is hers, as it must be.

But there was still more. Precisely because Lawrence was denied that utter fulfilment in a woman which would have given him the strength to bear his spiritual isolation, he needed a friend, needed friends – men and women who were his equals in spiritual development. And they did not exist; or, if they did exist, he did not know them. Here I speak with some authority, for it was to Katherine Mansfield and to me that he turned with longing in the crucial winter of 1915–16 after which *Women in Love* was written, and simply because I was a man, he turned primarily to me. And I failed Lawrence, not from any lack of love, or of will to avail him. I was never lacking in love towards Lawrence; but I lacked understanding, the understanding that is born of absolute experience, and can come from no other source whatever.

Yet it is plain to me now that, even if I had understood Lawrence, I should still have been bound to fail him, and that it was better to fail him in ignorance, than to be impotent to help him, in knowledge. If I had known his secret, I would have been his master, not he mine. And he needed to be the master. The effect of his own manhood which gnawed at him, demanded this spiritual compensation. If he had been able to accept the fact of his own dependence, Lawrence would never have been driven to his dire necessity. The man who can finally accept himself is a free man. If Lawrence could have accepted his own intrinsic dependence, then he would, by that very act, have become independent: his dependence would have fallen away from him. It sounds a miracle, perhaps it is a miracle, but this miracle is inevitable in the progress of the human spirit. If it is a miracle it is a natural miracle – that eternal rebirth of human soul without which life, to the sensitive spirit, must become an unendurable agony. This eternal rebirth of the soul Lawrence could not achieve: he fled from the naked isolation of self-knowledge without which it is inconceivable.

SOURCES: The review of *Women in Love* appeared in the *Nation and Athenaeum*, 13 Aug. 1921, entitled 'The Nostalgia of Mr D. H. Lawrence', and was collected in *Reminiscences of D. H. Lawrence* (1933); the second and third extracts are from *Son of Woman* (1931).

Mary Freeman

LAWRENCE AND FUTURISM

(1955)

IDENTIFICATION with social decay in *Women in Love* was the culmination of Lawrence's resolve to know suffering but to feel joy, to come to terms with life which he saw, as early as *The White Peacock*, as a brute with nice eyes. He had rejected Siegmund's contemplative ecstasy, with its uselessness in daily life, and now cultivated alert sensuousness toward the commonplace. It had seemed possible at the close of *The Rainbow* that a new and more satisfying world could be built if man recovered awareness of nature and reconstructed society in harmony with it. But at that point the pain and suffering of a war-torn world overwhelmed Lawrence, and he was tempted once more to find something satisfying in what repelled him: the divine in pain, the god in death.

The solution of this problem on a sensuous level involved him in subtleties that were unforeseen when he looked toward a new world at the close of *The Rainbow*. Nevertheless, it grew logically from his already marked concern with paradox, particularly as manifested in ambivalent emotions. Paul's love for his mother had covered rebellion and his hate for his father deep attraction. Most significantly, Lawrence had recognized in his earliest work that mild pain can be pleasant and that intense happiness can border on pain. Lettie had thought of the Druids and their blood sacrifices while she enjoyed the snowdrops in the ancient woods. Siegmund had connected the beauty of the sea with implacable fate. Paul's love for Miriam had been exquisite suffering and his fight with Dawes anguished consummation. The enhanced life that Lawrence had sought and found abundantly in nature was often as painful as passionate. If each day had seemed self-justified to Tom and Lydia, it was not because it was benign, but because it was living.

Of increasing interest to Lawrence were the obscure relations between the aggressor and the victim. This communion is explored in 'Rabbit Snared in the Night', as well as in 'The Prussian Officer'.

Why do you spurt and spottle
like that bunny?
Why should I want to throttle
You, bunny?

Yes, bunch yourself between
my knees and lie still.
Lie on me with a hot, plumb, live weight,
heavy as a stone, passive,
yet hot, waiting.

What are you waiting for?
What are you waiting for?
What is the hot, plumb weight of your desire on me?
You have a hot, unthinkable desire of me, bunny.

What is that spark
glittering at me on the unutterable darkness
of your eye, bunny?
The finest splinter of a spark
that you throw off, straight on the tender of my nerves!

It sets up a strange fire,
a soft, most unwarrantable burning,
a bale-fire mounting, mounting up in me.

'Tis not of me, bunny.
It was you engendered it,
with that fine, demoniacal spark
you jetted off your eye at me.

I did not want it
this furnace, this draught-maddened fire
which mounts up my arms
making them swell with turgid, ungovernable strength.

. . . .

It must have been *your* inbreathing, gasping desire
that drew this red gush in me
I must be reciprocating *your* vacuous, hideous passion,

. . .

It must be you who desire
this intermingling of the black and monstrous fingers of Moloch
in the blood jets of your throat.

Come, you shall have your desire,
since already I am implicated with you
in your strange lust.[1]

'The Prussian Officer' is a story of brutality and murder but it
rouses the most delicate nuances in sensation, even a forbidden
kind of understanding. Both the captain and his orderly find
satisfaction in violence whether given or received. From the
moment they recognize their mutual enmity, each feels fatally
bound to the other. When the captain slings his belt in his
orderly's face and sees 'the youth start back, the pain-tears in
his eyes and the blood on his mouth' he feels 'at once a thrill of
deep pleasure and of shame'. Later 'his veins, too, ran hot', when
he realizes that this 'was to be man to man between them. He
yielded before the solid, stumbling figure with the bent head.'
The orderly, for whom no one now exists but the captain, finds
killing him a profound gratification although 'his own life also
ended. . . . He was conscious of a sense of arrival. He was amid
the reality, on the real dark bottom.'[2]

Lawrence brought to this delineation of the satisfactions of
pain a deliberate naïveté resulting from real sophistication. He
described events but omitted labels. He did not care what they
were called but was concerned with what they exposed of the
nature of life.

Throughout *The Rainbow* the perverse twists, highly developed in *Women in Love*, were tentative and undeveloped, yet
unmistakably present. Skrebensky found the fear induced by
Africa a desirable fear. The wonderful controlled but unquenched
power of the horses drove Ursula to terror but also released her

from the shoddy conventionalities of mankind. Even Lydia
Lensky, after the death of her two children and first husband,
and before she met Tom, found that 'silenced, with a strange
deep terror having hold of her, her desire was *to seek satisfaction
in dread* [italics mine], to enter a nunnery, to satisfy the instinct
of dread in her, through service of a dark religion'.[3]

Such observations gathered and developed into the sensuous
acceptance of social decay in *Women in Love*. Lydia found release
from dread at Marsh Farm, but Lawrence, overwhelmed by the
aura of destruction and disintegration of a world at war, followed her rejected impulse to 'seek satisfaction in dread'. Believing that he was in a period of cultural decay, he felt it useless
to try to escape. A man was within it as it was within him. We
'roam in the belly of our era'. 'Our every activity is the activity
of disintegration, of corruption, of dissolution, whether it be
our scientific research, our social activity . . . our art, or our anti-
social activity, sensuality, sensationalism, crime, war. Everything
alike contributes to the flux of death, to corruption, and liberates
the static data of the consciousness.'[4] Need to absorb decay in an
acceptable view of life became the dominant motivation in his
writing at this time.

In *Women in Love*, and in other works where Lawrence tries
to raise death and pain to an ecstasy, he approached the attitude
characteristic of literary futurism. Behind the bombast of the
Italian futurists,* and their equivalents elsewhere, lay the same
need. Falling between the dying and the unborn world, they felt
it was necessary to wring some satisfaction out of this inchoate
state. Kenneth Burke in describing Nietzsche as an incipient
futurist remarked that he seemed 'to have forced himself to
welcome developments that he did not really like. . . . The result

* I have chosen to use the term 'futurist' as the most convenient
designation of an attitude not confined to those usually labelled
'futurists'. It is appropriate here not only because Marinetti has provided a relatively tangible credo and fascism brought out possible
social implications of the viewpoint, but also because Lawrence himself
recognised and commented on certain similarities between what he
sought and they asserted.

was a kind of *brutality* that is also apparent in his disciple, Spengler. We may note a strong ingredient of such brutality in the Futurists' frame of "acceptance".'[5]

When people are forced to see more suffering than joy, more ugliness than beauty, more death than life, it is not strange that men of acute sensibilities tend to become obsessed by the former and that those who can remain in one way or another life-loving should try to make suffering yield a perverse beauty.* This violation of convention, since it intimates evil and forbidden power, lends intense excitement to the effort and suggests stimulation as a positive value. Indeed, stimulation tends to become the sole value in wringing gratification from incongruity.

The futurists modernized this sensationalism – long a literary stock-in-trade, consciously exploited by many writers like Poe and Baudelaire – and dubbed it 'creative'. Lawrence, too, recognized sensationalism as a manifestation of our times, but not as a creative one. On the contrary, he saw it as a disintegrative process, symptomatic of cultural decay, and described it as 'a collective activity, a war, when within the great rind of virtue we thresh destruction further and further, till our whole civilization is like a great rind full of corruption, of breaking down, a mere shell threatened with collapse upon itself'. We go into actual war almost gladly 'to get once more the final reduction under the touch of death'. This 'sensationalism, this reduction back', this 'self-inflicted sadism', this singing death, had become, he thought, regretfully, the 'only form of life' for 'our civilized and still passionate men'.[6]

To achieve this alchemy Lawrence and the futurists took a number of similar steps. First, their effort to accept pain as pleasure, ugliness as beauty, death as life, proliferated into a general obsession with the obscure relations of apparent opposites. Both disparaged conventions that inhibited these associations and their assimilation of them. Both distrusted the mind

---

* Curzio Malaparte, one of the early Italian futurists, has given us in his book *Kaputt* an example *par excellence* of the futurists' alchemy through which the brutal, the terrifying, and the sickening can be made stimuli for exquisite sensuality.

with its rational procedure since they required what appeared
to be an irrational synthesis. The futurists exhorted one another
to let the unconscious bubble up freely; Lawrence asked us to
listen to the Holy Ghost. Psychologically naked, but steeled,
they plunged into the *mêlée* that they had found unsavory. Lost
in its intricacies, the futurist reported chaos, accepted it, and
deified it. Lawrence never lost his deep faith in some kind of
organization, but his own relationship to that organization was
often as obscure as Birkin's. Even the customary distinction
between the real and the illusory, the objective and the subjective,
is eroded in the work of the futurist, and, similarly, Lawrence's
most significant passages hover between vivid fact and elusive
symbols. This distinction is of little importance. Lawrence,
like the futurists, regarded all experience as valid because it
was.

This determination to accept whatever emerged from the
interplay of forces – to regard even pain as self-justifying – did
seem to transfigure moments that might otherwise have been
unquestionably disagreeable. But it had extremely disturbing
psychological and social implications. Both Lawrence and the
futurist regarded his own view as dynamic. But their efforts to see
both sides simultaneously, to observe and subserve life simultaneously, suggest an attempt to stabilize it, to catch it by a dash
of mystical salt. Just as the obsessional neurotic with aboulia
cannot cast off the possibility of acting in opposite directions
and hence tends to do nothing at all, so the futurist, in seeing
incongruous things as equally acceptable, tends to judge nothing
at all. Stimulation becomes its own end and the only good.
Action subserves it.* Lawrence's efforts to reconcile opposites,
his emphasis on the unpredictability of the lines of the future,
and his determination to live to the fullest in the present tempted
him to a similar comprehensive acceptance. Quite symptomati-
cally he thought 'awe' was one of our finest words and that to
know a thing fully was to lose it. He checked himself by frequent references to the emptiness of life without a belief, but he

* The futurist's intellectual and moral aboulia is perfectly illustrated
by Malaparte's *Kaputt*.

did not fully rule out the possibility that this belief might be belief in a stimulating chaos.

At the same time Lawrence's writing technique, which he had recognized as somewhat futuristic when he wrote *The Rainbow*, became more so when he wrote *Women in Love* where he sought ways of describing 'the static data of the consciousness' released by social decay. The transcendental sparkle evoked so successfully from ordinary experience in the former book is gathered in rapt concentration on disintegration and death in the latter. With the exception of Birkin's gambol in the birch wood, the big moments suggest the permeation of life by death and corruption. When stimulation went beyond the acceptable threshold, Lawrence found ways of cancelling the unbearable excess. Of greatest importance in neutralizing the despair rampant in *Women in Love* was the emphasis on identification with disintegrating society, of communion on a Black Mass level with mankind in some cosmic rite.* Individual suffering symbolized this identification.

Lawrence found also that the association of contradictory aspects of life often mitigated the disagreeable qualities of each at the same time that it, like contrasting colors, heightened sensation. Paul translated his mother's death into a mystery belonging to an incomprehensible but splendid universe. Birkin, by associating the 'mystic sources of corruption' with sexual intercourse, transfigured the potential morbidity of the flesh into 'flowers of corruption', thereby making mortality more attractive and procreation more imposing.† This association between creation and decay, established and underscored in transcendental moments, is represented throughout Lawrence's books by suggestive figures – lilies, swans, moonlight, reptiles, cold fire, ice, Aphrodite, and the sea – and insinuating adjectives – phosphorescent, salty, dark, electric. All call up their aura of flowering corruption.

---

* In *Days of Wrath* and *Man's Hope* André Malraux has neutralised the personal agony attending civil war by a similar sensuous communion.

† The love–death theme in *Tristan and Isolde* is a classic example of his transmutation.

Singly or together, they are shorthand indications of an entire perception – visual, aural, tactual, even intellectual – and, in spite of their surface obliqueness, they give an unusually solid sense of fact.

In his effort to reconcile incongruities in a blaze of ecstatic sensuousness Lawrence used another device characteristic of futurism. He frequently transposed attitudes and words conventionally appropriate in one context to quite another, for example, using the surcharged words commonly allotted to love in describing men, animals, flowers, and trees. (This practice roused rather lurid speculations regarding Lawrence's relations, not only with men, but also with birch groves and his cow Susan.) The futurists wrote love songs to crowds, machines, and death.

Lawrence succeeded in giving, with far fewer and less extreme language dislocations than Marinetti's, what the latter called 'a new way of feeling and seeing, a measuring of the universe as a sum of forces in motion'. In Lawrence's writing we are unusually aware of movement and conflict coupled with a strong sense of ultimate unity. The association of this skill with amoral sensationalism in both Lawrence and the futurists appears to arise from their common effort to relate in an intensive sensory experience that which is not rationally relatable.

However, it was precisely at this point that Lawrence tried to pull away from futurism. While the futurists spoke glibly of seeking new *dynamic* individuality in a new dynamic way of life, they were satisfied by a succession of intense but *disconnected* sensations.[7] Lawrence applauded the futurists for looking beneath conventional concepts to find a new 'physiology of matter', but at the same time he objected strongly that instead 'of looking for the new human phenomenon' they looked only 'for the phenomena of the science of physics to be found in human beings'. He, on the contrary, although more concerned with what a woman 'is' rather than what she 'feels – in the ordinary usage of the word',[8] tried to give the essence of human individuality, to describe an individual as a whole and unique being.

He used the same kinds of ambiguous symbols to suggest whole individuality that he used to suggest whole perception.

References to Ursula's 'dangerous helplessness', apotheosized in her experience with the horses, evoke the essence of her character, her potentiality, her 'deeper ego'. In the same way allusions to Gerald's 'clear northern flesh', his hair with its 'glisten like sunshine refracted through crystals of ice' and to the wolf as his totem and to Cain as his prototype establish and carry through the novel his cold desperation, born of his past and prophetic of his future. Hermione's futile struggle against a congealing doom is intimated thus: 'Her long pale face, that she carried lifted up, somewhat in the Rossetti fashion, seemed almost drugged, as if a strange mass of thoughts coiled in the darkness within her, and she was never allowed to escape.' Having once established the character of these individuals, Lawrence, by referring back – sometimes using only one adjective or noun from the original description or even a paraphrase of the original – carries individuality through its 'allotropic states'. Although it is the impact between persons and things that produces these 'allotropic states', it is also this impact and these allotropic states which reveal the 'deeper ego'. Lawrence felt that sensuous perception, by permeating the body to the very finger tips, unified the individual and apotheosized its uniqueness.

Lawrence did not intend to break his characters apart into 'psychological atoms', as Aldous Huxley has thought them to be.[9] It is the conventional 'moral scheme', not the characters, that he wished to split apart. There remains, not only a sequential unity of personality which he indicates in his totemic symbols, but even a new and fluid, though definite, moral scheme. It may take, as Lawrence wrote, a 'deeper sense than any we have been used to exercise' to discover this 'deeper ego', but he intended that it be there as carbon is present in diamond and coal. Gerald was a chained wolf in his relations with Pussums, in his reorganization of the mines, in his contempt for Loerke, and in his icy death. Gudrun's will-to-power, tested in modeling small animals, growing on her struggle with Gerald, found full expression in her final acceptance of sensation as self-justifying. Ursula's fluid sensibility, her 'dangerous helplessness', is behind her rebellion against her father, her hatred of Hermione, and her suspicion of Birkin. Birkin's chameleon flexibility led him to close searching relationships with persons as different as Hermione, Gerald, and Ursula.

If at certain points an experience of one character seems to resemble an experience of another, the resemblance is due largely to the coarseness of language itself. Lawrence, while sensitively aware of broad similarities of experience, was extraordinarily alert to the unique quality of each person that gives continuity to one's experiences. By expanding important moments in the life of a character he intended, not to break, but to enrich our sense of this specific continuity.

Despite lapses and the marked similarities of his technique to futurist techniques, Lawrence's characters remain human beings that are warm, vulnerable, and, even when lost, seeking to find their way. Futurists like Malaparte, and to a lesser degree, d'Annunzio, seem to use their men and women as instruments for receiving and producing intense but disparate, and ultimately meaningless sensations.

Not only did Lawrence criticize the futurists for losing the 'human phenomenon', but he objected even more strongly to their lack of discrimination. He liked them for saying 'enough of this sickly cant, let us be honest and stick by what is in us', but he disliked them for sticking by 'those things that have been thought horrid, and by those alone. They want to destroy every scrap of tradition and experience, which is silly. They are very young, college-student and medical-student at his most blatant. But I like them. Only I don't believe in them. I agree with them about the weary sickness of pedantry and tradition and inertness, but I don't agree with them as to the cure and the escape. . . . I love them when they say to the child, "All right, if you want to drag nests and torment kittens, do it lustily." But I reserve the right to answer, "All right, try it on. But if I catch you at it you get a hiding." '[10]

He was critical of similar manifestations in what he referred to as a futurist trend in American literature. 'The furthest frenzies of French modernism or futurism have not yet reached the pitch of extreme consciousness that Poe, Melville, Hawthorne, Whitman reached.' Melville could never 'accept the fact that perfect relationships cannot be'. He wanted to consider what 'is' as perfect. Melville was 'ironic, as the epicurean must be. The deep irony of your real scamp: your real epicurean of the moment.' 'It is the material elements he really has to do with. His drama is with them. He was a futurist long before futurism found paint. The sheer naked sliding of the elements. And the human soul experiencing it all. So often it is almost over the border: psychiatry. Almost spurious. Yet so great.' Thus Melville, dominated like the futurist by the conviction that even in contradictions one must find perfection, regarded man as an instrument on which life plays a mad but beautiful music. Lawrence recognized his own community of interest and attitude with Melville even while he was critical, and wrote:

> '. . . he stuck to his ideal guns.
> 'I abandon mine. . . .
> 'I say, let the old guns rot.
> 'Get new ones, and shoot straight.'[11]

Lawrence pointed to the dangers of a similar vein in Walt Whitman, 'Walt was really too superhuman. The danger of the superman is that he is mechanical.' . . . 'The difference between life and matter is that life, living things, living creatures, have the instinct of turning right away from *some* matter, and of blissfully ignoring the bulk of most matter, and of turning towards only some certain bits of specially selected matter.'[12]

In these objections to futurism Lawrence questioned his own trend that was unmistakably revealed in *Women in Love*. In spite of his effort to accept much that was unwelcome, he kept alive his discrimination toward many things. He tried to assimilate what he regarded as inevitable, but he vigorously condemned much that the futurists glorified. Even before the full development of his own futuristic mood he had written that the Alpine shrine commemorating accidents suggested 'something crude and sinister, . . . almost like depravity, a form of reverting, turning back along the course of blood by which we have come'.[13]

This ability to select was his most essential and far-reaching divergence from the futurist outlook.

Lawrence's most obvious difference from the futurists lay in his rejection of our industrial age. He felt that he must come in line with sun and storm, love and hate, life and death; but he could never see why man, having been vastly clever and constructed wonderful things, should now become a servant to his own creations. The futurist has been the prophet of the machine. He has not spoken of it as a means to an end, as a convenient arm of man, but as the crystallization of power before which man should prostrate himself in masochistic delight. He would minister to it as the totem of our age. Like Loerke, the futurist has held that 'Art should interpret industry, as art once interpreted religion'. It was a small step for him to lyricize war machines and mechanized destruction. Lawrence frequently tried to partake of nature's potency by symbolic identification with one of her aspects, much as the primitive tried to partake of the potency of his totem animal, but he could not share the futurist's predilection for enhancing himself through exaltation of, and sacrifice to, mechanical power. This dwarfing of mankind in the service of machines reinforced the futurist's amorality toward men and exaggerated his drive toward sensuous stimulation to the point of self-destruction. In order to live more fully he killed himself more or less literally.

Not only did Lawrence differ from futurists in respecting humanity, in admitting the inevitable partisanship of active man, and in denying the effectiveness of the machine for the enhancement of life, but also he avoided their complete cynicism by trying to see the end beyond the means. If all things hang together, as Birkin believed, then what the futurists regarded as self-justifying deeds Lawrence saw as forces applied toward a resulting effect. He wavered in this belief and often seemed to accept the moment as self-justifying. Yet his frequent glowering and the production of much of his best work in a mood of prophetic anger indicate his belief in some emerging future and in people as having some definite, although only vaguely definable, part in its emergence.

No matter how much he resembled the futurist, Lawrence went beyond him in extent and subtlety of thought. This is particularly true in his frequent explorations of the relationship of opposites and their part in some larger dynamic pattern. He was not willing to accept a confusion of opposites as a resolution of them. He wanted to distinguish between them, especially between the desirable and the undesirable, and yet be basically at one with some universal whole.

SOURCE: *D. H. Lawrence: a basic study of his ideas* (Gainesville, 1955).

NOTES

1. D. H. Lawrence, *Collected Poems* (1932) pp. 303–4.

2. D. H. Lawrence, *The Prussian Officer and Other Stories* (1914) pp. 1–33. Ursula also plumbed this 'real dark bottom' in her terror of the horses, and Loerke lived on 'the rock bottom of all life'.

3. D. H. Lawrence, *The Rainbow* (New York, Modern Library, n.d.) pp. 421, 43–4.

4. D. H. Lawrence, 'The Crown', in *Reflections on the Death of a Porcupine* (Philadelphia, 1925; London, 1934) pp. 5, 54.

5. Kenneth Burke, *Attitudes Toward History* (New York, 1931) I 37–8.

6. D. H. Lawrence, 'The Crown', in *Reflections on the Death of a Porcupine*, pp. 46, 69–76.

7. Friedrich Schürr, 'Die italienische Literatur von 1870 bis zur Gegenwart', a chapter from *Die romanische Literatur des 19 und 20 Jahrhunderts*, II (*c*. 1939), by Schürr and others, in the *Handbuch der Literaturwissenschaft*, ed. Oskar Walzel (Berlin, *c*. 1933–9) pp. 3, 4, 42, 50–69.

8. *The Letters of D. H. Lawrence*, ed. Aldous Huxley (New York, 1936) p. 200.

9. Huxley, Introduction to *Letters*, pp. xxi–xxiii.

10. *Letters*, pp. 197–8.

11. D. H. Lawrence, *Studies in Classic American Literature* (New York, 1930) pp. viii–ix, 208–13, 216.

12. It is interesting to note the similarity of Lawrence's ('Whitman', in *Studies in Classic American Literature*, pp. 243–4) and Kenneth Burke's (*Attitudes Toward History*, I 16–17) estimate of Walt Whitman.

13. D. H. Lawrence, *Twilight in Italy* (New York, 1916) p. 19.

Roger Sale

THE NARRATIVE TECHNIQUE OF
THE RAINBOW (1959)

You mustn't look in my novel for the old stable ego of the character. There is another ego, according to whose action the individual is unrecognisable, and passes through, as it were, allotropic states which it needs a deeper sense than any we've been used to exercise, to discover are states of the same single radically unchanged element.[1]

THIS passage of a letter from D. H. Lawrence to Edward Garnett is often cited in connection with *The Rainbow*, the novel to which it presumably refers. Yet the task of finding literary means to break down 'the old stable ego of character' would seem to be difficult, and it is surprising that no one, at least to the best of my knowledge, has ever attempted to analyze thoroughly the narrative method of *The Rainbow* to see if and how the expression of this 'deeper sense' is possible. We may have become so accustomed to interior monologues, objectifications of dream images, and other ways of accomplishing similar tasks that Lawrence's method, which is certainly unique, may have been accepted as accomplished fact before its constituent features have been identified.

The result of this silence might not be of any great importance were the problem a strictly aesthetic one. But despite the considerable attention that has been paid to various features of the novel, *The Rainbow* remains a relatively undefined quantity. Even worse, the reasons for the marked inferiority of the second half, the fact of which is widely enough accepted, have never been stated. This essay is designed not only to identify the narrative method of *The Rainbow* but also to find a measure of this achievement by discussing when and how the novel begins to deteriorate.

'Rhythm' is a critical term used to denote any movement which is not cumbersome, and I use the term in connection with *The Rainbow* only because the usual references to 'continuity' and 'blood consciousness' give no indication of the basic movements in the novel. There is the same general rhythm in a sentence or a paragraph that there is in the large movements from generation to generation, and it is this essential unity of movement that enables Lawrence to break down the 'old stable ego' and to assert the existence of a 'deeper sense' beneath.

The simplest declarative sentence is one of the main aids the novelist has in building up a stable ego, an identity. For instance: 'Morel found the photograph standing on the chiffonier in the parlor. He came out with it between his thick thumb and finger' (*Sons and Lovers*, ch. v). This makes no reference to egos at all, yet whatever qualities these sentences give to Morel, they are his and his alone. A series of such statements, especially if they form a pattern, create a 'character', a stable ego, however ill-defined this identity may be. In the short conversation that follows between Morel and his wife about the photograph of William's girl, Lawrence builds up a character by virtue of the fact that Morel is separate from his wife, and that he has his own attitudes and ways of speaking. We may infer the Morels' relationship from this conversation, but we do this on the basis of what we know of each person individually.

If we turn to a passage in *The Rainbow*, we can show how Lawrence tries there to break down this natural building-up process: 'And she loved the intent, far look of his eyes when they rested on her: intent, yet far, not near, not with her. And she wanted to bring them near. She wanted his eyes to come to hers, to know her. And they would not.' This is from 'Anna Victrix', the chapter that describes the early months of the marriage of Anna and Will Brangwen in their little cottage. Some differences between this passage and that quoted above from *Sons and Lovers* are clear immediately. It is not enough to be content with saying that one is external and objective and the other internal and subjective. The difficulty we have with the passage from *The Rainbow* is that we know nothing about the time in which it takes place. The verbs seem as though they would be, in a language that provided it, in the imperfect tense. The force of this is achieved by the simple 'when', which gains the sense of 'whenever' as the action proceeds without being temporally specified.

The issue becomes more complex in the next paragraph:

Then immediately she began to retaliate on him. She too was a hawk. If she imitated the pathetic plover running plaintive to him, that was part of the game. When he, satisfied, moved with a proud, insolent slough of the body and a half-contemptuous drop of the head, unaware of her, ignoring her very existence, after taking his fill of her and getting his satisfaction of her, her soul roused, its pinions became like steel, and she struck at him. When he sat on his perch glancing sharply round with solitary pride, pride eminent and fierce, she dashed at him and threw him from his station savagely, she goaded him from his keen dignity of a male, she harassed him from his unperturbed pride, till he was mad with rage, his light brown eyes burned with fury, they saw her now, like flames of anger they flared at her and recognized her as the enemy. (ch. vi)

Here we have a combination of the imperfect 'when', which removes the action from a specific time, and the metaphor of the hawks, which removes the action from its immediate spatial context. In establishing a causal 'when he, then she' relationship, Lawrence breaks down the specific time and replaces it with a tight unity of the two figures at a general time. This effect is enforced by the metaphor. Will sits on his perch; he is mounted on his wife. But in making 'perch' and the subsequent 'station' metaphorical, Lawrence makes the relationship metaphorical. Will is thus perched on Anna not only physically; he is generally in a position from which Anna can 'goad him from his keen dignity of a male'.

In the next short paragraph all time and space are missing: 'Very good, she was the enemy, very good. As he prowled round her, she watched him. As he struck at her, she struck back' (ch. vi). It is difficult to imagine another novel in which the complete withdrawal could be justified, and it is justified here only because the barriers between specific and general time and space have been gradually broken down in the preceding paragraphs. Here Will and Anna are only hawks, divorced from everything except themselves. This is followed by: 'He was angry because she had carelessly pushed away his tools so that they got rusty. "Don't leave them littering in my way, then," she said. "I shall leave them where I like", he cried. "Then I shall throw them where I like!"' (ch. VI). This is the same kind of world as that of *Sons and Lovers*; the time and place are unspecified but fixed. It is impossible to know how we arrived here or how much time has elapsed since the dialogue on the preceding page or since the scene in bed. By the end of the next paragraph, we have returned to general time and space: 'They would fight it out.' The force of this little dialogue comes in part from the fact that we must, despite its obvious specificity, see this too as a metaphor, part of a larger pattern, an action that may well have been repeated in essence many times.

Thus, in less than a page, we move from an action unspecified in time and space, to one in which time and space are ambivalent, to one in which they do not exist, to one in which they are very much present, and back again to one where they are unspecified. We learn not only about particular events, but also about a world in which there is nothing but Will and Anna. It is not enough to say that the particular here is an analogue for the general, because that is true in almost any novel. Will Brangwen ceases to be, for a time, a single person performing acts in a time sequence, and becomes part of something apart from time and of which Anna is a part. As the events become more generalized, the things that are not integral parts of the relationship gradually disappear. It is for this reason that scenes in *The Rainbow* always seem longer than they are. Time is suspended, we leave a scene only to return to it, we learn with some surprise that morning or evening or Sunday comes because much that takes place seems to be happening outside of time.*

* I have ignored here whatever theoretical interest Lawrence shows in this novel about time because it seems to me to have had sufficient attention while the technical uses of time have been almost ignored. On

This constant movement in time continuums, which is the essential narrative technique of *The Rainbow*, allows Lawrence to describe a large segment of time very quickly, and this, in turn, creates the impression that no time is left undescribed, that the sequence of events and relationships is never broken but is only made either more or less definite temporally. For instance, Lawrence says that when Anna was nine years old, she went to the dames' school in Cossethay. Soon she is 'about ten', and two pages later she is a 'lofty demoiselle of sixteen'. But we feel that no time has been skipped, that Lawrence is able to choose his definite times because the indefinite time is so full. The paragraphs which describe Anna from nine to sixteen begin with such sentences as 'For at the Marsh life had indeed a certain freedom and largeness', 'So Anna was only easy at home, where the common sense and the supreme relation between her parents produced a freer standard of being than she could find outside', 'At school, or in the world, she was usually at fault, she felt usually that she ought to be slinking in disgrace', and 'Still she kept an ideal: a free, proud lady absolved from the petty ties, existing beyond petty considerations.' The paragraphs are never complete in themselves; the same subject is approached from a number of different angles and, presumably, at a number of different positions in time. The effect is of great movement, yet of a constant thread of 'unstable ego' unifying the movement.

It is only after we have noticed this 'rhythm' in particular scenes and series of actions that we can see the rhythm of the larger components of the novel, the movements from one generation to another, from an individual towards the larger symbols that exist completely outside of time and space. I will make no effort to cover all of the book, but I should like to show some examples of the way in which the specific movement is expanded into a larger context.*

---

the use of stability in time and space to build up stability of ego, see especially Ian Watt, 'Realism and the Novel', in *Essays in Criticism*, II (1952) 376–96.

* Both F. R. Leavis (*D. H. Lawrence: Novelist* (New York, 1956)

Of the three generations in the novel, Tom Brangwen and Lydia Lensky have the most difficulty in establishing a relationship; yet their success is greater than that of their children or their grandchildren. Their greatest triumph comes when least expected. Tom cannot understand his wife's foreign language and manners and he finds it difficult to communicate with her. One evening he announces that he is going out and Lydia protests that 'You do not want to be with me any more.' He protests weakly, but she continues to attack him: ' "Why should you want to find a woman who is more to you than me?" she said. The turbulence raged in his breast. "I don't," he said. "Why do you?" she repeated. "Why do you want to deny me?" Suddenly, in a flash, he saw she might be lonely, isolated, unsure. She had seemed to him the utterly certain, satisfied, absolute, excluding him. Could she need anything?' (ch. III). They proceed from here to a knowledge of their uncertainty and fear: 'He did not understand her foreign nature, half German, half Polish, nor her foreign speech. But he knew her, he knew her meaning, without understanding' (ch. III). We believe this because of the constant insistence on the relationship to exclusion of time, space, and stability of ego. They reach out to each other in acknowledgment of their failure, and, in so doing, form a rainbow for their daughter:

Anna's soul was put at peace between them. She looked from one to the other, and she saw them established to her safety, and she was free. She played between the pillar of fire and the pillar of cloud in confidence, having the assurance on her right hand and the assurance on her left. She was no longer called upon to uphold with her childish might the broken end of the arch. Her father and her mother now met to the span of the heavens, and she, the child, was free to play in the space beneath, between. (ch. III)

---

pp. 108 ff.) and Mark Spilka ('The Shape of an Arch: A Study of Lawrence's *The Rainbow*', in *Modern Fiction Studies*, 1 (1955) 30–8) discuss at some length the values Lawrence finally asserts in the novel, and any further discussion of the ethics of personal relationships here would be an act of supererogation.

Although Tom and Lydia now join heaven and earth like the rainbow for Anna, the novel is, clearly, already focused on the daughter.

It is in terms of the success of Tom and Lydia that we come to Anna and Will in the next chapter. They realize their love in the scene in which they carry the sheaves across the field in the autumn moonlight:

> Then she turned away towards the moon, which seemed glowingly to uncover her bosom every time she faced it. He went to the vague emptiness of the field opposite, dutifully.
>
> They stooped, grasped the wet, soft hair of the corn, lifted the heavy bundles, and returned. She was always first. She set down her sheaves, making a pent house with those others. He was coming shadowy across the stubble, carrying his bundles. She turned away, hearing only the sharp hiss of his mingling corn. She walked between the moon and his shadowy figure. (ch. IV)

The failure of Will and Anna is implicit in their first love scene. The speed with which they come together contrasts with the painful slowness with which Tom courted Lydia. Anna, set afire by the moon, is always first, looking beyond, while Will follows, like a shadow. The motifs of woman in the light of the heavens-man in the shadow are used earlier in connection with Tom and Lydia and later with Ursula and Anton Skrebensky. Even though the time and place are specified completely here, the larger movement, the reassertion of the relationship between men and women, is apparent.

Through this emphasis on the larger action, individual scenes and generalized actions of different sets of characters become organized into a large single movement. As the second generation takes over, we can see how much of what they do is interpreted in the language used in describing Anna's parents. Their marriage, as indicated in the 'hawk' passage quoted previously, is frustrating and unhappy. Will turns away, tries to establish himself outside the home, and gradually 'his life was shifting its centre, becoming more artificial'. His response to marital frustration is to negate relationships whereas Tom's response was to insist on growth by acknowledging frustration. Anna gains control over Will, but this is fatal. Her 'triumph' comes when, eight months pregnant, she dances naked to the moon in her room, 'like a full ear of corn', and Will 'was burned, he could not grasp, he could not understand'. Lydia, in the face of similar victory, reached out to Tom, but now Anna taunts her husband, forces him from the room; and 'after this day, the door seemed to shut on his mind'.

As a result, 'Anna was indeed Anna Victrix':

Soon, she felt sure of her husband. She knew his dark face and the extent of its passion. She knew his slim, vigorous body, she said it was hers. Then there was no denying her. She was a rich woman enjoying her riches. . . . She forgot that the moon had looked through a window of the high, dark night, and nodded like a magic recognition, signalled to her to follow. Sun and moon traveled on, and left her, passed her by, a rich woman enjoying her riches. She should go also. But she could not go, when they called, because she must stay at home now. . . . If she were not the wayfarer to the unknown, if she were arrived now, settled in her builded house, a rich woman, still her doors opened under the arch of the rainbow, her threshold reflected the passing of the sun and moon, the great travelers, her house was full of the echo of journeying.

She was a door and a threshold, she herself. Through her another soul was coming, to stand upon her as upon the threshold, looking out, shading its eyes for the direction to take. (ch. vi)

The chapter to which this is the close represents one of the great moments in modern fiction. If the irony of 'settled in her builded house, a rich woman' carries anything like the force attributed to it placed as it is against the image of the arch of the rainbow, Anna's failure is a great triumph of Lawrence's method. We back off from a scene in which Anna is crooning to her baby as we back off from so many scenes in the chapter, only to discover that the action is assuming, gracefully and without specific warning, the book's larger symbols; the finality of this moment echoes the finality of the earlier one, and, at the same time, opens the door for the action to come.

In the next two chapters, Ursula comes to the fore as Anna did in chapters III and IV. As before, the parents' marriage, the terms of which have been made clear, is seen through the child, and both Will and Anna try to defeat the other by establishing the stronger relationship with Ursula. Will, defeated here, grows more and more ineffectual; he fails in his job, he fails in his fumbling attempts with other women, and he fails finally to hurt Anna as he would like.

Then, in 'The Marsh and the Flood' the scene shifts back to the home of the elder Brangwens. Tom is caught out in a cloudburst, and we see in his death the final success of his marriage, and, by implication, the final failure of Will and Anna's. But here, for the first time, the forward flow of the novel is checked; the preceding chapter does not lead into it as we have seen was the case in earlier chapters nor does the subsequent chapter lead away from it. At the end of the chapter Lydia describes to Ursula her first marriage, and she insists on the greatness of her love for both her husbands. Ursula cannot understand this, and neither can we see what it is doing here. We are told at the end: 'Ursula was frightened, hearing those things. Her heart sank, she felt she had no ground under her feet. She clung to her grandmother. Here was peace and security. Here, from her grandmother's peaceful room, the door opened on to the greater space, the past, which was so big, that all it contained seemed tiny; loves and births and deaths, tiny units and features within a vast horizon' (ch. IX). Having stopped the movement of the book, Lawrence also contradicts one of the novel's central symbols. The door here, instead of opening on to the 'beyond', the 'rainbow', and, always, the future, opens on to the past, the 'tiny units and features'.

In itself this contradiction might not be important. But it is indicative of more important changes in tone and method that are manifested in subsequent chapters. 'The Marsh and the Flood' serves as a watershed; before it Lawrence is in control, forcing our perception of each experience into a larger series of units, and after it, as we will see, he becomes more tentative and less careful. With Ursula we come to the period in the history which corresponds to Lawrence's own youth. Lawrence now begins to introduce small characters, names of people who are mentioned but who never appear, long conversations that are not worked into the fabric of the shifting verb tenses and the continuity of time. The reason, obviously, is that Lawrence is beginning to transcribe almost directly from his own experience. The twelve-page description of Ursula's conception of Sunday in the Brangwen household is clearly a recording of the Sundays of Lawrence's youth. Leavis writes of this: 'But if it should be necessary to show that there is more to be said about the place of the English Sunday in the history of English civilization, it would be enough to adduce this chapter of *The Rainbow*, so illustrating once again the incomparable wealth of the novel as social and cultural history.'[2] There is no reason, however, why we should demand that *The Rainbow* be a social history at all, and this long passage seems to be placed here as something that Lawrence was interested in – something, indeed, that is interesting – but as nothing that belongs. The very title of the chapter, 'The Widening Circle', illustrates how Lawrence has apparently lost interest in his central theme. What is widened here is completely different from what is widened earlier; both the matter and manner have altered.

There is an attempt to return to the novel's original terms in dealing with Ursula and Skrebensky. But even in the scene in which they make love in the stackyard, which echoes the sheaves-gathering scene with Will and Anna, something is out of control:

And timorously, his hands went over her, over the salt, compact brilliance of her body. If he could but have her, how he would enjoy her! If he could but net her brilliant, cold, salt-burning body in the soft iron of his own hands, net her, capture her, hold her down, how madly he would enjoy her. He strove subtly, but with all his energy, to enclose her, to have her. And always she was burning and brilliant and hard as salt, and deadly. Yet obstinately, all his flesh burning and corroding, as if he were invaded by some consuming, scathing poison, still he persisted, thinking at last he might overcome her. Even, in his frenzy, he sought for her mouth with his mouth, though it was like putting

his face into some awful death. She yielded to him, and he pressed
himself upon her in extremity, his soul groaning over and over.
(ch. XI)

We can applaud the use of the light woman–dark man motifs
of the earlier portions of the novel, but everything else seems
desperately wrong: the strident 'If he could have her, how he
would enjoy her!', the needless vagueness of 'subtly' and 'madly',
the vulgar flatness of 'even in his frenzy, he sought for her mouth
with his mouth', leading to the dismal last line. It is a blessing
that Lawrence had to cut Anton's subsequent, 'Let me come, let
me come' from the later editions. All this contrasts sharply with
the firmness and assurance of the scene with Will and Anna in
the field. The vagueness here is a real vagueness, all the worse
because it is offered to us as a great moment, and it is this kind
of writing that has led so many to impute all manner of disease
to Lawrence from homosexuality to the fascism of the dark gods.

But at the close of this scene, after Ursula tries to bring Anton
'back from the dead', we have this: 'Looking away, she saw the
delicate glint of oats dangling from the side of the stack, in the
moonlight, something proud and royal, and quite impersonal.
She had been proud with them, where they were, she had been
also. But in this temporary warm world of the commonplace,
she was a kind, good girl. She reached out yearningly for goodness and affection. She wanted to be kind and good' (ch. XI).
Here we have the old Lawrence. The insistent 'kind and good',
coming right after Ursula's enormous wilfulness in her subjection
of Anton earlier, is perfect. Like her mother, she has won, she
is now a woman with riches.

Unlike her mother, however, Ursula hates the victory, realizes
that Anton exists for her now 'in her desire only'. All this is the
proper expansion of the theme, the weakness of the shadowy man
and the wilfulness of the brilliant woman. But these terms are
used less and less as the novel proceeds, to be replaced either by
direct transcription from Lawrence's experience, as in the long
chapter dealing with Ursula as a school teacher, in which case the
ego is all too stable, or by the kind of passage quoted above, in

which there is hardly any ego at all – or anything else. Every now and again, as in the scene late in the book in which Ursula and Anton dance on the heath, we have a return to the classic form, and Ursula and her dark lover become, for a moment, the rightful heirs of the two preceding generations of Brangwens. Nevertheless, there is no constant movement of which this episode is a part, and without this the symbols seem pasted on and not, as before, a perfectly legitimate and exciting expansion of the central concerns of the novel.

It is not enough, I think, to say that the shift is justified because Lawrence had reached a period in history when he thought the failure in human relationships was closest to being absolute and that therefore some breakdown was necessary. For one thing Lawrence, if anything, handles the failure of Will and Anna better than he does the success of Tom and Lydia. But the whole vitality and enormous 'felt life' of the first half of the novel is the result of placing human relationships in the foreground; the social history is there, perhaps, but only when it can be utilized in the personal drama. In the second half, social history occasionally becomes an excuse for personal failure, and, even if Lawrence did not know better than this, such speculations have no place in this novel. The colliers, the woman's movements, the ennui of the university – these matters are thrust forward, the characters are moved into the background, and even Ursula becomes shadowy. Lawrence becomes a victim of that tentativeness Leavis has described so well in connection with the novels of the early twenties. He writes on and on, looking for a place to stop, almost as though he were mindless of the methods used and terms established in the first half of the novel.

This criticism, however, in no way mars our sense of the achievement of the first eight chapters. As long as Lawrence maintains his position *as a novelist*, as an artist with a new way to describe human experience, it is difficult to say too much for him. To use Leavis' terms, *The Rainbow* adds something as only a work of genius can. The assertion of the supreme importance of human relationships finds its formal counterpart in the flow, the constant motion in time, the dramatic description of eternal movement in human experience as it reaches outward, through the door, towards the rainbow.

SOURCE: *Modern Fiction Studies*, v (1959).

NOTES

1. D. H. Lawrence, *Selected Literary Criticism*, ed. Anthony Beal (New York, 1956) p. 18.
2. F. R. Leavis, *D. H. Lawrence: Novelist* (New York, 1956) p. 159.

S. L. Goldberg

THE RAINBOW:
FIDDLE-BOW AND SAND (1961)

> ... don't look for the development of the novel to follow the lines of certain characters: the characters fall into the form of some other rhythmic form, as when one draws a fiddle-bow across a fine tray delicately sanded, the sand takes lines unknown. (Lawrence to Edward Garnett, 5 June 1914.)

ALTHOUGH Lawrence himself warned us never to trust the artist but to trust the tale, or that 'there may be didactic bits, but they aren't the novel', with his own work it isn't quite so easy to distinguish. The common tactic, of course, is to try to split him into two Lawrences: such a good novelist, before he became a tiresome whiskery prophet. Yet really there was only one Lawrence, and the critic can't avoid dealing with him whole – even, indeed especially, in *The Rainbow* and *Women in Love*: if the Imagination is the whole soul of man in activity, the novelist's intellect partly shapes his work and his will guides it towards conclusions. 'Prophecy', in these two books particularly, is infused in the 'novel': to assess them we have to assess the total result, 'prophecy' and all – which means, in effect, discriminating the constructive forms of the art itself. For the 'prophecy' is compounded subtly and not always deliberately. It lies, for example, in the very disposition of the chapters, in narrative 'method', in the formal shape of plot, in the symbolic patterns: is more effective there, indeed, than in overt emphases and commentary. And it is these aspects of *The Rainbow*, the effects of the fiddle-bow on the sand, that I want to explore a little, not simply in order to underline their 'prophetic' function, but to weigh their relevance to the work as a whole. For the indisputable greatness of *The Rainbow* (indisputable, that is, since Dr Leavis showed what it is) is also, as Leavis himself suggests, in the end limited; and what limits it, I think, emerges most clearly if we examine the relation of form and idea in the book. It is not the prophetic vision, which inspires it throughout, nor Lawrence's experimental approach, which leads him to transgress against the accepted formalities of the novel, nor his attempt to render experiences that perhaps cannot be rendered at all; not his actual criticisms of modern society, nor even his uncertainty about what, finally, he wants to say. The limiting factor (which underlies some of these things) is rather his developing *over*-certainty about what he wants to say, the rising note of asserted will, his insistence on *putting* lines in the sand, which eventually comes to oversimplify his insight – in short, the drastic results of getting his prophetic vision (as he would say) 'in the head'.

I

Despite its general impression of spontaneous, exploratory freedom, *The Rainbow* is also constructed as an 'argument', solidly and intellectually wrought; but it is easy to overlook the most elementary way in which that argument is built up – the basic unit of the *chapter*. Each chapter of the book crystallizes one of Lawrence's fundamental intuitions about life, and their sequence embodies one kind of relation he sees between those intuitions – a kind of argumentative logic. Of course, the chapters do not crudely illustrate his 'beliefs' one by one, but establish, specify, define his insights in dramatic terms; if he generally adds more explicit commentary than a strictly 'dramatic' novelist in the line of Flaubert or James would, it is only offered *ex post facto*, as an intellectual summation of what is presented to the imagination. His 'philosophic' insights pervade and shape the action, and they do so in such a way that the individual chapters really perform a double function: to trace the unbroken line of natural growth, with its eddies and returns, over the generations of Brangwens, unfolding the stages of human experience; and at the same time, to unfold Lawrence's thematic purpose, to mark the stages in the total argumentative sweep of the novel.

As a 'story', the book is naturally divided by the three generations that form its subject-matter; as an 'argument', it also falls
into three main sections; but the two kinds of division overlap.
Again, where the over-all pattern of the story is a gradual opening
outwards, a widening range, the thematic pattern is a gradual
concentrating, a process of clarification and application. From the
opening chapter itself the Brangwens' life emerges as the image
of a human norm (a dynamic norm, not a static ideal), a richly
imagined symbol that assumes, in relation to the rest of the book
(and even to Lawrence's whole *œuvre*), the force of an argumentative premise: *here* is human being fulfilling itself within, and in
vital connection with, its context of impersonal natural forces
and social traditions. The following four chapters develop this
image; the 'dark' eternal forces of physical life, selfhood, marriage, the mutual implication of growth and decline, the relevant
social traditions, the limited consciousness of this rural generation, are all felt and realised, given a specific, though provisional,
definition. The thematic unfolding continues unbroken even
through the shift in the story at chapter IV, where Anna's spontaneous development begins to emerge, until it is at last recapitu-
lated in the wedding-scene at the end of chapter V. From there,
however, Lawrence begins the process of analysis he saw as his
new direction in this book, seeking now (through Anna and
Will) to clarify and define more explicitly terms that have become
problematical, have turned into issues. An earlier harmony of
forces collapses into a sterile victory for one; the natural and the
transcendental, the past and the present, tend to fall apart. Again
the thematic 'argument' is carried through the story's gradual
shift to Ursula (in chapter VIII) until it reaches (in chapter X) the
nature of the vital 'religious' sense she has absorbed from still
present traditions – a sense that will develop in her both as the
result, and as the touchstone, of her subsequent experience. And
at this point – heavily marked by an intruded, rather parsonical
rhapsody from Lawrence – the central theme has become clearly
manifest within the action. As the opening of chapter XI openly
indicates, this is the first major turn in the *thematic* progress of
the book: up to here, Lawrence has been concerned to define

modes of a genuinely organic, 'religious' vitality; from here, his subject is its present viability. He has now reached his destination – the critical exploration of the modern world.

This he undertakes through Ursula's experience of it, and particularly through her gradual penetration to the vital meaning of *love*. It is not, as she discovers, any merely sensual awakening (ch. XI); not the perverse, intellectualised, narcissistic indulgence to which our mechanical, collective society tends to corrupt it (ch. XII); not the fruitless idealism of personal relationships (ch. XIII); not the stagnant, in-turned warmth of the family (ch. XIV); not even a 'dark' sexual ecstasy which, engaging only part of the total self, is also doomed to sterility (ch. XV). And thus she (and the novel) reach a conscious articulation of the issues that guide the whole book. In the last chapter, her almost ritual trial crystallises one of its basic implications – the connection, and the difference, between vital moral consciousness and vital animal energy – and, concluding her *via negativa*, it leaves her at last clarified in herself, in a state of vital receptivity, as it were.

This argumentative drive of *The Rainbow* is of course only one of its various structures, and Lawrence manages it far more subtly, gives it far more life, than I have been able to suggest. But even to note it so briefly is perhaps enough to suggest how central a rôle his 'ideas' play in the work, how pervasive is his intellectual control of his material. The programmatic aspect of certain sections has often been noted; in fact, though it is not always equally obvious, Lawrence's control is continuous all through. (Considering his many rewritings, it would be surprising if it were not.) Even if we don't consciously notice its unremitting presence, nevertheless we feel it, for it is a large part of his characteristic intensity. He strikes straight to the basic realities as he sees them, and never lets go; the book bears a single-minded purposiveness, the concentrated force of a profoundly serious philosophic imagination. Clearly, his well-known remark in *Lady Chatterley's Lover* has a direct relevance to *The Rainbow*: properly handled, the novel can 'inform and lead into new places the flow of our sympathetic consciousness and can lead our sympathy away in recoil from things gone

dead. . . .' As always, the critical problems Lawrence raises are
those of an art deliberately and fully dedicated to *leading*.

II

At its most characteristic, Lawrence's narrative reaches through
outward behaviour, and even inner feelings, desires, or values,
to the unseen direction in which these things move, the ends they
express but also subserve. It is the texture and the flow of
vitality, the whole 'man alive', rather than the circumstances
and cruces of moral decision, that concern him; so that the Craft
of Fiction is less to his purposes than a responsive, plastic,
rhythmic *flow* which (as one critic has recently pointed out)
constantly shifts and submerges specific time and place in the
action, blends scene, narrative, analysis, description, and can
give appropriate weight to any manifestation of life in a living
universe. Nor is it only the sense of growth (as with Anna and
Ursula) that Lawrence can make us feel so subtly by this means;
the same flow also serves his more analytical purposes (as in
'Anna Victrix' or 'The Bitterness of Ecstasy'), where he renders
not only continuity in length, as it were, but continuity in depth
as well. The conventions of situation, climax, dénouement, are
largely replaced by a continuous interplay, a counterpointing, of
different 'levels' of experience – of the 'old stable ego' and the
impersonal 'carbon', for instance, or the everyday world and the
Sunday world, conventionally social 'realism' and visionary
depth – for Lawrence's theme is the whole organic complexity
of life (the rainbow, the arch), not the supreme importance of
any one element. And at his best, the various planes do interfuse:
the social realities of institutions and public relationships; the
moral realities expressed in traditions, memory, choice; the
individual realities of emotion, desire, growing awareness; and
the over-arching realities, the vast, impersonal forces of life and
death. The natural and the religious vision combine, the one
giving the other definition and executive power, the other in turn
(to use Forster's excellent term) *irradiating* the details of life
with the profoundest significance.

'The novel', as Lawrence said, 'is the highest example of subtle inter-relatedness that man has discovered'; and the real achievement of *The Rainbow* lies just where that organic view of art is given meaning in the organic view of life it expresses. In the first chapter of all, for instance, the dynamic inter-relations of life are both projected by and embodied in the art itself. The episode of Tom's proposal to Lydia, as Leavis has remarked, only crystallises the meaning of the whole: everything, from the weather and the falling dusk, the details of Tom's preparations, the curious personal suspension of the characters, to the final view of the night sky as Tom leaves, is – and is felt to be – integral to the chapter and the theme alike. Writing of this kind we can only perhaps compare vaguely with 'Myth', or call (in Leavis's sense) 'dramatic poem'.

Yet *The Rainbow* also includes a rather different sort of art. In other places, the action seems dominated by the determination to make some point conceived outside it, seems designed to embody that point and that point only, and therefore appears slightly factitious, manufactured. The landscape through which Ursula and Skrebensky walk just before their discussion of social issues in chapter XI – a passage Leavis praises for its symbolic subtlety – seems to me to reveal a touch of careful stage-management such as nowhere appears in, say, the first three chapters. Ursula and Skrebensky's visit to the barge after their discussion is another case. Leavis describes Lawrence's general method perfectly: statement and explicit analysis, as he says, are secondary, and 'owe their force, as they come in the book, to the dramatically and poetically rendered significances they resume. We have here, in fact, one of the characteristic methods (a triumphantly successful one) of *Women in Love*. The statement or analysis relates immediately to what has been said in the discussion of the same themes between the actors, discussion that comes with perfect dramatic naturalness and has its completion and main force in some relevant episode or enactment. We have an instance in the episode of the barge in the chapter, "First Love".' But these valuations (applied to *The Rainbow*) are perhaps more doubtful than Leavis allows. Leaving aside for the moment the question

whether Skrebensky is 'done' fairly as well as dramatically and
poetically, the phrase 'some relevant episode or enactment' surely
needs qualification. For is it not precisely the *quality* of the relevance that occasionally seems so limited? Such an episode as this
barge scene is certainly relevant; it is even rendered 'dramatically';
but it is a relevance that appears with a disconcerting promptness
and obviousness. Vivid and sharp though the scene is, its inter-
relations with its context are comparatively simple and clear-cut;
we feel the 'drama' as *instrumental*, a function of Lawrence's
argumentative intent. We must be careful not to confuse the
moral power of the 'argument' too readily with the imaginative
power of the art. For the confusion is possible, I think, with
many other passages as well – the scenes enacting Will's com-
pensatory use of Ursula, for example, or the values enacted by
Winifred Inger, uncle Tom Brangwen, Wiggiston, or Brinsley
St School. The writing here has a clarity, a broad, swingeing
effectiveness; the implicit values are pressed sharply home; but
whereas the sort of 'enactment' to be found in the first chapter,
despite its argumentative direction, seems to exhibit a genuine
'negative capability' – a capacity to let things be themselves and
speak in all complexity for themselves – this other seems to rely
on a different capacity, more intellectual but narrower – a
capacity to generalise by means of relevant particulars. It is a
difference that suggests some further distinctions.

III

If we have to call *The Rainbow* a 'dramatic poem', we also have
to see it as a novel. For a large part of the book we do not need
to bother about how faithful Lawrence is to social or psychological probability; as we can see, he is concerned to achieve a truth,
to explore human experience, at a profounder level than that.
His vision of life extends beyond any of its particular contin-
gencies – even though, of course, it is realised only by means of
them. But the book gradually shifts into another key as he also
begins to use that vision as a critical touchstone, and when it does
so we *do* have to bother about its accuracy to the social and

psychological facts it criticises. Lawrence enters the traditional
field of the novel – our familiar, everyday world, where we relate
people's values to what they are, and where the novelist has to
give people, beliefs, principles, forces, a socially representative
significance, and in simple honesty to confront them with the
recalcitrant facts, with representative opposing people, beliefs,
principles, and forces. Perhaps it is being unduly suspicious of
terms like 'dramatic poem' and 'myth' to insist on calling *The
Rainbow* a novel; but we do well to remember that the artist has
not only to dramatise his themes, but to do so with complete
integrity to his chosen material, his 'sand'. In directing *The
Rainbow* to the familiar social material of the novel, no doubt
Lawrence tried to achieve that integrity; I very much doubt,
however, whether he actually did. Beside the taut honesty of
Women in Love or many of the *Tales*, parts of *The Rainbow* –
and a great deal of its second half – seem to me (as they have
seemed to others) significantly weak in definition and in dramatic
power.

The first signs of this appear just where Lawrence begins to
shift key: most particularly, in the treatment of Anna and Will.
Brilliant as his presentation of their conflict is, he is hardly precise
about one important issue: how far his characters are morally
responsible for themselves or their common failure. His attention
is directed to the level of experience where we cannot finally
distinguish between necessity and freedom, between unconscious
forces that cause individual behaviour, and life-values that direct
it, values that are in some sense chosen. Hence the peculiar way
the characters seem to be both helpless and wilful. Yet there are
times when we may wonder if Lawrence isn't perhaps shuttling
between the two points of view rather than mediating between
them – treating his characters at some points as genuinely 'free'
individuals whose behaviour and values are convincing enough
to elicit our moral judgment, and at others as symbols embodying
irreconcilable forces of existence that we can only accept for
what they are. Of course, to present various life-values to us as
both necessary and in different contexts right, he must do both;
but one result (which he never took much pains to avoid anyway)

is that, in his double attitude to character, he may seem to be judging human essences with an arrogant God's-eye simplicity rather than merely urging certain values. In any case, by his very concentration on this level of experience – the level at which most of our ethical and social dilemmas have both their beginning and their end – he also raises an old familiar question, which is a more radical one than he seems always to realise. For if our life-values are somehow fated to us, can our conscious choice among competing life-values be real or effectual? To go on and insist, as Lawrence does, that such choice is not only effectual but urgently necessary, is to raise problems that need subtler thought – thought on what we may call a *political* level – than he offers in *The Rainbow*.

It is unresolved difficulties of this sort, I think, that cause a slight strain, a tremor, in the writing – a sense that his ultimate judgments (for example, that on Will Brangwen) seem rather arbitrary, that he is beginning to force the issues. At various points of the book the same kind of tremor appears as a stylistic flaw. Lawrence's peculiar jargon, his repetitions, his pseudo-Biblical cadences, and what is often called (obscurely, though always angrily) his 'sheer bad writing', have been frequently attacked; but in themselves they are only part of his characteristic idiom. It is where they obtrude very noticeably – and this happens only occasionally – that they indicate a real weakness: a degree of over-pitched insistence, an extravagant verbal energy that is devoted not to rendering the action dramatically, but to forcing a special sense of it. The most striking examples, of course, are some of the sexual encounters, like the kiss of Ursula and Skrebensky in chapter xv, after he returns to Nottingham; here the style, and the style alone, with an almost obsessive insistence, tries to convey the profound, dark, 'fecund' depths to which Ursula is carried, while the dramatic context (not to mention Lawrence's own criticisms of the characters' relationship) leaves no doubt just how unlikely they are to reach such profound levels of vitality at all. But the strain appears on other occasions as well: in the Resurrection sermon at the end of chapter x, for example, or in the rainbow vision in the last few pages of the book.

Obviously, more is involved than Lawrence's view of certain sexual experiences. Whenever he tries to impose a value on a dramatic situation other than the situation itself conveys, or tries to make sure we do not miss a point so important that he feels he can't trust the tale to convey it by itself – that is to say, whenever he relies on language instead of drama – the writing betrays the same over-excitement. His all-embracing vision of life constantly tends to reduce the action to a symbolic instrument; while the reduction is actually in process, the writing seems to be urging merely personal attitudes, to achieve only a compulsive, inspirational lyricism.

But if the style of *The Rainbow* suffers only intermittently, the effect on its social implications, deeply embedded as they are in the whole work, is more far-reaching; and in Ursula's vision of the rainbow at the end there culminates a weakness that is obviously more than stylistic and is also more than local. Again it begins to emerge at the point of modulation, in chapter VII ('The Cathedral'), where the social bearings of the action shift with a rather obscure logic: is it really clear how ecstatic, transcendental 'spirituality', the failure of nineteenth-century manhood to live with its own Industrialism, nineteenth-century Christianity, Christianity in general, and perhaps any universal system or institution, are related to each other? The uncertainty here isn't vital perhaps, but in the light of what follows it is at least symptomatic.

The other end of the process, the emotional falsity of the last few pages, is so glaring that every critic has remarked on it. Leavis, for example, mentions the limiting 'kind of commentary provoked by that ending', though he doesn't himself develop it or think it more than peripheral. He argues (as I understand him) that the 'radical mood' of those pages was left behind by Lawrence long before he reached the end of the book; that it is really only a momentary lapse, a sign of Lawrence's inability to find a suitable note, in the mood he was now in, to conclude what he had actually done; that the passage is so strikingly false, in fact, because its mood is incongruous with the rest of the book. But is it so incongruous or so incidental? Does not the same radical

mood pervade and weaken most of the second half? And is it not
built into the very structure of the whole?

No one has discussed better than Leavis himself the way
Lawrence develops the subtle, complex relationships between
each of the three Brangwen generations, the vividly realised
values and problems that recur and develop, the meaning of
continuity and change, the continuous influence of the past, the
widening circle of interest, the growing burden of consciousness
– in short, all the rhythms caught up in the book's triple-turning,
opening spiral. But of course Lawrence's object is not simply a
superior, profounder kind of 'realism' (beating the family-sagas,
the Arnold Bennett's, at their own game). He renders the processes of life as truly as he can, but he does so largely in order to
support upon that certain judgments about the modern world.
The book moves towards its argumentative conclusion in its
apparently *natural* turn to the 'modern' experience of Ursula.
(After all, what is there about the predicament of Anna and Will
that belongs so specifically, so exclusively, to *their* generation
and society?) The movement of natural growth is intertwined
with the movement of the argument, visibly so, indeed, at the
beginning of chapter XI. At the same point, moreover, the focus
of attention shifts from the interplay of life-values available to all,
to the conflict between the values of society and the deep, but
unformulated, religious sense of the individual.

Such a split between the individual and his society is simply
one of the facts of our age; nevertheless, a good deal depends on
how we define it and how far back we trace it. And Lawrence's
critique of modern society in *The Rainbow* develops with a
number of expectations, which are really assumptions, implicit
in its spiral structure. The tacit intention, if it can be called by so
definite a term, is for us naturally to expect the terms of Ursula's
problems to be at least similar to those of the earlier Brangwen
generations. We are to take her as the embodiment of the vital
process so subtly rendered earlier; the very impetus of the action
sweeping forward gives her a symbolic authority as the new
embodiment of life. We are not to question her basic vitality
even while we see it clarified by a series of experimental mistakes;

we are to endorse the underlying mood of her response to experience. And we are also led to expect that that experience, the values, forces, attitudes she meets, will be truly representative of the modern world. In short, her basic attitudes are to assume moral authority because they seem natural, inevitable. She is the chosen vessel of 'vitality'.

All this is obvious enough perhaps, and in itself only to say how Lawrence tries to give his social judgments moral force. The moral strategy of *The Rainbow* is not very complicated. Yet to put it so baldly may help, I think, to explain the dissatisfaction I feel with the *art* of the last five chapters of the book, a dissatisfaction that isn't simply an ideological objection to Lawrence's judgments (as it happens, I agree with most of them), or to the length of his treatment. It is rather closer to Leavis's observation that certain issues are proposed in *The Rainbow* that Lawrence was still incapable of dealing with. Certainly one reason why *Women in Love* is the finer book is its greater maturity, but these issues are just as central to *The Rainbow*, and what limits its achievement is surely Lawrence's belief that he was capable of dealing with them. The 'dramatic poem', in which he realises a timeless, universal vision of life, when it narrows down to criticise a particular society, where the specific facts of time and place are of the essence, becomes rather like a social *fable* – an application, an exposition, of values, rather than a dramatic exploration. As a critique of *society*, the second half of *The Rainbow* comes closer to *Hard Times* or *The Secret Agent* than to *Middlemarch* or *The Possessed*. The attitudes it endorses are not rigorously tested in dramatic opposition. Ursula has the world brought to her passively; it never kicks back hard; and of course the real judgment on it is already implicit in that very passivity. Her apparent freedom from the social phenomena she rejects also works to prejudge the issues. Lawrence's 'reverence for life', his sense of the organic complexity of experience and of natural continuity, magnificently realised as they earlier are, do not really validate either his specific judgments of modern society or the implicit assumption that genuine 'vitality' must be radically and totally at odds with all its values and institutions.

The truth is that *The Rainbow* offers not a critique of modern society, as Lawrence seems to have thought, but an explosive, outraged protest against it – with all the disturbing over-simplifications that implies. One is the over-simplification of representative fact. Skrebensky, for example, is little more than an illustrative collection of attitudes; he is certainly not realised fully enough to bear the weight of implication Lawrence tries to erect upon him. And some critics, even while prepared to agree with Lawrence that the values Skrebensky represents are vicious, have properly questioned if this is imaginatively established simply by associating them with a personal nullity as marked as his. But the issue goes even deeper just because that nullity seems so equivocal. For if Skrebensky were more fully realised, would this not involve a more subtle – but perhaps inconvenient – discrimination among his values? Winifred Inger is another case of the same kind: is Feminism or Humanism in itself only a symptom of perversity, to be rejected *in toto*? Could such attitudes not express, in however limited a way, vitality in some people, sterility in others? Does Brinsley St School represent all that modern society could permit in education? Once again, Lawrence is not entirely wrong, but discriminations that need to be made are not made. To Ursula, he says at one point (with no apparent irony), 'the vote was never a reality. She had within her the strange, passionate knowledge of religion and living far transcending the limits of the automatic system that contained the vote.' The vote won't save us, we can agree; yet does Lawrence show it so totally irrelevant to social life that we have to dismiss it as part of an 'automatic system'? A transcendence that takes so little along with it on so ambitious a flight seems a curious form of 'vitality'.

That vitality *is* imaginatively realised in Ursula's progressive rejections of merely sensual or merely intellectual experience, in her gradual conscious realisation of what she is seeking, and in the two important scenes by moonlight with Skrebensky. Even so, Lawrence tends to give her specific feelings far more authority than they warrant. She sweeps Winifred Inger's liberal humanism aside as she sweeps the vote aside: she cannot desire mere 'love' or mere power; she wants to be like lions and wild horses rather than lambs or doves; yet, although her desires echo Anna's and the story later on endorses them, they don't in themselves focus the critical light very sharply. She comes to feel critical of Nottingham University College: 'the religious virtue of knowledge was become a flunkey to the god of material success'; perhaps so, but nothing we are actually shown supports her feeling, and nothing really qualifies it. This tendency sometimes appears with an almost disarming frankness, as when Ursula ponders her past: 'She did not know what she was. Only she was full of rejection, of refusal. Always, always she was spitting out of her mouth the ash and grit of disillusion, of falsity.' Lawrence, indeed, all too often presents an asserted disillusion in the character for an evident falsity in society.

Of course he continually criticises her mistakes, her *affaires* with inadequate values, her immature, inarticulate thrashings about. On the other hand, however, her underlying attitudes, her 'good heart' as it were, escape criticism altogether. Her characteristic Luddite reaction to industrialism, for instance, ranges from impotent fury to tearful sentiment, but it is never critically placed; nor is the equally sentimental violence that catches, in the surrounding darkness, at the gleam of savage animal eyes, of flashing swords of overpowering 'angels', like fangs, 'not to be denied'. The wholesale destructiveness she unleashes on Skrebensky is just this radical, apocalyptic mood in action. And what is remarkable is not her adolescence, but Lawrence's readiness to identify himself with her. The 'vitality' this part of the book offers, in fact, seems so opposed to industrial society that it doesn't prompt any fine awareness of its complexities or those of the people who try to live in it. (Poor Skrebensky! it turns out, after all, that *God* had created him that way and you can't make an angel of the lord out of a sow's ear.) Even apart from the question of how far the individual can change his own life-values is the more immediate question of his power to affect the society of which he is a part. Against those who represent their society fully, the Skrebenskys, the Winifred Ingers, the uncle Tom Brangwens, the irrevocably lost, are the Ursulas, alienated and struggling towards full humanity. But what about the horrible Harbys or the people of Wiggiston, those who are shown to be very much of the system and yet, as Lawrence occasionally insists (he certainly doesn't demonstrate), are mainly its victims: 'like creatures with no more hope, but which still live and have passionate being, within some utterly unliving shell'? Is it too much of a parody to sum up his pervasive suggestion as, that the 'unliving shell', the whole 'automatic system that contains the vote', has to be smashed open (somehow); it *will* be (somehow), by human vitality itself; and although (somehow) it has no visible social embodiment, that vitality still lies deep (somewhere) inside (some) people? Applied to modern society, metaphors of eggs and nuts, however 'organic' they are, can involve a grievous fuzziness.

It may seem absurdly irrelevant to press Lawrence in this way when he is only urging questions, not writing a political programme. But we can't avoid the terms in which he puts those questions; and it is precisely these same romantic assumptions, this impatience and vagueness, that reach their culmination in the last pages of the book. The hollow rhetoric there emerges inevitably from the social attitudes of the last five chapters or so; and through them it is also related, I think, to certain aspects of the whole work. If we were to look at the opening pages, for example, as the actual representation of English society, could we deny a significant golden, paradisal haze about it, a touch of nostalgic softening . . . ?

IV

Not all the lines in the sand are equally unknown or equally deep; and we may gauge the depth of Lawrence's imaginative insight by the symbols it creates no less than by the inter-relatedness of the action or its social implications. The broad distinction, I think, lies between programmatic symbolism like that of the rainbow (or arch or doorway), or the Cathedral (church, spire), and other symbols, equally recurrent, but less visibly manipulated, more organic. The first sort seem rather like leitmotifs, which provide a kind of unity only at the expense of a certain artificiality. They are given meaning by the action; they are carefully used; but their power to concentrate and radiate meaning is limited by the air of conscious deliberation that accompanies them. The chapter on 'The Cathedral', for example, partly does, as Leavis claims, create and explore its own significance. Yet beneath its subtlety, the writing seems rather too sure about its final destination, rather unresponsive to other possible attitudes (which isn't, of course, incompatible with vagueness elsewhere); so that, despite the fact that the Church, the pointing spire, is part of the Brangwens' life from the beginning, or that it is at Rouen, for instance, with its cathedral 'which knew no transience nor heard any denial', that Ursula begins to break from the sensual bond with Skrebensky, the symbol itself still seems something of a *device*. So, too, with the rainbow-arch-doorway imagery, even though early on it arrives as organic metaphor and then recurs through the whole book; or the wild horses, where early metaphor later becomes rather obvious symbol. The effect here is less of rhythm than of design.

Other symbols, however, do seem to arise spontaneously and to continue to work more flexibly. The imagery of *birds*, for example, which runs all through the Anna–Will section, is never heavily underlined (even in its most explicit use, the episode of the fighting blue-caps), but its effective meaning is established with a delicate strength that maintains it through the book. Again, the three or four major scenes involving the *moon* have a disturbing power characteristic only of Lawrence: the capacity to create symbolism of this order is at the centre (though it is by no means the whole) of his imaginative achievement. He makes no attempt here to comment discursively or even to probe. We could cite his *ex post facto* remarks about the moon in *Fantasia of the Unconscious*, but the novel itself actually weaves together the human sexual rhythms and the corn glistening in the darkness or the movement of the sea, while the moon beats down its signal, its challenge, of 'almost malignant apartness'. If the scene with Anna and Will is less wrought-up than those with Ursula and Skrebensky, all enact quite explicit themes, yet they do so with no contrived or superficial relevance. In the end, we can't explain their meaning in other terms any more than Ursula or even Lawrence could; their power derives from a full, firm grasp of experience, a vision that remains irreducibly poetic.

The related symbolism of *darkness* illustrates how Lawrence can successfully evolve prophetic argument from within prophetic vision so long as his use of the symbol – urgent and insistent as it is sometimes – remains faithful to what is deeply imagined, never committing it to a significance narrower than he has in fact created. That significance emerges from the total action of the early chapters particularly: at the end of chapter 1, Tom's apartness from Lydia and the passion that draws them together to their long, dark, marital embrace, are reflected in the dynamic elements themselves – in the flying darkness of the clouds and the terrible liquid-brilliance of the moon. In the next chapter, darkness is the element of withdrawal, and of birth, fecundity, a sensual vitality in harmony with a deep moral vitality as well; Tom, in the pain of loss, watches Anna and Will embrace by night in the fowl-loft; at night, he is overborne by the flood: the symbol assumes meaning without strain, apparently without conscious intent. Yet it gradually becomes more explicit, deployed more openly, as in 'The Cathedral', or when Ursula and Skrebensky kiss, or in the 'darkness' surrounding present consciousness, or in the constant juxtaposition of 'dark' with 'fecund', 'flame', and the like. Nevertheless, Lawrence's desire to generalise and direct does not here falsify the organic wholeness of his grasp. The symbol expresses complexities that still remain complex; emphatic insistence and repetition do not destroy its felt significance, a poetic rhythm genuinely there.

The actual discriminations to be made in *The Rainbow* are not simple. As I have tried to suggest, Lawrence's 'prophetic' impulse doesn't simply overtake and then wholly dominate his imagination. *The Rainbow* is profoundly original and profoundly meaningful because of, not in spite of, the pervasive presence of intellect; and 'prophecy' – radical insight, judgment, emphasis – is its very condition. Nor is it simply that the art weakens when Lawrence turns, in the second half, from universal to local issues.

That is broadly true perhaps, but not entirely, for Lawrence is right to insist on their vital continuity and only provokes criticism when he fails to realise that continuity imaginatively – when, in fact, he falls victim to the very situation he attacks. The elements of the whole 'man alive', alive in his social relations as in his individual, passional consciousness, fall apart; 'blood-relationships' become 'mere spirit or mind'. Sometimes Lawrence seems to know our situation so well that he wants only to refuse it; exploration of it from within lapses into analysis of it from without; and so he comes to over-simplify the subtle inter-relatedness even of our life, however sick. The result – an art of serious 'fable' – usually demands both attention and respect (though it only adumbrates the success of *Women in Love*). Occasionally, although we can understand and even endorse his mood, his undifferentiating violence compromises the values it is meant to serve, and the art fails to integrate insight and moral intent on any level. Where Lawrence is most deeply at one, however, *The Rainbow* does possess a magnificent and challenging vitality. In the end, Lawrence's greatness is that he gives us the reality by which we can judge him.

SOURCE: *Essays in Criticism*, XI, no. 4 (1961).

G. Wilson Knight

'THROUGH...DEGRADATION TO A NEW HEALTH'–A COMMENT ON *WOMEN IN LOVE (1961)*

THE public ratification of *Lady Chatterley's Lover* must not be allowed to obscure the book's sexual challenge. Lawrence is too often regarded as an apostle only of a revitalised normality; but his meanings are sometimes less simple, and after narrating a number of normal sexual encounters between Lady Chatterley and Mellors the story reaches its climax in an engagement of a different kind.

Earlier engagements have been given the natural sexual associations of softness, peace and fluidity, of floods, waves and undulatory motion (x 138–9; XII 181; my page numerals refer to the 1960 Penguin edition). The new engagement has associations of earth, rock, the metallic, heavy ore, smelting, fire and savagery. The contrast is precise.

We have been carefully prepared for it by a repeated emphasis on the posterior locations which will appear to be involved (x 130; XII 180, 182, 184; XIV 218; XV 229), leading up to thought of the woman's buttocks during a dance as being 'offered in a kind of homage' to the man, followed by the man's caress of 'fire' on the two 'secret *entrances*' of and 'openings *to*' her body (my italics, XV 230–3). Then the new consummation is attained (XVI 258–9). The experience is to be distinguished from 'love' and even 'voluptuousness' and associated instead with 'sensuality', 'fire', 'death', and – applied to the man – 'devil'. Through assaulting the 'oldest shames' in 'the most secret places' the man mines into the 'bed-rock' of the woman's physical being; and we are told that it is good so to 'burn out false shames and smelt out the heaviest ore of the body into purity'. There is a penetration into the 'very heart of the jungle' where exist the being's 'roots'; this, 'the core of the physical jungle' of herself, is also 'the last and deepest recess of organic shame'. That an entrance other than the normal is intended is suggested by the phrase 'this phallic hunting out'; and depth by saying that 'the phallos alone could explore it'. The 'sensuality' is 'awful', but cathartic: Lawrence once, on 12 February 1915, wrote in a letter to Bertrand Russell that the use of another's body for 'mere sensation' led naturally to sodomy, and though the vein was there one of disapprobation, the theme is the same and similarly associated with 'rock' (Harry T. Moore, *The Intelligent Heart* (Penguin, 1960) III 235, I 83). This experience Lady Chatterley now realises that she has always unconsciously desired 'at the bottom of her soul, fundamentally'; the words are exactly chosen. The writing has compression, density, and precision.

The integration of this episode within the story's structure shows a more studied and patterned artistry than is usual in Lawrence's major designs. It is carefully prepared for, and reverberates afterwards. Now that the meaning has been poetically established, it is driven home by Mrs Bolton's letter on the rumours regarding Mellors' past actions of 'sensuality' with his separated wife, which Lady Chatterley immediately relates to her own experience with him (XVII 276). Even more explicit is her husband Clifford Chatterley's letter (XVII 277–82) on these 'unspeakable things' which include 'unusual sexual postures' and using a wife, 'as Benvenuto Cellini says, "in the Italian way" '. Under the embarrassment of these scandalous rumours in which he appears to be regarded as a second 'Marquis de Sade' – the letter also associates him with Rabelais – Mellors, he says, now goes about like a dog with a tin can tied to his tail, and though he pretends unconcern must be inwardly repeating 'like Don Rodrigo in the Spanish ballad: "Ah, now it bites me where I most have sinned!" ' 'Tail' is used in *Lady Chatterley's Lover* as a precise synonym for rump (XV 232; also XVII 277 and XVIII 290). This quotation from the Spanish ballad (entitled 'The Penitence of Don Roderick' in J. G. Lockhart's *The Spanish Ballads*), together with the whole description of sensual encounter in chapter XVI, was omitted from the expurgated edition.

At the conclusion of *Apropos of Lady Chatterley's Lover*

Lawrence refers to conversations of his with Italians regarding the book's publication. One of them asks, 'What does it describe?' and when told, though what was told is not reported, wonders at Lawrence's anxiety, remarking, 'But we do it every day.' Another, more cautious, asks, 'You find it really necessary to *say* it?' In these conversations 'it' denotes a definite action.

An interesting passage in Clifford's letter sees humanity and its lusts as existing at 'the *bottom* of a deep ocean' (Lawrence's italics: the connotations are not those of the floods and waves noted above). Here we 'prey upon the ghastly subaqueous life of our fellow-men, in the submarine jungle of mankind'; but 'our immortal destiny is to escape' again 'into the bright ether' of our 'eternal nature'. The writing is not wholly unsympathetic; Clifford is perhaps the most objectively created person in the book; and it is arguable that his is a more complete survey than anyone's.

Clifford's image of subaqueous life might have been drawn from Middleton Murry's review of the earlier novel, *Women in Love*, in 1921, not 1931 as stated when reprinted in his *Reminiscences of D. H. Lawrence* (1933; IV 218–27). This novel describes in imaginative terms certain sexual encounters of an abnormal kind, and Murry was violently antagonised. Lawrence's people, he wrote, 'grope in their own slime to some final consummation, in which they are utterly "negated" or utterly "fulfilled" '; his is a 'protozoic god' and he is 'passionately obscene in the exact sense of the word'; 'man and woman are indistinguishable as octopods in an aquarium tank'. Only Lawrence's 'passion', that is his prophetic fervour, can clear him of the charge of 'the crudest sexuality'; and yet 'not one person in a thousand' would decide that the actions in question 'were anything but the crudest kind of sexuality'. He admits that they may not be, but how, he does not know. Murry's apparent indecision is probably dictated by a reluctance to speak more openly. 'After all,' he says, when defending this review against Mrs Carswell's attack, 'I had known Lawrence intimately'; his stature he recognised, and yet 'perhaps I knew what Lawrence *meant* by his writing far better than other men'. And:

Therefore I cried, with vehemence and passionate sincerity, over
the débris of a broken friendship: 'Ecrasez l'infame'. (*Reminiscences*, IV 239–40.)

Murry discusses the end-chapters of *The Rainbow* and the important chapter 'Excurse' (XXIII) of *Women in Love* in *Son of
Woman* (1931; II 88–92, 106–22). His acute commentary has
assisted my understanding.

In 'Excurse' the woman, Ursula, denounces Birkin's sexual
propensities in a passage associating his 'sex life' with 'death'
and 'foulness' and calling it a mixture of 'spirituality' and 'dirt'.
She calls him 'obscene', *'perverse'* and 'death-eating' (XXIII 344–6;
my page numerals refer to the Penguin edition of *Women in Love*).
Birkin admits it, recognising that he was 'perverse, so spiritual
on the one hand, and in some strange way, degraded on the
other'; 'he knew that his spirituality was concomitant of a process
of depravity, a sort of pleasure in self-destruction' (XXIII 347–8).

The theme of 'Excurse' has been prepared for earlier (XIII
162–4; XIX 282–3, 285–6; XXII 330–1). Lawrence, says Murry,
seems to be 'demanding a new kind of physical contact' accom-
panied by 'fear and terror' (*Son of Woman*, II 111). Though
fearful, for it is to involve 'the last physical facts, physical and
unbearable' (XXII 331), it is honoured above the 'mingling' (XIII
164; XVI 225) of normal union, 'this horrible fusion of two
beings' which 'every woman and most men', despite its being
so 'nauseous and horrible', insisted on (XXIII 348). There is
instead talk of fingers, loins, back, flanks, downward movement
of the hand, electricity and darkness; and the word 'mystic'
recurs. Frontal, phallic, sexuality is surpassed, and an otherness
touched 'more wonderful than life itself' – a deathly otherness –
'the very stuff of being' at 'the darkest poles of the body' by
the 'rounded' loins, 'the darkest, deepest, strangest life-source
of the human body at the back and base of the loins' (XXIII
353–4; and see XIV 203–4).

First the man, Birkin, is the active partner:

He had taken her at the roots of her darkness and shame – like a
demon, laughing over the fountain of mystic corruption which
was one of the sources of her being. . . . As for her, when would

she so much go beyond herself as to accept him at the quick of death?' (XXIII 343)

Then we have the woman's tentative approach:

· She had thought there was no source deeper than the phallic source. And now, behold, from the smitten rock of the man's body, from the strange marvellous flanks and thighs, deeper, further in mystery than the phallic source, came the floods of ineffable darkness and ineffable riches. (XXIII 354)

'With perfect fine finger-tips of reality she would touch the reality in him' (XXIII 360). 'Roots', 'shame', 'demon', 'rock', all point ahead to *Lady Chatterley*; so, if we have regard to its one excremental reference and the later word 'foundations' (*Lady Chatterley's Lover*, XV 232; XVI 258), do 'the fountain of mystic corruption' as 'one of the sources of her being' and the man's 'marvellous fountains' (XXIII 354). In *Women in Love* the implements are fingers; but, as again in *Lady Chatterley*, it is a matter less of love than of deliberate and 'impersonal' (XXIII 343) 'sensual reality' (XXIII 361; and see III 48; VII 87; XIX 285–6), and is to this extent 'inhuman' (XIII 162–3; XXIII 361). It touches the inmost non-human being of the person 'mystically-physically' (XXIII 354); as Murry observes (*Reminiscences*, IV 222), 'it does not admit of individuality as we understand it'. In what Murry calls this 'ultra-phallic realm' (*Son of Woman*, II 118) sexual distinctions are transcended 'beyond womanhood' in a dark 'otherness' at once 'masculine and feminine' (XXIII 353, 361; and see XIII 164; XIX 282). The technique may be called 'ambisexual' in that either man or woman may be the active partner:

And he too waited in the magical steadfastness of suspense for her to take this knowledge of him as he had taken it of her. He knew her darkly, with the fullness of dark knowledge. Now she would know him, and he too would be liberated. (XXIII 360)

Each, while remaining sexually inviolate, becomes semi-sexually empowered and integrated: 'They would give each other this star-equilibrium which alone is freedom' (XXIII 360; and see XIII 164, 168–70; XVI 225; XIX 287). Through touch of the impersonal roots, the centres of corruption and death, death itself being an 'inhuman otherness' (XV 217), the true integration is accomplished. In his essay 'Pornography and Obscenity' (*Phoenix* (1936) III 176) Lawrence distinguishes between the sexual and excretory functions in terms of creation and dissolution, opposing their confusion as a mark of degradation. The terms ('dirt', 'flow', 'degraded') correspond with those used in *Women in Love*, though the concern is different. In his more imaginative and fictional excursions he is trying to blast through this degradation to a new health. Death and darkness – though darkness is used by Lawrence for more general purposes too – are natural associations, since the locations in question are those of expelled poisons and the non-human. So the deathly is found to be the source of some higher order of being; contact with a basic materiality liberates the person.

Murry correlates his discussion of *Women in Love* with three of Lawrence's poems: 'New Heaven and Earth', 'Elysium' and 'Manifesto'. In the first it is the man who puts his hand out 'further, a little further', touches the otherness, and is ignited. In the second the man is the passive partner:

> Ah, terribly
> Between the body of life and me
> Her hands slid in and set me free.

The true personality 'me' is liberated from the weight of the 'body of life', its material 'matrix' or life-basis, and the true self, which we must call in some sense a 'spirit-self' – in *Fantasia of the Unconscious* (Secker, New Adelphi ed. 1930; XI 120) it is called 'soul' – is now born. 'Manifesto' is yet clearer:

I want her to touch me at last, ah, on the root and quick of my
  darkness
and perish on me, as I have perished on her. . . .
When she has put her hand on my secret, darkest sources, the
  darkest outgoings,
when it has struck home to her, like a death, 'this is *him*!'
she has no part in it, no part whatever,
it is the terrible *other*,
when she knows the fearful *other flesh*, ah, darkness unfathom-
  able and fearful, contiguous and concrete,
when she is slain against me, and lies in a heap like one outside
  the house,

when she passes away as I have passed away,
being pressed up against the *other*,
then I shall be glad, I shall not be confused with her,
I shall be cleared, distinct, single as if burnished in silver,
having no adherence, no adhesion anywhere,
one clear, burnished, isolated being, unique,
and she also, pure, isolated, complete,
two of us, unutterably distinguished, and in unutterable con-
    junction.
Then we shall be free, freer than angels, ah, perfect.

The italics are Lawrence's. Such is this strange achievement,
neatly matched by the thoughts of W. B. Yeats' 'Crazy Jane
Talks with the Bishop', where we are told that 'fair and foul are
near akin', that the one needs the other, and so

> . . . Love has pitched his mansion in
> The place of excrement;
> For nothing can be sole or whole
> That has not been rent.

The correspondence is close.

Murry did not like it; but it seems that he has suffered some
injustice from admirers of Lawrence. Granted his knowledge,
he was very reticent. There were obvious reasons why he could
not speak so clearly as we can today.

After *Women in Love* Lawrence passed on to the male in-
terests of *Aaron's Rod*, *Kangaroo*, and *The Plumed Serpent*,
though sexually little is made of these. In *Lady Chatterley's
Lover* he composed a final and comprehensive sexual statement.
Such a man as Lawrence will not retreat; the abnormal claim
staked out remains, with a dual and lucid emphasis, corresponding to the diverse sexual engagements in *Women in Love* of
Gerald and Birkin (for Gerald, XXIV 388–90; XXIX 451–2; XXX
499–500), on (i) normal engagements and (ii) an abnormal
penetration, the phallos replacing the fingers of *Women in Love*;
that is the point of 'the phallos alone could explore it'.

SOURCE: 'Lawrence, Joyce and Powys', in *Essays in Criticism*,
XI, no. 4 (1961).

Julian Moynahan

RITUAL SCENES IN
THE RAINBOW (1963)

THESE scenes are 'rituals' because they dramatize, frequently in solemn ceremonial gesture and in a ceremonious prose, the ultimate relation of the 'essential' man or woman – usually it is a woman – to what Lawrence calls the 'unknown'. As such they are analogous with religious rites in which the relation of the human soul to God is celebrated. In these scenes 'the old stable ego' of the character shatters, and the individual becomes unrecognizable in his everyday aspect. 'Daytime consciousness' is suspended; the individual is described as coming under the direct influence of irresistible forces of life. Behavior under these circumstances may be assumed to express an ultimate of the human condition, the inhuman 'isness' of the self. These scenes present an artistic proof that essential being exists and indicate its nature. In them the individual is created anew, in a set of terms distinct from the dramatic and descriptive language used to define the same character as a social being.

There are five of the scenes altogether: the extended description of Lydia's slow emergence from the state of quiescent withdrawal she had suffered after the death of her first husband (ch. I); the dancelike gathering of the sheaves performed by Will and Anna on a moonlit night during their courtship (ch. IV); the scene in which Anna Brangwen, pregnant and naked, dances before the 'Unknown' as David danced before the Lord (ch. VI); Ursula's 'moon-consummation' in the stackyard (ch. XI); Ursula's encounter with the horses (ch. XVI). They are composed for the most part through the narrator's descriptions; there is little opportunity for the use of a dramatic method, since the characters are not primarily interacting with one another but with mute natural forces. Now I should like to examine three of these scenes in detail.

Lydia's 'new parturition' does not result from any conscious aim to make a new attempt after happiness. She wants to rest, but the Life Force, working in the succession of the seasons and making itself manifest in flowers, bees, and thrushes' eggs, causes 'her soul' to rouse itself to attention. She cannot help herself. Although she consciously prefers withdrawal from life, Nature reaches out for her and brings her up from her walk in 'the Underworld, where the shades throng intelligibly but have no connection with one'. Lawrence's images define the essential Lydia, who cannot break her organic bond with life even though she wishes to die, in terms of a perennial flower which withdraws under the surface of the earth into its seed and is reborn according to ineluctable biological necessity, under the beneficent influence of a warm spring. His metaphor of the Underworld merges Lydia with the figure of Persephone, who in the vegetation myth returns to the upper world after her sojourn in Hades. When the reader comes to view Lydia in these metaphorical terms, his understanding of her and her plight becomes transformed. The *gestalt* of her moral-psychological character becomes indistinct. As her outlines dissolve she flows into the greater life of organic nature.

These images of the flower and the seed are not sentimental metaphorical projections of a psychological condition. The suggestion is that the essence of Lydia and the essence of the flower are the same; and it is implied that if she is to flourish once again in the daytime world she must be returned temporarily to the organic, instinctual source of creation, there to be recharged with vitality. Lawrence had begun as early as his first novel to suggest through images and metaphors an intimate connection between the outer world of nature and the inner world of the individual. But it was still possible in *The White Peacock* for the reader to assume that the author was exploiting sentimentally the great Pathetic Fallacy of romanticism. Here we have passed beyond loose analogy to a position which identifies concretely the essence of the human with the essence of the

natural. Lydia 'inhumanly' and both Lydia and the flower
'physiologically' respond to the mysterious Will of life, which
replaces the Will of God as prime mover. Hulme's prophecy is
exactly fulfilled.

The artistic strategy of the sheave-gathering scene involves
the use of incremental repetition in combination with vivid
imagery to suggest that Will and Anna enact in their sensual
pursuit of and retreat from one another the larger rhythms of the
'living cosmos'. Will wishes to kiss Anna. This desire arises in
ordinary consciousness. But in reaching after her he is seized
upon by the Life Force. His ordinary will is replaced by 'a low,
deep-sounding will in him, which vibrated to her, tried to set her
in accord, tried to bring her gradually to him, to a meeting, till
they should be together, till they should meet as the sheaves that
swished together'. This inscrutable will becomes the agent, and
the young man becomes the instrument of its massive urge
toward 'accord'. As long as this will continues to vibrate, the
dancelike approaches and retreats of the two lovers are controlled
by a power outside themselves, a power whose operation blurs
the distinction between the sexual impulses of two young lovers
and the general dynamic relation which all parts of living nature
hold to one another.

This scene in no way prepares us for the ensuing narration
of the frequently unhappy, even sordid, marital relations of Will
and Anna. There is little reason why this experience should have
happened to them rather than to some other characters. In other
words, whatever happy meaning we choose to read from this
scene, it is not one that is continuously supported and amplified
by later developments in the careers of the two characters. As
husband and wife, mother and father, Will and Anna fail to
live up to the inhuman selves they expose in this scene. As a
design, the sheave-gathering scene remains a thing in itself; its
actors are really symbols, and the meaning of the symbols has
little to do with the actual couple who live out their marital
career and raise seven children in the village of Cossethay and
in the provincial town of Beldover.

Ursula's encounter with the horses cannot be criticized from exactly the same point of view. It seems a meaningful outcome of experiences she has already undergone as an ordinary human being. Ursula in *The Rainbow* is a sort of female Quixote who passes through one experience after another in quest of her 'true self'. Her activities cover a considerable range: an adolescent love affair, a Lesbian attachment, two years as pupil-teacher in a grade school, a broken engagement, three years as a university student. In each circumstance Ursula finds that the elusive goal of self-realization and the elusive definition of the true self are still beyond her. At last, when she has discovered that she is with child by her discarded lover, she comes to realize that she has been pursuing a will-of-the-wisp:

What did the self, the form of life matter? Only the living from day to day mattered, the beloved existence in the body, rich, peaceful, complete, with no beyond, no further trouble, no further complication. (ch. XVI)

She then writes a letter to Skrebensky, humbly asking him to take her back, and when she has finished it she feels 'that now, now she was at the depths of herself. This man was her true self forever. With this document she would appear before God at the Judgement Day.'

Perhaps for many novelists such a point of moral awareness would be sufficient, but the two-phased Laurentian moral imperative is directly opposed to this attempt at compromise. As Ursula goes walking in the woods after writing the letter she becomes dimly conscious of 'a gathering restiveness, a tumult impending within her'. This tumult we must take as the voice of her submerged 'essential' nature signaling her that she must continue her search after wholeness. As the scene continues the inner turbulence is projected outside Ursula and becomes embodied in the herd of horses which races up and down before her until, on the verge of physical and nervous collapse, she manages to escape from the field where she has encountered them. Her escape is in some sense an exit from the wilderness of instinctive experience, back to the 'ordered world of men'. Whether these horses are a hallucination or really there, they symbolize the power of the life of instinct, the life which underlies the upper layers of the self, underlies the accretions of moral and psychological conditioning that hide the deep, turbulent impulses of 'flesh' and 'blood' in every individual. Ursula is harried by her own interior horses, grotesque as that may sound, but we must assume that the image of the trampling herd is a valid symbol for the deep instinctive life of all of us.

She was aware of their breasts gripped, clenched narrow in a hold that never relaxed, she was aware of their red nostrils flaming with long endurance, and of their haunches, so rounded, so massive, pressing, pressing, pressing to burst the grip upon their breasts, pressing for ever till they went mad, running against the walls of time, and never bursting free. (ch. XVI)

These anarchic, archetypal horses must be confined, but they and their pressure are real enough. Ursula's compromise is a denial of the life inside her. She is punished by suffering this visionary confrontation and simultaneously she is 'saved' by being brought face to face with a truth about herself and about life, the denial of which could only lead to a kind of death-in-life. For it is clear that although these horses are profoundly dangerous to 'the ordered world', the power they symbolize is to be taken as the ultimate energic source of man's vitality, his creativity, and of whatever is vital in civilized society as well.

This compelling scene is disappointing only in the aftermath. Ursula's experience was designed to illuminate for her the paths of error into which she had wandered in the conduct of her life. Deeply corrupted by her experience in the daytime world, she had lost touch with vital instinct and now the structure of her character must be broken down. She must be reduced to a surd of elemental being, later to be reconstituted as a wholesome human individual:

As she sat there, spent, time and the flux of change passed away from her, she lay as if unconscious upon the bed of the stream, like a stone, unconscious, unchanging, unchangeable, whilst everything rolled by in transience, leaving her there, a stone at rest on the bed of the stream, inalterable and passive, sunk to the bottom of all change. (ch. XVI)

The reader awaits impatiently the account of some new growth which must come to this person who has adventured so much and suffered so much in the past. But Lawrence cannot, or at least does not, even begin to indicate the mode of this new growth. We are told that Ursula now possesses 'a deep, inalterable knowledge'. We view the first stirrings of her renewal in the familiar metaphor of a 'naked, clear kernel thrusting forth the clear, powerful shoot', and we hear that Ursula has reached the shore of the unknown land 'after crossing the void'. Finally, we are given the vision of the rainbow arching over the world's corruption, and the novel sings itself out with no definition of the new Ursula, or description of the unknown land she has entered.

The Rainbow is in a sense Lawrence's sacred book. It is therefore not surprising that he should have adapted material from religious tradition* to his secular but visionary ends, especially since Lawrence saw religious myths as 'images of human experience'. The succession of familial generations which the novel describes, its theme of continuity through change, its embodiment of the notion that in ordinary, everyday experience the individual is called to work out his salvation – all these features establish a significant parallel between the Brangwens ('a curious family, a law to themselves, separate from the world, isolated, a small republic set in invisible bounds') and one of those ancient

---

* The rainbow metaphor is borrowed from Genesis, where it is a sign of the new covenant between God and Noah. Tom Brangwen, patriarch of the family, is symbolically associated with Noah. In ch. II his drunken speech on marriage at the meal following Anna's wedding corresponds to the biblical episode in which the drunken Noah is exposed before his sons. The biblical flood is reproduced in transposed position as the flash flood which bursts over the Marsh farm and drowns Tom. See ch. IV, 'The Marsh and the Flood'.

biblical families like the clan of Noah or Abraham which carried
God's promise in its table of genealogy. When the young Ursula
dreams of that giant race before the flood, of the Sons of God
who came in 'unto the daughters of men and they bore children
unto them', the image of these Old Testament titans is apt to
blend in a reader's imagination with the former generations of
Brangwen men who 'lived full and surcharged, their senses full
fed, their faces always turned to the heat of the blood, staring
into the sun, dazed with looking toward the source of generation'.

Certainly the pulsing, incantatory prose rhythms of *The Rainbow* constantly recall the King James Version. Even the narrative
quality of the novel shares some characteristics with the Bible
stories. According to Erich Auerbach,[1] 'in the Old Testament
stories, the sublime, tragic, and problematic take shape precisely
in the domestic and commonplace'; 'the peace of daily life in the
house, in the fields, in the flocks, is undermined by . . . the
promise of a blessing'; 'the two realms of the sublime and everyday are not only unseparated but basically unseparable'. In his
general summary of biblical style Auerbach goes on to mention
'certain parts brought into high relief, others left obscure, abrupt-
ness, suggestive influence of the unexpressed, "background"
quality'. This last refers to what Auerbach calls the 'multilayered-
ness' of the characters in Old Testament narrative. It results
from the fact that they are involved simultaneously with daily
life and in a developing relation to God the issue of which is
salvation or perdition.

Up to a point these descriptions may be extended to *The
Rainbow*, for in this novel a fictional world is created in which the
possibility of transfiguration is always present in the round of
daily life; where multilayered characters like Tom, Lydia, or
Ursula stand ready to respond to the call from the Unknown
with the poignant affirmation of a 'Here am I.' But there are
difficulties, as soon as we remind ourselves that *The Rainbow* is,
after all, a secular book, and that Lawrence's inscrutable will of
life is not the same as the mysterious Divine Will of the Judaeo-
Christian tradition. I said earlier that Lawrence's concern with a

real livingness within the person was a concern for the freedom
and integrity of people. While *The Rainbow* immensely deepens
one's sense of vital human realities as they exist within history
and society, and of vital forces of nature underlying civilization,
it sometimes accomplishes this at the expense of Lawrence's
original concern with freedom.

On a cynical view, it might be argued that Lawrence has
invented a group of ordinary people, removed from them the
power of moral choice and described them as being pushed
toward an unknowable goal of self-realization by influences
over which they have no control. While the characters sometimes
obey imperatives recognizably moral, their obedience is often
dictated to them from outside themselves. As we have seen, it is
often difficult to compose into a single image Lawrence's vision
of a transformed life and the 'actual' lives of the characters.
Beginning with the intention of revealing essential truth about
the self Lawrence succeeds only in dissociating his characters
into two incompatible levels of being.

On a view more adequate to the generous spirit of Lawrence's
fundamental intention, it is certainly true that Lawrence did not
fully succeed at the enormously difficult task of clarifying the
relation of his 'inhuman selves' to social roles on the one hand
and to vital forces on the other. The difficulty was partly technical; after all, Lawrence had to invent numerous new aesthetic
forms in order to reveal new aspects of reality and the drama of
essential being. In the process he sometimes lost sight of the
fact that salvation may seem a meaningless outcome unless
consciously and vigorously sought. The outlook of the modern
reader who sides with Anna against the Cathedral is still colored,
or ought to be, by the ethical strenuousness of Christianity,
which rings out in such pronouncements as 'Seek and ye shall
find!' We hesitate to judge Will Brangwen severely when we
know so little of his 'folded centres of darkness', to admire
Ursula when the coming to pass of her new life, as described at
the end, so closely resembles a state of deep neurotic depression.
Nevertheless, except for this single clouded issue *The Rainbow*
is one of the great advances in the art of the twentieth-century

novel, conquering as it does vast new territories in the realm of human reality and creating new images of human destiny.

SOURCE: *The Deed of Life: the novels and tales of D. H. Lawrence* (Princeton, 1963).

NOTE

1. See *Mimesis: The Representation of Reality in Western Literature,* trans. Willard Trask (Princeton, 1953) pp. 12–13, 22–3.

H. M. Daleski

WOMEN IN LOVE: 'FIRM SINGLENESS AND MELTING UNION' (1965)

Pace Leavis, who says it seems to him that 'the position for which Birkin contends in his wooing of Ursula does emerge from the "tale" vindicated, in the sense that the norm he proposes for the relations of man and woman in marriage has been made, by the varied resources of Lawrence's art, sufficiently clear, and, in its intelligibility, sufficiently cogent, to compel us to a serious pondering',[1] I must confess that I find the norm Birkin proposes, in so far as it is defined by the values he advocates rather than by those he rejects, neither clear nor cogent. I think that Lawrence's attempt to portray Birkin and Ursula's achievement of 'the pure duality of polarization' (with all that the phrase, in its context, implies) is as unsatisfactory and unconvincing as the 'doctrinal' passages in which he makes a frontal attack on our credence, and as the 'symbolic' scenes in which he presents external support for his position. The means by which they achieve 'polarity' are detailed in a crucial chapter called 'Excurse'; the title, it seems, serves as an announcement, among other things, of a fresh sortie.

Some ten pages of 'Excurse' are devoted to a description of the special kind of experience Birkin and Ursula have together and of its effect on them; I quote a representative passage, of manageable length:

She looked at him. He seemed still so separate. New eyes were opened in her soul. She saw a strange creature from another world in him. It was as if she were enchanted, and everything were metamorphosed. She recalled again the old magic of the Book of Genesis, where the sons of God saw the daughters of men, that they were fair. And he was one of these, one of these strange creatures from the beyond, looking down at her, and seeing she was fair.

He stood on the hearth-rug looking at her, at her face that was upturned exactly like a flower, a fresh, luminous flower, glinting faintly golden with the dew of the first light. And he was smiling faintly as if there were no speech in the world, save the silent delight of flowers in each other. Smilingly they delighted in each other's presence, pure presence, not to be thought of, even known. But his eyes had a faintly ironical contraction.

And she was drawn to him strangely, as in a spell. Kneeling on the hearth-rug before him, she put her arms round his loins, and put her face against his thighs. Riches! Riches! She was overwhelmed with a sense of a heavenful of riches.

'We love each other,' she said in delight.

'More than that,' he answered, looking down at her with his glimmering, easy face.

Unconsciously, with her sensitive finger-tips, she was tracing the back of his thighs, following some mysterious life-flow there. She had discovered something, something more than wonderful, more wonderful than life itself. It was the strange mystery of his life-motion, there, at the back of the thighs, down the flanks. It was a strange reality of his being, the very stuff of being, there in the straight downflow of the thighs. It was here she discovered him one of the sons of God such as were in the beginning of the world, not a man, something other, something more.

This was release at last. She had had lovers, she had known passion. But this was neither love nor passion. It was the daughters of men coming back to the sons of God, the strange inhuman sons of God, who are in the beginning.

Her face was now one dazzle of released, golden light, as she looked up at him and laid her hands full on his thighs, behind, as he stood before her. He looked down at her with a rich bright brow like a diadem above his eyes. She was beautiful as a new marvellous flower opened at his knees, a paradisal flower she was, beyond womanhood, such a flower of luminousness. Yet something was tight and unfree in him. He did not like this crouching, this radiance – not altogether.

It was all achieved for her. She had found one of the sons of God from the Beginning, and he had found one of the first most luminous daughters of men. (ch. XXIII)

The ostensible meaning of this experience in the parlour of the inn is, I think, sufficiently clear – it is the means by which Birkin and Ursula establish their 'unison in separateness' – but the experience, as described, is one in which, to say the least, it is difficult to participate imaginatively, and which leaves us both dissatisfied and puzzled. There is, for instance, the confusing issue of individual singleness. The delight they take in each other's presence, 'pure presence', suggests that what we have here is the realization of the hopes that are set out in Birkin's reflections on the relations of men and women; but it is not clear whether the achieved 'purity' is a product of the experience, or whether it is antecedent to it and merely ratified by what happens. On the one hand, even before Ursula touches Birkin, she sees him as one of 'the sons of God': the reference to the mysterious passage in the Book of Genesis, it seems, does not only serve to assert Birkin's established independence of being* but obscurely implies that his pure presence is also a matter of pure maleness, for the man who is 'no son of Adam' can be assumed to be free from any contamination of the other sex. This, I take it, is what underlies the related assertions that he is 'a strange creature from another world', and that he is 'not a man' but 'something other, something more'. Similarly, Ursula is 'beyond womanhood'. If, then, the achievement of 'pure individuality' is antecedent to the experience, we would like to know, for we are not told, just how it is that they are 'metamorphosed'.

On the other hand, it is later stated that their 'accession into being' is directly due to the experience itself: 'She seemed to faint beneath, and he seemed to faint, stooping over her. It was

---

* A passage in *The Rainbow* provides a gloss on the overt meaning of Birkin's identity with the biblical giants: '[Ursula] laid hold of [Skrebensky] at once for her dreams. Here was one such as those Sons of God who saw the daughters of men, that they were fair. He was no son of Adam. Adam was servile. Had not Adam been driven cringing out of his native place, had not the human race been a beggar ever since, seeking its own being? But Anton Skrebensky could not beg. He was in possession of himself, of that, and no more. Other people could not really give him anything nor take anything from him. His soul stood alone' (ch. XI).

a perfect passing away for both of them, and at the same time the most intolerable accession into being . . .' (ch. XXIII). If the experience described were a phallic one, an accession into pure male and female being would be acceptably in line with typical Lawrencean thought, but the fact that it is not raises further difficulties. In the first place, though the non-phallic nature of the experience is stressed, it seems that we are intended to attribute to it the sort of transcendent value that is usually associated in Lawrence with the sex act: Ursula discovers 'something more than wonderful, more wonderful than life itself', but what she discovers is 'neither love nor passion'. The 'floods of ineffable darkness and ineffable riches', we are later told, that spring from 'the smitten rock of the man's body, from the strange marvellous flanks and thighs', come from 'deeper, further in mystery than the phallic source' (ch. XXIII). I do not wish to suggest, of course, that the experience is represented as a substitute for sexual intercourse; on the contrary, once supreme value is attached to it and not to intercourse, sex, so to speak, is put safely in its place and ceases to be a menace. It is as if the experience is a means of controlling the 'old destructive fires' which, as was earlier intimated in relation to Birkin's stoning of the moon's reflection, can never be entirely extinguished. Birkin and Ursula, indeed, after they have had tea at the inn, drive off into Sherwood Forest and, on a moonless night – 'It was a night all darkness, with low cloud' (ch. XXIII) – consummate their union in a more usual fashion. If what transpires in the forest, as the following quotation suggests, cannot be said to be analogous to the satisfaction of thirst in a world of plenty of water, its 'perfection', I think, is intended to be viewed as a consequence of the revelation at the inn and its significance as subordinate to it:

She had her desire of him, she touched, she received the maximum of unspeakable communication in touch, dark, subtle, positively silent, a magnificent gift and give again, a perfect acceptance and yielding, a mystery, the reality of that which can never be known, vital, sensual reality that can never be transmuted into mind content, but remains outside, living body of darkness

and silence and subtlety, the mystic body of reality. She had her
desire fulfilled. He had his desire fulfilled. For she was to him what
he was to her, the immemorial magnificence of mystic, palpable,
real otherness. (ch. XXIII)

If this analysis is acceptable, then it must further be urged that
the experience at the inn is presented, rather too obviously, as an
expedient by which the paradoxes inherent in Birkin's position
are resolved; it is presented from one point of view, that is to
say, as the means by which 'pure' male and female being are
attainable outside of sexual intercourse, and at the same time, in
regard to the careful avoidance of any suggestion of 'mingling
and merging', or of any sense of containment, it is offered as a
kind of sexual contact which, by its nature, cannot be either
destructive or subversive of singleness. That it is an expedient is,
in part, suggested by the poor quality of the writing. There is no
call, I should say, for a detailed analysis of this weakness, for it is
plainly evident in the passages I have cited, and there is general
critical agreement, moreover, that the combined vagueness and
stridency of the style hardly does Lawrence credit.[2] The special
pleading is also betrayed by the ridiculous lengths to which
Lawrence is driven in attributing significance to the experience:
after it, Ursula, who is said to be 'usually nervous and uncertain
at performing . . . public duties, such as giving tea', is 'at her ease,
entirely forgetting to have misgivings', and 'the tea-pot [pours]
beautifully from a proud slender spout' (ch. XXIII); similarly,
when they are driving to Sherwood Forest, Birkin is described as
sitting still 'like an Egyptian Pharaoh, driving the car. He felt
as if he were seated in immemorial potency, like the great carven
statues of real Egypt, as real and as fulfilled with subtle strength,
as these are, with a vague inscrutable smile on the lips' (ch. XXIII),
but lest there should be any doubt as to his ability to steer the
vehicle, it is hastily asserted that the Egyptian in him is duly
tempered by a touch of the Greek:

But with a sort of second consciousness he steered the car
towards a destination. For he had the free intelligence to direct

his own ends. His arms and his breast and his head were rounded and living like those of the Greek, he had not the unawakened straight arms of the Egyptian, nor the sealed, slumbering head. A lambent intelligence played secondarily above his pure Egyptian concentration in darkness. (ch. XXIII)

Even if we consider the description of the ultra-phallic revelation not so much as an expedient on Lawrence's part as a failure to communicate a genuine mystical experience, it seems open to serious objection. The failure in communication means that, at best, the experience remains the author's own, personal and not transmuted into the imaginative terms which alone could secure it a rightful place in a work of art; we are left, consequently, with little, if any, idea of what it is that actually happens to Birkin and Ursula at the inn. G. Wilson Knight attempts to relate the incident to the later account of anal intercourse in *Lady Chatterley's Lover*. He writes – I omit his parenthetical page references:

Frontal, phallic, sexuality is surpassed, and an otherness touched 'more wonderful than life itself' – a deathly otherness – 'the very stuff of being' at 'the darkest poles of the body' by the 'rounded' loins, 'the darkest, deepest, strangest life-source of the human body at the back and base of the loins'. . . . In *Women in Love* the implements are fingers; but, as again in *Lady Chatterley*, it is a matter less of love than of deliberate and 'impersonal' 'sensual reality', and is to this extent 'inhuman'. . . .[3]

Though I think we cannot be sure of the meaning of certain references in *Women in Love* if we attempt to explain them as they stand, there are passages which appear to be related to the description of 'the shameful natural and unnatural acts of sensual voluptuousness' of Will and Anna in *The Rainbow** and which, when read in the light of *Lady Chatterley's Lover*, would seem to confirm Wilson Knight's argument. Before Birkin and Ursula go to the inn, for instance, he thinks of how 'he [has] taken her at the roots of her darkness and shame – like a demon' (ch. XXIII); and later, Ursula is glad to realize 'they might do as they

* See the final pages of the chapter 'The Child'. C.C.

liked. . . . How could anything that gave one satisfaction be excluded? What was degrading?' (ch. XXIX). Nevertheless, I do not believe that the incident at the inn should be interpreted in this way. It is not merely that it is difficult to reconcile Wilson Knight's interpretation with the description, as we have it, of what transpires in the public parlour of the inn; after Birkin and Ursula leave the inn, we are told that he is still waiting 'for her to take this knowledge of him as he [has] taken it of her' (ch. XXIII). Nor, as I have already pointed out, does it seem to me that the description of the intercourse which follows (ch. XXIII) suggests anything unconventional.*

The failure in communication, then, would seem to preclude the relationship which Birkin ostensibly succeeds in establishing with Ursula from being regarded as in any sense normative, the norm which he proposes being, in the crucial instance of their sexual relations, if in no other, neither exoteric nor intelligible. Moreover, even if we assume, for the moment, that the description of the experience at the inn succeeds in suggesting the means by which a 'pure stable equilibrium' between the lovers is to be assured, we cannot help noticing that the state of balance supposedly attained is precarious, if not equivocal. The scene, as Ursula kneels before Birkin, is a little too reminiscent of the wild cat and the Mino to be quite comfortable, and though it is said that Birkin does 'not like this crouching, this radiance – not altogether', the disavowal, in its half-heartedness, is a disquieting intimation of what we are to expect in the next phase of Lawrence's writing, the phase which culminates in the blatant one-sidedness of the main relationships in *The Plumed Serpent*.

Ostensibly secure in their singleness, Birkin and Ursula are now ready for marriage, ready, that is, to be 'transcended into a new oneness', to consummate their separate being in 'a new, paradisal unit regained from the duality' (ch. XXVII). The kind of marriage they wish to make, however, is more expressive of revolt against the established order, against 'the horrible privacy of domestic and connubial satisfaction' and 'the hot narrow

---

* A discussion of the more certainly established unorthodoxy in *Lady Chatterley's Lover* is to be found later in Daleski's book. C.C.

intimacy between man and wife' (ch. XVI), than is the liaison of
Gerald and Gudrun, and it implies no surrender to the society
they despise. Indeed, it is over tea at the inn, immediately after
the climactic revelation, that Birkin declares they must 'drop
[their] jobs', that 'there's nothing for it but to get out, quick'; and
it is 'when they [wake] again from the pure swoon' which ensues
on Ursula's '[pressing] her hands . . . down upon the source of
darkness in him', that they decide 'to write their resignations
from the world of work there and then' (ch. XXIII). Even fighting
the old, as Ursula later tells Gudrun (ch. XXIX), means belonging
to it, and their rejection of the world they know is absolute. It
extends to a renunciation of all possessions, for Birkin maintains
that 'houses and furniture and clothes' are 'all terms of an old
base world, a detestable society of man' (ch. XXVI), and in their
determination to avoid having things of their own, they refuse
to be bound even by a chair they have bought at a jumble market
and give it away. Just what they will do and where they will go
is not precisely defined. Birkin, who is fortunately possessed of a
private income, suggests that they should 'wander away from
the world's somewheres into [their] own nowhere', contending
that it is possible 'to be free, in a free place, with a few other
people', though he admits that it is not so much 'a locality' he is
seeking as 'a perfected relation between [them], and others'
(ch. XXIII).* In the event, they embark, together with Gerald

* Here, plainly, is the first expression in the novels of the project
which Lawrence cherished in his own life; and his 'wandering' from
country to country after the war is, of course, reflected in the novels
which follow *Women in Love*, all of which, until *Lady Chatterley's
Lover*, are set, either in whole or in part, outside of England. Lawrence
remarked on the project in a letter early in 1915: 'We will also talk of
my pet scheme. I want to gather together about twenty souls and sail
away from this world of war and squalor and found a little colony
where there shall be no money but a sort of communism as far as
necessaries of life go, and some real decency. It is to be a colony built
up on the real decency which is in each member of the community. A
community which is established upon the assumption of goodness in
the members, instead of the assumption of badness.' Letter to W. E.
Hopkin (Jan. 1915), *Letters of D. H. Lawrence*, ed. Aldous Huxley
(1932) p. 215.

and Gudrun, on the Alpine holiday. Though their decision to
leave the mountain resort should be viewed, in contrast to the
enthusiasm which Gerald and Gudrun evince for the cold white-
ness, as indicative of the bid they are making for life, Gerald's
death nevertheless forces them to return. It is with his death, so
ominous in its implications for the 'world' from which they are
fleeing, that ultimately they are faced.

I have stressed Birkin and Ursula's desire to withdraw from the
world because, in so far as Lawrence's feelings in this respect can
be identified with theirs, their attitude represents a significant
reversal of the attempt, begun in *The Rainbow*, to come to terms
with it. In the earlier novel, it will be remembered, the realization of 'man-being' was seen to be dependent on effective 'utter-
ance' in the 'man's world', and Tom and Will and Skrebensky
were, in different measure, condemned for a failure in manhood;
it was only Ursula who could be said to have achieved full individuality. At the opening of *Women in Love* the prior struggles
for integrated being of *The Rainbow* are, so to speak, taken for
granted, in the sense that none of the four leading characters is
subject to the limitations of 'blood-intimacy': they are articulate,
self-conscious, and intellectual; and all are active in the 'world of
work'. The problem Lawrence apparently set himself was that of
exploring the development of individuality with ever more and
more complex characters, of proceeding, as it were, to a Birkin
and an Ursula and a Gerald and a Gudrun through a Tom and a
Lydia and a Will and an Anna. In *Women in Love* it becomes
evident, however, that true being is more than a matter of having
a day, as well as a night, goal. In the end, as I have previously
pointed out, Gerald's work in the mines and Gudrun's art are
revealed as 'disintegrative', as an abuse of organic life; and the
black sensuality of their relationship is productive of the violence
which, in the novel, is seen as an inevitable concomitant of any
process of 'dissolution'. What, then, of Birkin and Ursula? What
are we to make of the fact that their 'accession into being' is
followed at once by their resignations from the 'world of work'?
Whether or not we are inclined to accept their ostensible achievement of genuine individuality, their withdrawal from the world

— though it may perhaps be justified by the hopeless state of the society in which they would have to live if they did not withdraw from it — must be deemed, in the context of the two books, a serious qualification of their fullness of being. Accordingly, it should come as no surprise that, in the next phase of his writing, Lawrence should assiduously seek to determine the conditions under which a return to the world is possible, and that, given the collapse of the pre-war world of *The Rainbow* and of *Women in Love*, such a return should ultimately necessitate the emergence of a leader who will try to refashion it.

With the crucial Hardy essay in mind, we may also view the arduous movement to the world and away from it and then back again as having a different, though of course related, motive force. Unlike the main male protagonists in *The Rainbow*, who strive to reconcile their male and female elements but who fail to do so, and who are on the whole dominated by tendencies which, in the essay, are said to exemplify the female principle, Birkin, a most Lawrence-like figure, is presented as believing in an unadulterated masculinity. The distinguishing quality of his manhood, however, his insistence on the primacy of being, turns out (again in terms of the essay) to be disconcertingly feminine in character. This insistence manifests itself as the most pronounced feature of his relationship with Ursula: separateness of being is a prime condition of their unison, and it is because the maintenance of individual being is paramount that he urges her to withdraw with him from the world.* 'Doing', 'Public Good', and 'Community' are typical attributes of the male principle as opposed to female 'Being' and 'Self-Establishment'.† It is therefore on essentially female terms, though in the name of a clear

---

* Cf. Lawrence's own view: 'One must forget, only forget, turn one's eyes from the world: that is all. One must live quite apart, forgetting, having another world, a world as yet uncreated. Everything lies in *being*, although the whole world is one colossal madness, falsity, a stupendous assertion of not-being.' Letter to Lady Ottoline Morrell (Apr. 1916), *Letters*, ed. Huxley, p. 344.

† The importance of this distinction in Lawrence's writing (see in particular the essay on Thomas Hardy in *Phoenix*) is discussed earlier in Daleski's book. C.C.

and determined manhood, that Birkin is set to live his life with Ursula. Again, it should not be found surprising that, in the next phase, there ultimately evolves the stern and relentless male who, in his personal relations with a woman, is an assertive and dominating figure, and who plays his part in the world as a leader of men.

Male elements in Birkin, which I think we must now view as existing in a state of insidious war with female elements rather than in a condition of triumphant and uncontaminated assumption, are manifested in his relationship with Gerald. He tells Gerald that he believes in 'the *additional* perfect relationship between man and man – additional to marriage', and that this relationship should be 'equally important, equally creative, equally sacred, if you like' (ch. xxv). His desire for such a relationship may be regarded as expressive of his revolt against the conventional relations of men and women, of defiance of the 'whole community of mistrustful couples insulated in private houses or private rooms, always in couples, and no further life, no further immediate, no disinterested relationship admitted' (ch. xvi); but it also suggests, as I shall now try to show, that he is urged to satisfy longings which, in relation to a woman, he feels compelled to resist. This is indicated when he proposes to Gerald that they should swear a *Blutbrüderschaft*. He makes the proposal when he realizes that he must face 'the problem of love and eternal conjunction between two men', and when he first admits to himself that 'to love a man purely and fully' has been 'a necessity inside himself all his life':

'You know how the old German knights used to swear a *Blutbrüderschaft*,' he said to Gerald, with quite a new happy activity in his eyes.

'Make a little wound in their arms, and rub each other's blood into the cut?' said Gerald.

'Yes – and swear to be true to each other, of one blood, all their lives. That is what we ought to do. No wounds, that is obsolete. But we ought to swear to love each other, you and I, implicitly, and perfectly, finally, without any possibility of going back on it.'

He looked at Gerald with clear, happy eyes of discovery. Gerald looked down at him, attracted, so deeply bondaged in fascinated attraction, that he was mistrustful, resenting the bondage, hating the attraction.

'We will swear to each other, one day, shall we?' pleaded Birkin. 'We will swear to stand by each other – be true to each other – ultimately – infallibly – given to each other, organically – without possibility of taking back.' (ch. XVI)

Birkin later adds, as Gerald shows less and less inclination to accept the offer, that what he wants is 'an impersonal union that leaves one free' (ch. XVI), but it is noticeable that he actually lays more stress on unison than on separateness: they, like the German knights, should be 'of one blood'; they should be 'given to each other, organically'. Moreover, though Birkin strenuously opposes (albeit not always successfully) Ursula's efforts to make him declare his love for her, since the word is tainted in his mind with connotations of 'mingling and merging', he proposes a swearing of love as the oath of brotherhood. In other words, the typically 'male' desire for a 'melting into pure communion', for a 'fusing together into oneness', is allowed expression only in relation to a man; for in such a relation, it seems, there is no defensive compulsion, as there is in regard to a woman, to realize the 'otherness' of the partner.

I suggest that strong confirmation of this intepretation is to be found in the description of the well-known wrestling bout between Gerald and Birkin, which functions as a non-bloody, if not altogether acknowledged, pledge of brotherhood. The two men strip naked and begin 'a real struggle', driving 'deeper and deeper against each other, as if they would break into a oneness':

So the two men entwined and wrestled with each other, working nearer and nearer. . . . [Birkin] seemed to penetrate into Gerald's more solid, more diffuse bulk, to interfuse his body through the body of the other, as if to bring it subtly into subjection, always seizing with some rapid necromantic foreknowledge every motion of the other flesh, converting and counteracting it, playing upon the limbs and trunk of Gerald like some hard wind. It was as if Birkin's whole physical intelligence interpenetrated into Gerald's body, as if his fine, sublimated energy entered into the flesh of the fuller man, like some potency, casting a fine net, a prison, through the muscles into the very depths of Gerald's physical being.

So they wrestled swiftly, rapturously, intent and mindless at last, two essential white figures working into a tighter, closer oneness of struggle, with a strange, octopus-like knotting and flashing of limbs in the subdued light of the room; a tense white knot of flesh gripped in silence between the walls of old brown books. Now and again came a sharp gasp of breath, or a sound like a sigh, then the rapid thudding of movement on the thickly-carpeted floor, then the strange sound of flesh escaping under flesh. Often, in the white interlaced knot of violent living being that swayed silently, there was no head to be seen, only the swift, tight limbs, the solid white backs, the physical junction of two bodies clinched into oneness. Then would appear the gleaming, ruffled head of Gerald, as the struggle changed, then for a moment the dun-coloured, shadowlike head of the other man would lift up from the conflict, the eyes wide and dreadful and sightless.

At length Gerald lay back inert on the carpet. . . . (ch. xx)

We can be reasonably confident, I think, that Lawrence did not intend this description to be overtly homosexual in character, though there is not much evidence of what he thought about homosexual practices. Cecil Gray, who is for the most part hostile to Lawrence, reports that in 1916 he read the typescript of an unpublished work called *Goats and Compasses*, which he describes as 'a bombastic, pseudo-mystical, psycho-philosophical treatise dealing largely with homosexuality'; but since the only two copies of the 'treatise' were destroyed, one by Lawrence himself and the other by Philip Heseltine, Gray's description of it testifies to nothing more than that Lawrence was interested in the subject – though Gray found his interest 'suspiciously lively'.[4] In *The Rainbow*, however, Lawrence is clearly critical of the 'perverted life' of Winifred; and in his essay on Whitman he unequivocally states: 'For the great mergers, woman at last becomes inadequate. . . . So the next step is the merging of man-for-man love. And this is on the brink of death. It slides over into death.'[5] Moreover, Catherine Carswell, who knew Lawrence well, records his detestation of sexual 'perversion',[6] and Knud Merrild, who lived for some time with him in New Mexico, insists on his undoubted 'normality'.[7] It would seem, therefore, that the distinct homosexual colouring of the description of the wrestling bout – and of other scenes (such as the bathing scene in *The White Peacock*, the sick-room scene in *Aaron's Rod*, the scenes in which there are physical encounters between Somers and Kangaroo in *Kangaroo*, and the initiation scene in *The Plumed Serpent*) in which Lawrence portrays a close physical intimacy between men with one of whom he is more or less identified – is evidence of the pronounced feminine component in his make-up, of a latent or repressed homosexual tendency, rather than of any overt homosexual intention on his part.

The emotional force of the quoted description, however, suggests that the bout is meant to have an extra-physical significance, and indeed we are told that the wrestling has 'some deep meaning to them – an unfinished meaning' (ch. xx). It seems to me that we should regard it as parallel in function to the means by which Birkin and Ursula establish contact at the inn, though in the case of the man and the woman, of course, the occasion marks their full acceptance of the bond between them; whereas here the pledge to brotherhood – Birkin's reply to Gerald's question as to whether this is the *Brüderschaft* he wants being a noncommittal 'Perhaps' (ch. xx) – is only tentatively affirmed. If there is a parallelism between the scenes, then the differences between them are striking. First, the description of the wrestling is not marred by any of the mystical fogginess which clings to the account of what happens at the inn. Second, whereas the contact between man and woman preserves their separateness, that between man and man knots them together. It might be argued that 'knotting' is an inescapable consequence of wrestling, but the references to their 'oneness', as they wrestle 'rapturously', are too insistent and (in the context of the book as a whole) too charged with meaning to be limited in their application to the merely physical facts of the tussle: they seem to drive deeper

against each other, 'as if they would break into a oneness'; as
they 'entwine', Birkin seems 'to interfuse his body through the
body of the other'; Birkin's 'sublimated energy' casts 'a fine net,
a prison, through the muscles into the very depths of Gerald's
physical being'; they work into a 'tighter, closer oneness of
struggle' as they become a 'white interlaced knot of violent living
being'; and, finally, there is to be seen only 'the physical junction
of two bodies clinched into oneness'.

It is scarcely surprising that this pledge of brotherhood should
come to nothing, for Birkin and Gerald obviously stand for
radically different ways of life – virtually, indeed, for life as
opposed to death. Nevertheless, at the end of the novel, Birkin
is left to regret the fact that Gerald's death has put an effective
end to his hopes of union with a man:

'Did you need Gerald?' [Ursula] asked one evening.
'Yes,' he said.
'Aren't I enough for you?' she asked.
'No,' he said. 'You are enough for me, as far as a woman is
concerned. You are all women to me. But I wanted a man friend,
as eternal as you and I are eternal.'
'Why aren't I enough?' she said. 'You are enough for me. I
don't want anybody else but you. Why isn't it the same with
you?'
'Having you, I can live all my life without anybody else, any
other sheer intimacy. But to make it complete, really happy, I
wanted eternal union with a man too: another kind of love,' he
said.
'I don't believe it,' she said. 'It's an obstinacy, a theory, a perversity.'
'Well – ' he said.
'You can't have two kinds of love. Why should you!'
'It seems as if I can't,' he said. 'Yet I wanted it.'
'You can't have it, because it's false, impossible,' she said.
'I don't believe that,' he answered. (ch. XXXI)

The 'two kinds of love' which Birkin says he wanted should
not be distinguished simply as love for a woman and love for a
man: what is involved, as I have tried to show, is a need on his

part both for firm singleness and for melting union. That Lawrence believes it is possible to reconcile these needs is suggested by the closing words of the novel, which, in their inconclusiveness, are anticipatory of the further consideration this problem is given in the next phase of his work. After the rigorous trial of *The Rainbow* and *Women in Love* he has, at last, in his portrayal of the relationship of Birkin and Ursula, ostensibly established the conditions of fruitful marriage; in *Aaron's Rod* we are, so to speak, invited to support Birkin's contention that a married man's desire for 'eternal union with a man too' is not an obstinacy, nor a theory, nor a perversity.

SOURCE: *The Forked Flame: a study of D. H. Lawrence* (1965).

NOTES

1. *D. H. Lawrence: Novelist* (London, 1955; New York, 1956) p. 176.
2. See, for instance, Leavis, *D. H. Lawrence*, p. 148, and Graham Hough, *The Dark Sun* (1956) p. 82.
3. 'Lawrence, Joyce and Powys', in *Essays in Criticism*, XI (Oct. 1961) 406–7.
4. *Peter Warlock* (1934) p. 114.
5. *Studies in Classic American Literature* (New York, 1923; London, 1924) p. 251.
6. *The Savage Pilgrimage* (1932) p. 95.
7. *A Poet and Two Painters* (1938) p. 208.

George H. Ford

WOMEN IN LOVE:
THE DEGENERATION OF
WESTERN MAN (1965)

AMONG the African fetish statues he had seen in Halliday's London apartment, Birkin remembers one of a woman, a 'slim, elegant figure from West Africa, in dark wood, glossy and suave. . . . He remembered her vividly: she was one of his soul's intimates.' Why is it that the statue had haunted Birkin so persistently? Like many of his generation in the western world, Birkin enjoys African carving for its aesthetic satisfactions, yet it is obvious that his almost obsessive concern is not motivated by a search for beauty. It is what these statues tell him about the history of civilization and of his own future.

He remembered her: her astonishing cultured elegance, her diminished, *beetle face*, the astounding long elegant body, on short, ugly legs, with such *protuberant buttocks*, so weighty and unexpected below her slim long loins. She knew *what he himself did not know*. She had thousands of years of purely sensual, purely unspiritual knowledge behind her. It must have been thousands of years since her race had died, mystically: that is, since the relation between the senses and the outspoken mind had broken, leaving the experience all in one sort, mystically sensual. Thousands of years ago, *that which was imminent in himself* must have taken place in these Africans: the goodness, the holiness, the desire for creation and productive happiness must have lapsed, leaving the single impulse for knowledge in one sort . . . in disintegration and dissolution, knowledge such as the beetles have. [Italics mine.]

Birkin's reflections serve as a flashback to the earlier scene in Halliday's apartment when another African statue was seen, this time through the eyes of Gerald. He, too, is disturbed by the

statue (it is of a woman in labor), and although he finds no aesthetic pleasure he nevertheless senses what Birkin associated with
it. It conveys to Gerald 'the suggestion of the extreme of physical
sensation, beyond the limits of mental consciousness'.[1] The early
scene of the breakfast party is memorably staged with the four
naked men standing round the statue and commenting on the
'terrible face, void, peaked, abstracted almost into meaningless-
ness by the weight of sensation beneath'. And the affair of the
preceding night is also effectively incorporated by Gerald's
significant discovery that the statue makes him think of the
Pussum, the 'violated slave' still asleep in the adjacent bedroom.
But Gerald makes one blunder in his response to the statue. He
thinks it is crude and savage. Birkin hastens to correct him:

There are centuries and hundreds of centuries of development in
a straight line, behind that carving; it is an awful pitch of culture,
of a definite sort.

Gerald's mistake is one often made by those readers of Lawrence who overlook what Birkin calls the 'astonishing cultured
elegance' of the statue and assume that he is evoking a work by a
savage. Such a reading blurs the main point of his soliloquy.
Lawrence had learned from his reading (and his subsequent study
of Leo Frobenius's *The Voice of Africa* confirmed the point) that
long before the coming of Europeans there had existed great city
states in Africa which had produced highly sophisticated works
of art and established a tradition of fine craftsmanship.[2] A slow
decline, not a cataclysm, finished off this civilization, and it is the
nature of this decline that Birkin tries to conjure up as he
contemplates what the statue symbolizes for him.

Parenthetically it should be added that, so far as our appreciation of *Women in Love* is concerned, it does not matter fundamentally whether Birkin is right or wrong in his information about
disputed points of Africa's past. Nor does it matter fundamentally
whether his assumptions about one of the ways a civilization may
decline are accurate or inaccurate. They are part of the given
world of this novel and essential to an understanding of it. The

basic assumption, and one developed in the parody scene at the
Pompadour when Birkin's letter is read aloud by Halliday, is that
a civilization having evolved out of its savage beginnings may
lose its creative urge and lapse into decadence before becoming
simply extinct. 'There is a phase in every race – . . . when the
desire for destruction overcomes every other desire.' As intoned
by the drunken Halliday for the amusement of London's Bo-
hemia (this 'menagerie of apish degraded souls'), the effect of
the pronouncement is painfully comic – painful because no other
direct statement in *Women in Love* is more significant or more
serious – and astringently comic because of the setting in which it
is framed. If the social process so conceived is unchecked a
civilization declines to a stage which may have some resemblance
to the original savage stage; it suffers a 'reduction' – an abstract
term upon which Lawrence leans often and hard in his fiction and
letters.

Writing to his Jewish friend Mark Gertler, whose 'obscene'
painting seems to have inspired the account of Loerke's frieze of
the drunken workers in the novel, Lawrence uses the same historical formula: 'You are of an older race than I, and in these
ultimate processes, you are beyond me. . . . At last your race is
at an end – these pictures are its death-cry. And it will be left
for the Jews to utter the final . . . death-cry of this epoch: the
Christians are not *reduced* sufficiently.'[3] And in *St Mawr* he
restates more explicitly the assumptions on which these gloomy
predictions are based:

Every new stroke of civilization has cost the lives of countless
brave men, who have fallen . . . in their efforts to overcome the
old, half-sordid savagery of the lower stages of creation, and
win to the next stage. . . . And every civilization, when it loses
its inward vision and its cleaner energy, falls into a new sort of
sordidness, more vast and more stupendous than the old savage
sort.

During the composition of *Women in Love* Lawrence discovered some living illustrations much closer at hand than the

Africans for his theory of cultural degeneration. His Cornish neighbors impressed him as a surviving pocket of a once impressive 'pre-Christian Celtic civilisation' which had degenerated. In view of the beetle-like face of the African statue, the following description of the Cornish people (whose souls, he said, were like black beetles) is especially interesting:

The aristocratic principle and the principle of magic, to which they belonged, these two have collapsed, and left only the most ugly, scaly, insect-like, unclean *selfishness*. . . . Nevertheless . . . there is left some of the old sensuousness of the darkness . . . something almost negroid, which is fascinating. But curse them, they are entirely mindless.[4]

This cluster associating the Celtic and African reappears in *Lady Chatterley's Lover* in a description of another Celt, the Irishman Michaelis:

She saw in him that ancient motionlessness of a race that can't be disillusioned any more, an extreme, perhaps, of impurity that is pure, . . . he seemed pure, pure as an African ivory mask that dreams impurity into purity, in its ivory curves and planes.

That the African statues signify for Birkin a whole process of decline and fall, and that however aesthetically pleasing they evoke for him the impurity of a degenerated civilization, are points I have been laboring partly because of an extraordinary discussion of these statues by Horace Gregory in his *Pilgrim of the Apocalypse*. According to Gregory, Lawrence found his principal characters of less interest than the statue of the West African woman, 'for him, perhaps the most important figure in the book'.

She is positive, concrete, the perfect representation of life as opposed to the imperfect human beings surrounding her. . . . What the statue is made to represent is the *normal* essence of Gudrun and Ursula combined – their deviation from the statue's norm . . . is the perversion imposed upon them by their individual existence. . . . In all four characters, male and female, the statue sets the standard, never fully realized by any of them.[5]

And Mr Gregory concludes his analysis by asserting that 'the image of the West African savage' was a fragment of hope in the midst of death. When a perceptive critic blunders into stating something so fantastically wrong as this (and other critics share his view) one is led to labor a point. Birkin's reflections in his soliloquy, developing like Keats, in his address to the Grecian urn, continue, and we may well ask what fragment of hope is there here:

There is a long way we can travel, after the death-break; . . . We fall from the connection with life and hope, we lapse . . . into the long, long African process of purely sensual under-standing. . . . He realised now that this is a long process – thousands of years it takes, after the death of the creative spirit. He realised that there were great mysteries to be unsealed, sensual, mindless, dreadful mysteries, far beyond the phallic cult. How far, in their inverted culture, had these West Africans gone beyond phallic knowledge? Very, very far. Birkin recalled again the female figure: the elongated, long, long body, the curious unexpected heavy buttocks . . . the face with tiny features like a beetle's. This was far beyond any phallic knowledge.

Only when Birkin makes his resolution to repudiate the direction pointed by the statue does the rhythm of hope make itself felt.

This much is clear, but the passage of Birkin's reflections remains one of the most puzzling in the novel. What is meant by the repeated references to some kind of knowledge 'beyond phallic knowledge'? What is it that the woman knew that Birkin does not yet know but dreads he will know? The horror for Birkin is not the state of mindlessness itself. The term *mindlessness* appears often in Lawrence's writings to describe the state of darkness in which the Brangwen farmers live or the coal miners in *Sons and Lovers*. That a degenerating culture loses contact with the values of light and abandons the quest for intellectual effort (the quest portrayed in *The Rainbow*) may be deplorable but not terrifying and threatening, as in Birkin's reflections about the 'dreadful mysteries far beyond the phallic cult'. The latter seems to be the horror, the horror, in *Women in Love*. Whatever

it is, three things may be said of it which call for more extended
discussion. It involves some form (or rather forms) of sexual
perversion; Birkin is strongly attracted to it (as the Pussum said
of Birkin's sermon, 'Oh, he was always talking about Corruption.
He must be corrupt himself, to have it so much on his mind').
And thirdly, its culmination is death itself, or more specifically
some form of suicide, individual and national.

The first point, about sexual perversions, is the most difficult
to establish, and even raising the question is enough to rouse the
ire of some brands of Laurentian admirers. The difficulty is that
the novel itself is not explicit, could not be explicit, in this area,
and we have to grope our way up a rickety ladder constructed of
image-clusters and scraps of information. Halliday's mistress, the
Pussum for example, is explicitly associated with the corruption
when Lawrence says of her: 'She was very handsome, flushed,
and confident in dreadful knowledge.' Less explicitly, a link is
established by references to marsh flowers (she is 'soft, unfolded
like some red lotus in dreadful flowering nakedness'), and she is
associated with the beetle-faced statue not so much by her fear of
beetles but by her very appearance as in this remarkable passage:

There was something curiously indecent, obscene, about her
small, longish, dark skull, particularly when the ears showed.

Like many of the characters in *Women in Love* the Pussum is a
vividly realized fictional creation yet at the same time, as representative of the corruption which the book treats, she is tagged by
the novelist with evaluative terms such as *obscene*.

Gudrun Brangwen, a more highly complex character, is
similarly presented. Her wood carvings were thought by Gerald
to have been made by the same hands as those which created the
African statues, and indeed Gudrun's affinities with what the
statues suggested to Birkin are referred to many times. Most explicitly there is a passage near the end of the novel which is a kind
of commentary on the earlier soliloquy. The passage consists of
reflections (virtually a soliloquy again) on the difference between
what Gerald offers as a lover of Gudrun and the kind of experi-

ence that Loerke could give her. Gerald's love-making has many
qualities of perversity, but because he still has some 'attachment'
to moral virtues, 'goodness' and 'righteousness', he cannot provide the special sexual thrills that Loerke promises:

Was it sheer blind force of passion that would satisfy her now?
Not this, but the subtle thrills of extreme sensation in reduction.
It was ... the last subtle activities of ... breaking down, carried
out in the darkness of her.

She reflects further that she no longer wants a man such as Gerald
but a *'creature'* like Loerke (who had been described by Birkin
as a sewer rat and by Gerald as an insect):

The world was finished now, for her. There was only the inner,
individual darkness ... the *obscene religious mystery* of ultimate
reduction, the mystic frictional activities of diabolic reducing
down, disintegrating the vital organic body of life. ... She had
... a further, slow exquisite experience to reap, unthinkable
subtleties of sensation to know, before she was finished. [Italics
mine.]

Before an attempt is made to explicate Gudrun's soliloquy a
word should be interjected about Loerke himself. Better even
than the Pussum and Gudrun, Loerke illustrates Lawrence's bold
technique of creating characters who are fully alive and so elo-
quently self-assertive that they may engage our sympathies, and
yet, in terms of the book's overall theme, of exposing them as
appalling examples of social corruption. It is almost a tightrope-
walking performance, and one can see why some of these creations have aroused divergent responses in his readers. Loerke
was even described by Nathan Scott (who sees Lawrence through
the spectacles of Denis de Rougemont) as a 'Laurentian saint'.
And to Anaïs Nin also, simply because he is an artist, he is the
man to be admired. Of the fact that at the end of the book Gerald
is dead and Loerke alive, Miss Nin says:

So it is Gerald who dies, not Loerke. It is the 'mindless sensuality' which dies. Yet it has been said that Lawrence in *Women in Love* had urged us to mindless sensuality and disintegration.[6]

The title of Miss Nin's book is *D. H. Lawrence: An Unprofessional Study*, and one wonders just how far the saving clause of her subtitle can be extended. Perhaps the most important equipment for a reader of Lawrence is just a nose. After his affair with the Pussum, Gerald admitted to Birkin:

There's a certain smell about the skin of those women, that in the end is sickening beyond words – even if you like it at first.*

Lawrence surely expects us to be similarly responsive, and a reader who concludes that Loerke is a Laurentian saint would seem to be lacking in a sense of smell. 'He lives like a rat, in the river of corruption, just where it falls over into the bottomless pit', says Birkin. Mankind, he adds, wants 'to explore the sewers', and Loerke is 'the wizard rat that swims ahead'. His very name evokes his negativism, the Loki of the sagas and of William Morris's *Sigurd the Volsung*: 'And Loki, the World's Begrudger, who maketh all labour vain.'

What is it then that this ruthless little 'creature' can provide that Gerald cannot offer? Both men have sadistic propensities and can presumably furnish the masochistic satisfactions that Gudrun craves. When she sees a picture of Loerke's nude statue of the young girl art-student on horseback (his preferences in girl-flesh anticipate those of the hero of Nabokov's *Lolita*), a girl who had to be subdued by his slapping her hard, 'Gudrun went pale, and a darkness came over her eyes, like shame, she looked up with a certain supplication, *almost slave-like*.' The counterpointing here is extremely intricate, for we are reminded that perhaps the two high points of Gudrun's earlier appreciation of Gerald had been when she watched him subdue a rabbit by force

* Cf. a reference to the women of the South Sea Islands whose skin he could not conceive of touching: 'flesh like warm mud. Nearer the reptile, the Saurian age'. (*Studies in Classic American Literature* (New York, 1923) pp. 202–3.)

or, more pertinently, when he drove his spurs into the flanks of his mare. . . . And the phrase *almost slave-like* also flashes back to the Pussum whose submissive response to Gerald was similarly described.

Both men, then, have this capacity in common. What Loerke is capable of beyond it is the provision of some perverse pleasures, and the cluster of associations is consistently hinting at some exploitation of the anal and excremental areas. The recurring references to the abnormally prominent buttocks of the African statue and to sexual relations in which the connections with 'creative life' are severed (anal intercourse has long been practised as a mode of avoiding conception), the traditional association of beetles with excrement, and the allusions to Loerke as a creature of the sewers all contribute towards some explication of both Birkin's soliloquy and that of Gudrun.

The hints concerning anal relations between men and women do not, however, indicate the full extent of the 'further sensual experience' which Birkin contemplated. Gudrun's soliloquy, in particular, refers to some 'obscene *religious* mystery of ultimate reduction'. What is the term *religious* meant to suggest to us? Are we supposed to conjure up some Black Mass? Loerke, one might add, is well named to make a celebrant in such a rite, for in some Norse myths *Loki* is the devil. Perhaps it is merely the Bacchic festivals that are hinted at, or bestial erotic ceremonials,* or blood-sacrifice ceremonies such as the Druids had performed, or so Lawrence believed, in Cornwall. Somers in *Kangaroo* recalls his experience during 1916 in Cornwall of drifting into a 'blood-darkness'. 'Human sacrifice! – he could feel his dark, blood-consciousness tingle to it again, the desire of it, the mystery of it.' Again Conrad's *Heart of Darkness* provided a model (if a somewhat obscure one) in its allusions to Kurtz's participation in 'certain midnight dances ending with unspeakable rites, which . . . were

* So far as I know there is no record of Lawrence's being exposed to some library of erotic literature such as Swinburne was exposed to under the guidance of R. M. Milnes. His distaste for such writers as Casanova ('he smells') is well known. (*The Letters of D. H. Lawrence*, ed. Aldous Huxley (1932) p. 523.)

offered up to him'. All that can be indicated about the introduction of the term *religious* into Lawrence's account of cultural degradation is that it reinforces a sense of the sinister without clarifying the nature of the corruption.

A further set of associations is less obscure but for Lawrence equally sinister, one that suggests that a declining society will revert to homosexuality. Loerke's perversities might include his love–hate relationship with his 'companion' Leitner – they had for long shared a bedroom and 'now reached the stage of loathing' – but this remains undeveloped. The problem of homosexuality takes us back from Gudrun and Loerke to Birkin's soliloquy and its expression of anxieties.

Unlike Proust, whose novels of this period also treat of the Cities of the Plain, Lawrence elected to avoid any direct representation in *Women in Love* of what Ezekiel calls the 'abomination' of Sodom; he offers us no study of a M. de Charlus. The Bohemians are described as 'degenerate', and there is some emphasis on the men being effeminate in manner with high-pitched squealing voices, but if London is to be likened to Sodom it is more because of its probable future fate than its present condition in this respect. If for the moment we shift from the novel to the novelist, however, we may detect a figure in this carpet. Lawrence's letters of 1915 and 1916 contain a remarkable number of references to his horror of beetles which is related, in most instances, to a horror of homosexual relations. In the Moore edition of the letters alone there are eighteen references to beetles and insects during the years 1915–16. On 30 April 1915, he reported his disgust after seeing an 'obscene' crowd of soldiers:

I like men to be beasts – but insects – one insect mounted on another – oh God! The soldiers at Worthing are like that – they remind me of lice or bugs.

Most revealing are passages referring to a visit paid by Francis Birrell to the Lawrences (in the company of David Garnett):

These horrible little frowsty people, men lovers of men, they

give me such a sense of corruption, almost putrescence, that I
dream of beetles.[7]

On this particular occasion his revulsion took form in an incident
that as reported by Garnett, seems fantastic. So wrought up was
Lawrence by Birrell's visit that he struggled to cast a spell over
him, and the young man actually woke up at night with his
tongue swollen so abnormally that he was in great pain.[8] As
Lawrence himself reported, such young men 'are cased each in a
hard little shell of his own', and 'they made me dream of a beetle
that bites like a scorpion. But I killed it.' One may associate the
incident with Kafka, but much more striking is a similarity to the
situation in Genesis when the men of Sodom gather outside Lot's
house and demand that his guests, two angels, be delivered to the
crowd 'that we may know them'. The guests retaliate on the men
of Sodom by striking them with blindness – this on the night
before the destruction of their city.

Francis Birrell was not the only man to provoke the beetle
nightmare in Lawrence at this time. For some reason his unhappy visit to Cambridge led to his associating Keynes and the
whole group there with beetles and corruption, and also with
Cambridge were linked such Bloomsbury figures as Duncan
Grant.* In a letter to Henry Savage in December 1913, in which
he frankly aired his feelings about homosexual relations, Lawrence concluded:

One is kept by all tradition and instinct from loving men, or a
man – for it means just *extinction of all the purposive influences*.

It may be noted that the phrase which I have italicized is almost
identical with the words used by Birkin in confronting the beetle-
faced statue. As he contemplates the possible lapse from 'the

* See Nehls, *D. H. Lawrence*, 1 269, 301, 302. The beetle image
reappears in Lawrence's play *David*. King Saul, in a mood of black
despair, prophesies that David's God will be devoured by a beetle
which hides in the bottomless pit. *The Plays of D. H. Lawrence* (n.d.)
p. 261.

desire for creation and productive happiness', he speaks of the fall 'from the connection with life and hope'.

In this reconstruction of what is implied in Birkin's fearsome sense of the slow degeneration of western man, nothing so far has been said about machinery. So much has been written by others about Lawrence's vitalistic dislike of industrialism (and I shall add my mite in discussing Gerald Crich) that it is perhaps a useful corrective to see that the horror in *Women in Love* is not exclusively industrialism, against which Lawrence's nineteenth-century predecessors in this role, Carlyle, Ruskin, Morris, had already expended themselves in valiant invectives. It is manifested rather in various forms of sexual corruption. The degeneration of the African civilization, or of Sodom, did not depend upon the discovery of power-operated lathes or steam shovels. Industrialism may accelerate and will certainly complicate the process, but from his study of history and legend, Lawrence was aware of patterns of human propensities that were independent of how coal and iron are worked, and the differences between what he calls the African process and the Arctic process are not crucial. The end of the slow process of degeneration of past societies was extinction, and a degenerate contemporary society would descend the same slope.

The image of the death-slope is Lawrence's of course rather than mine. It crops up in the novel and also in several of his war-time letters. In August 1915, he commented brutally on the kind of young man who joins the Roman Catholic Church, or the army, in order to enjoy obeying orders as a 'swine with cringing hindquarters'.* 'I dance with joy when I see him rushing down the Gadarene slope of the war.' In the Biblical story (about which Gladstone and T. H. Huxley had had their celebrated controversy) a community infected with evil spirits gains some relief by Christ's intervention, the evil spirits being driven out and

* *Letters*, ed. Moore, 1 360. Cf. *Reflections on the Death of a Porcupine*, pp. 83–4. In a Leconte de Lisle-like passage about baboons and their 'unthinkable loins', vultures and other creatures, Lawrence pictures the carrion-eating hyena with the same striking phrase: 'his cringing, stricken loins'.

into a herd of their swine. The swine, like a horde of lemmings, plunge down a slope into the sea and perish.

For Lawrence's purposes in 1916–17, the story of the Gadarene swine was richly suggestive. Not only did it provide one more analogue for the annihilating plunges taking place between the trenches across the Channel but an image suggesting the combination of swinish sensual corruption with a herd madness, an inexplicable propulsion towards self-destruction. The degenerate society, after exhausting all the possibilities of perverse sensuality represented by Loerke, finds its final thrill, its 'voluptuous satisfaction' – a phrase describing Gerald's sensations as his fingers tighten on Gudrun's soft throat – in death itself.

In his wartime essay, 'The Crown', Lawrence tried to formulate the connections between what he calls 'perversity, degradation and death', especially death in war:

So that as the sex is exhausted, gradually, a keener desire, the desire for the touch of death follows on. . . . Then come . . . fatal wars and revolutions which really create nothing at all, but destroy, and leave emptiness.

Those who prefer to lay the sources of war conveniently at the door of the munitions-makers will derive little satisfaction from Lawrence's recognition of destructive madness: 'we go careering down the slope in our voluptuousness of death and horror . . . into oblivion, like Hippolytus trammelled up and borne away in the traces of his maddened horses'.[9]

The most effective use of the image of the slope occurs during the coming together of Ursula and Birkin on the night before their marriage. After a violent quarrel with her father about her proposed marriage, she arrives at Birkin's cottage in tears:

He went over to her and kissed her fine, fragile hair, touching her wet cheeks gently.

'Don't cry,' he repeated, 'don't cry any more.' He held her head close against him, very close and quiet.

At last she was still. Then she looked up, her eyes wide and frightened.

'Don't you want me?' she asked.

'Want you?' His darkened, steady eyes puzzled her and did not give her play.

As in scenes from stories and novels already discussed, the exchange of feelings through the eyes is emphasized, and the ascent from the downward slope culminates in a poignantly rendered coming together:

'Do I look ugly?' she said. And she blew her nose again.

A small smile came round his eyes. . . . And he went across to her, and gathered her like a belonging in his arms. She was so tenderly beautiful, he could not bear to see her, he could only bear to hide her against himself. Now, washed all clean by her tears, she was new and frail like a flower just unfolded. . . . And he was so old, so steeped in heavy memories. Her soul was new, undefined and glimmering with the unseen. And his soul was dark and gloomy, it had only one grain of living hope, like a grain of mustard seed. But this one living grain in him matched the perfect youth in her.

'I love you,' he whispered as he kissed her, and trembled with pure hope, like a man who is born again to a wonderful, lively hope far exceeding the bounds of death. She could not know how much it meant to him, how much he meant by the few words. . . . But the passion of gratitude with which he received her into his soul, the extreme, unthinkable gladness of knowing himself living and fit to unite with her, he, who was so nearly dead, who was so near to being *gone with the rest of his race down the slope of mechanical death*, could never be understood by her. He worshipped her as age worships youth, he gloried in her because, in his one grain of faith, he was young as she, he was her proper mate. This marriage with her was his resurrection and his life. [Italics mine.]

The poignancy of the release from loneliness is similar to the effect of scenes in *Love Among the Haystacks*, *The Rainbow*, *Lady Chatterley's Lover*, and *The Man Who Died*, but perhaps most moving of all in this novel because of the overpowering nature of the destructive rhythms and the variety of ways in which they have been made to sound throughout the action. The hero is not a mere visitor full of righteousness; he is himself a citizen of Sodom, infected with a society's hatreds, degeneracy, and desire for death. Whatever the African statue stood for, as I suggested above, attracts all the characters, even at times Ursula, who usually insisted that she was a 'rose of happiness' and not one of the Baudelairian flowers. And for Birkin the attraction had been a powerful one. 'You are a devil, you know, really', Ursula says to him early in their relationship. 'You want to destroy our hope. You *want* us to be deathly.' And later: 'You are so *perverse*, so death-eating.'

The perversities associated with the statue take in more than being half in love, as Birkin was, with easeful death. What the 'further sensual experience' might be which prompted him to his soliloquy, and which he decides to repudiate, has already been indicated. As for the 'horror' of homosexuality, there have been readers, beginning with the early reviewers of the novel, who find the 'Gladiatorial' and 'Man to Man' chapters in this respect obscene. And if Lawrence had included the 'Prologue' chapter with which he had originally opened the novel, with its account of Birkin's realization that he likes the bodies of men better than the bodies of women, such readers would have had even more cause for alarm. The problem is extraordinarily complex and (not in the mere squeamish sense) delicate, calling for a nice discrimination between an 'abomination' and an ideal relation, a discrimination that some readers may be too impatient to make. In his 1918 essay on Whitman, Lawrence himself struggled to clarify the differentiation which had been assumed in his novel. For having sung of the 'love between comrades' Whitman is highly praised by Lawrence as one who had made pioneering efforts on behalf of a great cause. Such a love, provided that it never acts 'to destroy marriage', is recommended as healthy and life-giving. If it becomes an alternative to married love instead of a supplement, it is, on the contrary, deathly.[10] The *Blutbrüder-schaft* that Birkin wanted to establish with Gerald was supposedly a life-giving relationship not to be confused with the deathly degeneracies evoked in his soliloquy.

With the help of the Whitman essay, this distinction can perhaps be grasped, although as the final page of the novel shows, Ursula herself adamantly refused to grasp it. 'I wanted eternal union with a man too: another kind of love', Birkin says wistfully.

'I don't believe it,' she said. 'It's an obstinacy, a theory, a perversity.'

More difficult to grasp, however, is the parallel differentiation between some of the corruptive relations suggested by the statue and the innocence of exploratory relations between men and women as lovers. And here Ursula can, herself, be the spokeswoman for the innocence. At the ski-resort she reflects as she is going to sleep:

They might do as they liked. . . . How could anything that gave one satisfaction be excluded? What was degrading? . . . Why not be bestial, and go the whole round of experience? She exulted in it.

This passage is only slightly veiled and offers few problems. What was puzzling is the earlier scene at an English inn when Ursula discovers in Birkin's body 'the source of the deepest life-force'.

She had thought there was no source deeper than the phallic source. And now, behold, from the smitten rock of the man's body, from the strange marvellous flanks and thighs, deeper, further in mystery than the phallic source, came the floods of ineffable darkness and ineffable riches.

In 1961 G. Wilson Knight set out to explain what Lawrence was picturing in this curious scene by citing lines from the love poems in which the woman 'put her hand on my secret, darkest sources, the darkest outgoings'. As might be expected, Knight's explanation prompted an outburst of angry articles in the maga-

zines, most of them concerned with *Lady Chatterley's Lover.*
Indeed the novel went on trial, in effect, for a second time. A
lawyer, the Warden of All Souls at Oxford, discovered that in
one of the several sexual encounters described in that novel,
intercourse in the Italian style had been practised.[11] It had also
been occasionally practised, it seems, by Will and Anna in *The
Rainbow* and by Birkin and Ursula in the scene in the Tyrol
referred to above.

For the present discussion I am not going to be concerned with
the legal or even the aesthetic aspects of the practice beyond
simply endorsing Mark Spilka's comment (made several years
before the controversy became prominent) that Lawrence treats it
as an act having a limited function which, as a Puritan, he seems
to have thought can serve as a kind of 'discovery and purifica-
tion'.[12] What is relevant here is not whether some sort of Ovidian
Ars amatoria could be compiled from Lawrence's writings, but
whether the passages cited from *Women in Love* represent a serious
artistic blunder on the part of the novelist, creating such a blur
that the theme of the novel, and the drama of the hero's development, are both hopelessly obscured. More specifically, if the
'dreadful mysteries, far beyond the phallic cult' associated with
the beetle-faced statue are represented in one scene as degenerate
and in another scene (with only a slight shift in terminology) as
redemptive – when Ursula is transfigured by her discovery of a
'source deeper than the phallic source' – how is a reader supposed
to respond to what seems like a total contradiction?

Of the many critical discussions of *Women in Love*, the only
one which I have encountered that even raises some of the questions that I have been trying to grapple with here is that by Eliseo
Vivas. Vivas's conclusion is that Lawrence introduced a contradiction which is seemingly not resolved, because the novelist
has pictured Birkin as rejecting 'the African process' and then
shown him as, in effect, succumbing to it.[13] On these grounds we
might throw up our hands and say of Lawrence himself what
Ursula, in a fit of pique, said of Birkin: 'He says one thing one
day, and another the next – and he always contradicts himself.'
What may be enjoyed as a colorful trait in a fictional character is

not necessarily a commendable asset in the artist who created the fictional character. Fiction can be great when it is tentative and exploratory, making us aware of the puzzling complexities of choice confronting the characters, but if it is merely muddled it will not stand.

As when discussing the cathedral scene in *The Rainbow* I myself suggest again that although Lawrence may be asking too much of us in his account of Birkin's development, the sequence itself is not a muddled one. We are being expected to discriminate between sensual experiences enjoyed by a pair of loving men and women (which are regarded by the novelist as innocently enjoyed) on the one hand, and degenerate indulgences of a society which has cut all connections with spiritual values on the other. Perhaps like the comparable discrimination we were expected to make between a full-fledged homosexual relationship and *Blutbrüderschaft* we may, despite the cluster of horrors associated with the statue, find the distinction too fine, too naïve even, for the stretch of our patience. Yet if we are to understand the development of the characters as well as the social background against which their relations are worked out, the effort to establish the distinction is one worth making. Again, as with the discussion of Whitman, we can derive some help from one of Lawrence's essays. In 'Pornography and Obscenity' he writes:

The sex functions and the excrementory functions in the human body work so close together, yet they are, so to speak, utterly different in direction. Sex is a creative flow, the excrementory flow is towards dissolution, de-creation, if we may use such a word. In the really healthy human being the distinction between the two is instant, our profoundest instincts are perhaps our instincts of opposition between the two flows. But in the degraded human being the deep instincts have gone dead, and then the two flows become identical. . . . It happens when the psyche deteriorates, and the profound controlling instincts collapse.[14]

The discriminatory effort required in this instance, it may be added, is called for in many other places of this story, for *Women in Love* is one of the most demanding of novels. The kind of complexities encountered in discussing the two soliloquies, Birkin's and Gudrun's, which I have been treating expansively here, could be demonstrated again in connection with what Vivas has called the 'constitutive' symbols of which the novel is full – the great scene of Birkin stoning the moonlit water for example,[15] or the winter scenes in the mountains culminating in Gerald's confronting another statue, a Tyrolian Christ sticking up out of the snow 'under a little sloping hood, at the top of a pole'.

What I have been stressing myself is that the complexities derive much of their density from Lawrence's choosing to portray Birkin in particular not as a White Knight, incorrupt and incorruptible, but as a suffering character dramatically involved in extricating himself from a death-loving world to which he is deeply, almost fatally, attracted. Like Conrad in similar presentation of Kurtz and Marlow, Lawrence in this way perhaps doubles the difficulties confronting his readers, but the clear gain in the overall effectiveness of his novel as a novel is beyond measurement. In a society made up of 'a herd of Gadarene swine, rushing possessed to extinction',[16] Gerald Crich is clearly infected with the madness and perishes. Birkin himself is a near casualty. As Wilfred Owen says in his haunting late fragment, 'Strange Meeting': 'Foreheads of men have bled where no wounds were.'

SOURCE: *Double Measure: a study of the novels and stories of D. H. Lawrence* (New York, 1965).

NOTES

1. In this discussion I am quoting from the original version of *Women in Love* (1921) before Pussum was changed into Minette. The revisions which Lawrence introduced into his later edition were prompted by the threat of a libel suit, and although a few of them might reflect a more significant change of intention most of them are mere insulators, and not being consistently changed they also lead to confusion. Because Heseltine, who was threatening the libel suit, had

African statues in his apartment, Lawrence obliged by changing the one referred to in chs. VI and VII into a statue from the West Pacific and by deleting the references to negroes. But in ch. XIX he left these unchanged. See also his reference in an essay to 'an African fetish idol of a woman pregnant' (*Reflections on the Death of a Porcupine* (Bloomington, 1963) pp. 140–1). At least from our present perspective, one detail of these revisions is an amusing example of Lawrence's humour. The name *Pussum* was changed to *Minette* presumably because Heseltine's mistress had been known as the Puma, but the name of Heseltine's wife, whom he married in Dec. 1916, was *Minnie* Channing.

2. On 18 Apr. 1918 Lawrence wrote that he had read 'two ponderous tomes on Africa' by Frobenius, and in *Aaron's Rod* he pictures Lilly reading the same author. See also Basil Davidson, *The Lost Cities of Africa* (Boston, 1959) and André Malraux, *The Voices of Silence* (New York, 1953) p. 132.

3. *The Collected Letters of D. H. Lawrence*, ed. Harry T. Moore, 2 vols (1962) I 477–8. (Italics mine.)

4. *Letters*, ed. Moore, I 418, and *The Letters of D. H. Lawrence*, ed. Aldous Huxley (1932) pp. 303, 329.

5. Horace Gregory, *D. H. Lawrence: Pilgrim of the Apocalypse* (New York, 1933) pp. 45–6, 49.

6. Anaïs Nin, *D. H. Lawrence* (Paris, 1932) p. 110. See also Nathan A. Scott, Jr, *Rehearsals of Discomposure* (New York, 1952) p. 157.

7. *Letters*, ed. Moore, I 333.

8. Edward Nehls (ed.), *D. H. Lawrence: A Composite Biography*, 3 vols (Madison, 1957–9) I 269, 301.

9. *Reflections on the Death of a Porcupine*, pp. 66–7, 80.

10. D. H. Lawrence, *The Symbolic Meaning*, ed. Armin Arnold (1962) p. 263.

11. See John Sparrow in *Encounter*, Feb. 1962, pp. 35–43, and June 1962, pp. 83–8; and replies by Colin MacInnes and Stephen Potter in *Encounter*, Mar. 1962, pp. 63–5, 94–6. See also Wilson Knight in *Essays in Criticism*, Oct. 1961, pp. 403–17, and Andrew Shonfield in *Encounter*, Sept. 1961, pp. 63–4, and a letter to the editor, *Times Literary Supplement*, 4 Aug. 1961. An earlier controversy provoked by Colin Welch's accusing Lawrence of witchcraft can also be found in *Encounter*, Feb. 1961, pp. 75–9, and Mar. 1961, pp. 52–5. Also relevant are Middleton Murry's comments in his *Reminiscences of D. H. Lawrence* (1933) pp. 223–7.

12. Mark Spilka, *The Love Ethic of D. H. Lawrence* (Bloomington, 1955) p. 100.

13. Eliseo Vivas, *D. H. Lawrence* (Evanston, 1960) pp. 261–7.

14. *Phoenix* (1936) p. 176.

15. Again Vivas's account (*D. H. Lawrence*, pp. 257–61) is especially helpful. For a contrasting interpretation of the scene, see Murray Krieger, *The Tragic Vision* (1960) pp. 37–49.

16. *Letters*, ed. Moore, I 520.

Ronald Gray

WOMEN IN LOVE AND THE GERMAN TRADITION IN LITERATURE (1965)

LAWRENCE'S relationship to Germany was both more intimate and more critical than that of any other English writer – he was perhaps the first of these to marry a German wife – and yet his opinions of German writers were hostile when they were not contemptuous, as they were of Goethe[1] and Thomas Mann.[2] More than this, he instinctively recoiled both from the German nation and from the very atmosphere of Germany: 'Out of the very air', he wrote of a post-war visit, 'comes a sense of danger, a queer, *bristling* feeling of uncanny danger.' It was not that the people were actually planning or plotting or preparing; there was nothing conscious in what Lawrence saw already in 1924 as the ancient spirit of prehistoric Germany coming back, 'at the end of history'. Nor, needless to say, was he thinking in terms of rival nationalisms, having opposed the war of 1914–18. Rather, it was that 'the northern Germanic impulse is recoiling towards Tartary, the destructive vortex of Tartary'. And, in a German mood himself, 'it is a fate; nobody now can alter it. It is a fate.'[3]

Lawrence's sense of this fatal course in German and thereby in European history is reflected nowhere better in his work than in *Women in Love*, a novel which must strike every reader familiar with German literature as almost cast in a German mould. It is not in fact cast – Lawrence does no more than make use of the ambivalent systems in giving his work structure; he does not write from out of a settled *Weltanschauung*, as Thomas Mann or Hermann Hesse do. He remains essentially an explorer. Yet a discussion of *Women in Love* in its more German aspects may be useful not only in drawing attention to features that may be ignored, but also in indicating the contribution the novel may make to the European culture of the future.

One thing likely to be noticed by anyone with a mainly German background is the number of German words the novel contains – *Wille zur Macht, Blutbrüderschaft*, the *Glücksritter* desired by Gudrun – and the fact that, unlike most of the other foreign words in it, these refer to essential concepts in the novel. More important, however, is the role played in the whole structure by the concept of 'polarity', one rarely found in English literature but a commonplace in German. Structurally, although in no other respects, no novel corresponds so closely with *Women in Love* as does Goethe's *Elective Affinities*. Here there is the same pattern of two pairs of lovers, Eduard and Ottilie, Charlotte and the Captain, the same occult affinity bringing the one pair together and towards a spiritual union, the other towards a lower and less rewarding one, as there is, although with different implications, in Rupert Birkin and Ursula, Gerald Crich and Gudrun Brangwen. It is not merely that Lawrence chooses to write of two pairs – that in itself is undistinctive. It is rather that, like Goethe, he is writing of the attraction and repulsion within the pairs and between them, in terms of what he explicitly calls 'polarity', a hidden magnetism. Again, it is not that the two novels point to a similar conclusion. Goethe's is concerned with 'resignation': the awareness that the impulse to love can have no real fulfilment until after death. It also treats of love as making the lovers unconsciously reach towards closer and closer identity with one another, in the spirit of that 'synthesis' which was always one of Goethe's preoccupations. Ottilie's handwriting comes to resemble Eduard's more and more, her whole personality grows like his, so that the ultimate union beyond the grave, spoken of in the final lines, must seem meant as a final and complete transubstantiation of the woman in the man. Moreover, the man himself, Eduard, is so passive and dull a character (for whom Goethe himself had little regard) that the prospect of fulfilment remains bleak. For Rupert Birkin on the other hand, the desire for assimilation in the other lover is a way to catastrophe. The differences between the two selves are not to be overcome or whittled away. On the contrary, they are to be heightened, intensified; the woman to become more herself as a

woman and the man more himself as a man; only then may they
come together, not in fusion but in distinct selfhood, the man
keeping the woman 'single within himself, like a star in its orbit'.[4]
It is not identity with the mystery of the other's presence that
matters, but apartness in the awareness of mystery, the 'palpable
revelation of living otherness'.[5] In this formulation, which Lawrence was evidently attached to more passionately than to many
others in his novel, he was, whether he knew it intellectually or
not, reiterating a tradition of considerable antiquity.* He was
also affirming the essential difference he felt between himself
and Goethe, for whom, as he believed, there was never any
capacity for '*development* of contact with other human beings'.
'Goethe *began* million of intimacies, and never got beyond the
how-do-you-do stage, then fell off into his own boundless ego.'[6]
That incapacity, on Lawrence's interpretation, was the counterpart of the desire for identity, the inability to respect otherness.
He might have quoted Faust's desire to enjoy all the joys and
sufferings of all mankind, and thus to extend his selfhood to
embrace all selfhood:† this has the same boundless egoism and
the same barrenness of contact, for Faust as a rule feels no joys
or sorrows but his own, and when he does feel *for* someone else
(Gretchen is the only instance) he at once ascribes universal
importance to the fact.

The insistence on diversity within unity is one characteristic of
Women in Love, but the novel is not solely concerned with the
struggle of Rupert and Ursula towards fulfilment – a fulfilment
which is in any case only felt intensely for a moment, to become
after that a source of life, a sense of having the pulse 'beating
direct from the mystery'.[7] The story also contains the struggle of

---

* Heinrich Suso, the medieval mystic, writing of the man who is
'entirely lost in God', adds the paradox that the same man's being
'remains, though in a different form, in a different glory, and in a
different power' (quoted in R. C. Zaehner, *Mysticism, Sacred and
Profane* (1957) p. 21). Lawrence's 'human' mysticism, in which the
male lover often seems close to the God of Suso, retains this old tradition of a distinctiveness in identity.

† 'Und so mein eigen Selbst zu ihrem [der Menschheit] Selbst
erweiten'.

Gerald and Gudrun towards their own fulfilment, their perfection, as Lawrence calls it, and this is to Rupert's and Ursula's fulfilment as negative to positive. The love of Gerald and Gudrun is a purely self-annihilating one, without immediate relationship to the mystery beyond or in the lovers. And being self-annihilating in this sense it is also self-assertive, perhaps because when the self is dead without recourse to any fertility beyond it, it is faced with sheer nothingness, an intolerable void from which it recoils on itself with even greater avidity. This is how it is with Gerald, the 'Dionysus' of the story (whereas Rupert is more often compared with Jesus, and spoken of deprecatingly as a would-be 'Salvator Mundi'). It is Gerald whom we most often see assertive, dominating his mare, digging his spurs into her at the level-crossing to force her to obey his will as the frightening locomotive rumbles past.* It is he who cows the struggling rabbit with a vicious blow on the back, and he who runs his factory with a ruthless disregard for the old and infirm. But it is also Gerald who, ultimately, is terror-struck at the awareness of death, and who goes to Gudrun as a suppliant, to be perfected not in distinctness from her but in complete self-yielding to her. The love between Gerald and Gudrun is always one of self-assertion on the one hand and self-surrender on the other, now the man, now the woman being dominant. There is never fulfilment for both together, but always for one only, while the other lies awake and conscious, hatred growing within. And as Lawrence shows it, this attempted violation of the other's mystery is destructive, nihilistic, ultimately disastrous. Gudrun begins the destructive progression when she hits Gerald in the face, saying with little awareness of her own meaning that she has struck the first blow. Gerald ends it when, unable any longer to assert his will over Gudrun, he first tries to strangle her and then, realizing that he has not enough truly positive will to accomplish even that, goes off up the mountain to fall unconscious and freeze to death.

These are the two pairs, corresponding, but very distantly corresponding, to the two in Goethe's novel. Lawrence does not,

* Gudrun thinks 'Gerald would be freer, more dauntless than Bismarck'.

however, take sides, he does not condemn Gerald as though
he thought him capable of choosing another course. Rupert
continues to love Gerald in death, he even conceives of himself
as on the same path to destruction. The fulfilment of Gerald and
Gudrun is spoken of as their perfection, and perfect it must seem
from that 'inhuman' plane where Rupert meets Ursula – 'there
can be no calling to book, in any form whatsoever', he tells her,
'because one is outside the pale of all that is accepted, and nothing
known applies. One can only follow the impulse, taking that
which lies in front, and responsible for nothing, asked for nothing,
giving nothing, only each taking according to the primal desire.'[8]
This is a kind of fatalism which sees the two courses, the two
forms of perfection, the creative and the destructive, and follows
them through to their goals, each in its way a fulfilment of the
mysterious purpose in creation which embraces them both.
There are times when the book seems to be written on that
inhuman plane, as though the savage descriptions of the mountains and the tender evocations of flowers were issuing from a
superhuman creator. But that is not the whole story. Lawrence
is tempted towards the superhuman, and yet remains essentially
human and sane.

It is at this point that the name of Nietzsche most readily
springs to mind, and it is indeed only a few pages after the
passage I have just quoted that the *Wille zur Macht*, the 'will-to-
power' is mentioned. Lawrence ranges up and down Nietzsche's
ideas, the Dionysian and the Apolline; Dionysus and Christ; the
'master-morality' of Gerald Crich displayed in the organizing
of his industry; the need for man to be surpassed in the course
of evolutionary creation; the achievement of a state beyond good
and evil; the dominance of the male over the female; the aristocratic temper contrasted with the slave-temper; the need for self-
annihilation in order to transcend the self. He is as paradoxical
as Nietzsche, as full of contradictory beliefs and ideals; when he
writes of Gerald's brutalities one is inclined to see in him just
such an admirer of the 'blond beast' as Nietzsche has often been
held to be. Yet there are two essential distinguishing features.
First, Nietzsche's thought is entirely aphoristic. One aphorism

will often contradict another, and there are times when contradictions follow one another within the compass of a short passage. There is no comprehensive pattern, no exposition, development, climax, catastrophe, and taking stock, as there is in the novel. 'I am not a man', Nietzsche wrote, 'I am dynamite', and the truth of that can be seen in the form of his writing. The thoughts explode into the air with the force of an eruption, the individual blocks soar out and sink down, and one looks in vain for a coherent aim or purpose. It is on this account, I believe, that Nietzsche has been held responsible for the disaster which overtook Germany thirty years after his death. Whether or not Nietzsche would have welcomed the Nazi seizure of power, the destructive impact of his thought, its incoherence and lack of creative direction did, as I think, insidiously undermine humane thinking in Germany, and thus seriously weakened resistance to the Nazi movement. Lawrence on the other hand, while treating of just the same ideas, places them within the framework of a novel where their particular juxtapositions are significant. In the chapter curiously entitled 'Excurse' we see the union of Rupert and Ursula; in the immediately following chapter 'Death and Love' we see that of Gerald and Gudrun, and from then on their progressive hatred and unwilling isolation. We are not asked to 'call to book' any of these characters, and yet as we take the impulse, take 'that which lies in front', we see the full nature of their loving. It is not a choice, not a decision, but a horrible awareness of the implications of the ideal, of all that has led up to it and is likely to stem from it. This Lawrence achieves, where Nietzsche does not achieve it, by virtue of the impulse which brings him to place this event after that one, the Gerald and Gudrun chapter after the Rupert and Ursula chapter, to balance one against another and let the scales rise or fall as they will. There is a humane morality in Lawrence which takes cognizance of Nietzsche's inhuman or superhuman morality and the morality of master and slave, and which does not condemn it, any more than Rupert condemns Gerald, but yet *shows* a contrast so plainly as to resolve our hearts and minds.

Moreover, and this is the second point I referred to, Lawrence is able as a novelist to introduce that detachment which is so lacking in Nietzsche. One is aware that Nietzsche is self-critical, intensely self-critical. Yet how seldom does a note of humour enter: the note is solemnly intense, apart from such dull flashes of Voltairean wit as those in the 'Lieder des Prinzen Vogelfrei'. Nietzsche admired Aristophanes and Petronius, yet his own prose runs on burdened feet of seriousness. He is too intent on impressing us with the awful terror of his message to strike the more light-hearted note of indifference which his doctrine sometimes implies. Lawrence, on the other hand, while he certainly uses Rupert Birkin as a mouthpiece, is not identified with him. Rupert is properly contrasted with other characters who find him priggish and sanctimonious, over-concerned to put his ideals into words; he is worsted in arguments and his lapses are seized on and defined by others in a way that shows how much Lawrence himself was aware of them.

This kind of detachment is not in Nietzsche, nor is Rupert Birkin's tenderness with flowers and animals and women. Nietzsche remains abstract; Lawrence would have said that he was all intellect, despite his Dionysianism, and he seldom writes of the natural scene or of individual human beings. Thoughts are his real concern; myths and generalizations, not minute particulars, are his means of communication. He could not spare time to spend a chapter near the climax of a work to describe the buying of an old chair.*

With Rilke it is a different matter. In Rilke there is, especially in his middle period, much time to spare for the detail of things – flamingoes, a panther, a hydrangea, a cathedral, a statue. And Rilke shares with Lawrence an antipathy to Christianity, a concern with love between men and women, a determination to love in a world in which there is no God, and indeed most of

* I had not, at the time of writing, read R. L. Drain's dissertation, 'Formative Influences on the work of D. H. Lawrence' (Cambridge, 1962). I am glad to find myself agreeing with Dr Drain on the idea that Nietzsche was for Lawrence a point of departure, but that Lawrence at his best put aside the egotist for the sake of taking 'our decent place' in the whole (op. cit. p. 223).

the Nietzschean preoccupations. In many ways they are quite surprisingly alike, and I find it a hard task to put in a small compass the distinctions I still find between them. It can perhaps be put like this. There is a quite remarkable similarity between the final image of Rilke's *Duino Elegies*, of a man setting out to walk further and further into the increasing darkness of total death, up into the mountains of Primal Pain, and the final image of Gerald Crich moving away from the half-strangled Gudrun to climb higher and higher to his death among frozen rocks. The *Elegies* and the novel were written at about the same time,[9] and it is as though each writer saw and knew the reality of the destructive way in his age. Lawrence, as I noted earlier, saw both this way and a way represented in Rupert and Ursula, although he had sympathy with, knew himself close to, both ways. And Rilke also saw two ways. He saw the way which led to the never-ending *impasse* of the *Elegies*, and he saw the way to which he gave expression in the companion-piece to the *Elegies*, the *Sonnets to Orpheus*. In the *Sonnets* there is a gaiety, a refreshed enjoyment which is only announced, scarcely ever realized in the *Elegies*, and I am tempted strongly to say that, just as Lawrence knew himself to be in both Rupert and Gerald, so Rilke knew himself both as the desperate lamenter of the *Elegies* and as the rejoicing singer of the *Sonnets*. But I cannot feel that is quite the case. For Rilke does not present the final image of the *Elegies* as a tragic ending, as Lawrence presents the death of Gerald. It is rather an end desirable in itself: true happiness is to know this increasing destruction of oneself, to realize more and more fully the death that is bearing in. And the Orphic image is equally a realization of 'true' happiness, the refreshment and the acceptance in the *Sonnets* is as much true as the decomposition and the pain and lament. The *Elegies* and the *Sonnets* seem to me to stand over against each other in pure contradiction, just as so many of the lines they contain are contradictory even down to adjoining words and phrases. One is left at the last rather with the sense of contradiction, of an unresolved polarity, rather than with the pattern within a single work, the clear impulse towards one end, which there is in *Women in Love*.

Rilke's and Lawrence's way of feeling about love is similarly close and yet distant. Rilke's ideal of love without reciprocity, love that does not ask for love to be returned, is remarkably close to Lawrence's twin stars, 'asked for nothing, giving nothing'.[10] Like Lawrence, Rilke despised the give and take of love which was no more than mutual support over a void; lovers, he said, 'hide from each other their lot'. Yet Rilke's lovers are totally isolated, set over against one another as the *Elegies* are set over against the *Sonnets*, each complete in himself or herself – Narcissistically complete, like Gudrun near the lowest point in her course. 'It seemed to [Gerald]', Lawrence writes, 'that Gudrun was sufficient unto herself, closed round and completed, like a thing in a case. In the calm, static reason of his soul, he recognized this, and admitted it was her right, to be closed round upon herself, self-complete, without desire. . . . He knew that it only needed one convulsion of his will for him to be able to turn upon himself also, to close upon himself as a stone fixes upon itself, and is impervious, self-completed, a thing isolated.'[11] And such a condition is surely that of Eurydice in Rilke's poem, who has no need of Orpheus but turns back into the livid paths of Hades: 'sie war in sich, und ihr Gestorbensein erfüllte sie wie Fülle'. 'She was within herself, her having died fulfilled her like full harvest' – a condition dreadful and yet in its way perfected. But there is in Rilke's conception of love no way out from this total isolation. There is no awareness of otherness, the 'immemorial magnificence of mystic, palpable, real otherness'.[12] There is nothing that could lead to such a dialogue as that at the end of Lawrence's novel, after Gerald's death.

'It's a bitter thing to me,' [Rupert] said.
'What – that he's dead?' she said.
His eyes just met hers. He did not answer.
'You've got me,' she said.
He smiled and kissed her.
'If I die,' he said, 'you'll know I haven't left you.'
'And me?' she cried.
'And you won't have left me,' he said. 'We shan't have any need to despair, in death.'[13]

Rilke's lovers have no such knowledge, for they have only the isolation, not the living contact of realized selves. They are 'constellations' (*Sternbild* is a key-word in Rilke), not stars together in orbit. Ultimately, they are all one within the transcendent order of Rilke's Angels, yet each one separate and alone in its consciousness, incapable of reaching out to others except by the way of the Angels, that is, by themselves embracing all in one totality. Thus it is that in Rilke's life there were many lovers; he is like Gerald in that, and unlike Rupert, or Lawrence for that matter, for whom marriage was a relation between chosen man and chosen woman. The all-embracing love, seeing the many as one, denying to the one its individual distinctness, leads to that isolation where there is only the one self and, as Lawrence so clearly saw, to ultimate destruction not only for the individual but for the civilization in which that mode of loving prevails.

This concern of Lawrence's both for a union and for distinctness is one of the features that marks him off from many of his predecessors in the main German tradition of thought and literature. In this he resembles Hölderlin – at least in one of his moods – the Hölderlin who wrote the distich entitled 'Root of all Evil':

Einig zu sein, ist göttlich und gut; woher ist die Sucht denn
Unter den Menschen, daß nur Eines und Einer nur sei?

'To be at one is divine and good, whence comes then the yearning of men that only the One, only Oneness should be?' This yearning has been marked in Germany for two centuries; it appears in a variety of forms. It can be expressed in Faust's attempt at embracing all human experience – 'and so extend my self to cover all their selves' – as well as in Fichte's vision of the world created by the self – in each case there is a Oneness which does not permit and does not want the existence of anything outside the self. It can be expressed in Hegel's 'world-historical man' who is held to be the very embodiment of the age in which he lives, and is thus entitled to draw along with him even his opponents. It is in all the attempts at fashioning a *Weltanschauung*,

establishing a final truth about the world, valid for all men, all
the attempts at establishing a point of vantage outside history,
from which the writer speaks with a quasi-divine authority. It is
not in Kant, who remained conscious of the otherness of the
'thing-in-itself'. But then Kant, as Stefan Zweig observed, is the
'arch-enemy of all German poets'. It is in Schopenhauer, who
tried to bridge the gap between the inner and the outer world by
declaring 'we *are* the thing-in-itself'. It is not in Hölderlin when
he writes 'einsam / Unter dem Himmel wie immer bin ich' – to
be *beneath* the sky, yet in touch with its mystery, is essential to
his way of feeling. On the other hand, the yearning is in Kleist,
Kleist who was so shattered by Kant's insistence on otherness
that he portrayed the Amazon lover Penthesilea literally tearing
at the breast of Achilles with her teeth, almost devouring him in
her need to consume him wholly within herself, as Gerald later
seeks to consume Gudrun. And it is not unjust to associate *that*
form of the yearning with the striving for political unity in
Germany in the last century and a half. In politics also there has
been on the one hand the desire for autarky, for a Narcissistic
isolation shorn of all contact with the outside world, and on the
other a determination to obliterate the distinctiveness of the
outside world, to consume it and assert the essential *Deutschtum*
of everything it contains. That has not been the whole story, it is
perhaps needless to say. There have been Germans, less able to
make their voice heard, for whom the Faustian image is completely
inappropriate, and recent developments in the Bundesrepublik
encourage the hope that the whole spirit of the all-inclusive
Weltanschauung is diminishing.[14] But Kleist's Penthesilea,
coupled with Kleist's insane and brutal nationalism, is an apt
image of the link between the yearning for oneness in sexual
love and in social organization.

Lawrence must have been aware of the implications his novel
had for Germany. It is unlikely to be mere chance that the novel
moves from England in the final chapters towards Germany –
to the Austrian Tyrol, in fact, to a place near Innsbruck. Nor does
it seem insignificant that Gudrun, becoming incapable of enduring Gerald's love any longer, falls in love with the sculptor

Loerke from Düsseldorf. By now Gudrun's repleteness in herself has reached the point of almost complete indifference to the outside world. She cannot bear to experience Gerald's need for her, and indeed his desire has now become a voluptuous ecstasy in the thought of destroying her. In Loerke, the satirical gnome-like figure, diabolically free in his own indifference to everything, she finds a new lease of life – 'she was happy like a child, very attractive and beautiful to everybody, with her soft, luxurious figure, and her happiness. Yet underneath was death itself.'[15] With Loerke she can enjoy a pure game, neither giving, neither taking, each engaged in an intellectual delectation of himself through the other. Gudrun's indifference is so great that her fulfilment with Loerke seems perfect. 'You are going away tomorrow?' he asks her. ' "*Wohin?*" That was the question – *wohin?* Whither? *Wohin?* What a lovely word! She *never* wanted it answered. Let it chime for ever.'[16] It is as though Lawrence had read Rilke's words in the *Sonnets to Orpheus* (i xxiii): 'Erst wenn ein reines Wohin' – only when some 'pure whither' is learned will fulfilment come. Impatience, the desire to dictate one's own path, leads astray. The wind blows where it lists, and for Gudrun, as Loerke tells her, the wind 'goes towards Germany'.[17] After Gerald's death she leaves for Dresden, and we hear no more of her. It is as though Lawrence had perceived that her deathly wish for isolation and domination would find a natural environment there.

Lawrence does not write detachedly of Gudrun, any more than he does of Gerald: he does not point a warning finger. On the contrary, Gudrun's feelings and thoughts are as persuasively set down as though they were Lawrence's own. The sense of a disaster in her life that is still to come arises rather from its juxtaposition with that of Rupert and Ursula, pure juxtaposition. Gudrun is given over to Loerke, of whom she knows that 'he admitted no allegiance, he gave no adherence anywhere. He was single and, by abstraction from the rest, absolute in himself.'[18] He has the same self-repleteness as there is in Gudrun, as there is in Rilke's Eurydice, he is just as satisfied as she is with a 'reines Wohin'. And yet – isn't there something in this very similar to

Rupert Birkin's passage about having one's pulse beating direct from the mystery? Isn't that the same kind of dependence on the wind that blows where it wants to? It *is* dependence, it is the same in the sense that it yields up personal control. It is different, in that what Loerke and Gudrun yield to is nothing, pure arbitrariness, and what Rupert speaks of is 'having the faith to yield to the mystery'.[19] Gudrun, like one of Rilke's lovers, runs on past the other, 'auf Nichts zu'. Rupert, remembering the other, gains faith in the mystery, grows warmer with a new trust in living. There is this essential difference.

But this is not a tract about Germany, it is a novel. If I have drawn attention to German aspects of it, it has been at best in the hope that I might draw attention to particular features of Lawrence's work, make clearer what they are by pointing out how they differ from others that resemble them in a general way. I said earlier on that to define a pattern, a skeletal form, might seem inappropriate in talking about so spontaneous a writer as Lawrence, and that still holds true. For *Women in Love* is not a novel with a message, it is not instructing us to adopt one course rather than another. It can only present us with an imitation of life, and it will be more or less of a fine work as it gives more or less of a balanced picture. Had Lawrence written about Rupert and Ursula alone, or Gerald and Gudrun alone, without including the other pair, his picture would not be balanced, he would have written a tract. In fact, he has written a tragedy. The mood at the end of the book is not one of condemnation but of bitter sorrow for the death of Gerald, and there cannot be sorrow or tragedy where a message is being imparted or a lesson taught. There is neither message nor system nor *Weltanschauung* here – Lawrence uses the mechanism of systems and *Weltanschauungen* to build the structure of his novel, but he surrenders himself as he writes to the spontaneity of the moment, and that means surrendering as much to the spirit of one pair of lovers as to that of the other. There is, of course, what Ursula calls the 'Salvator Mundi touch' about Lawrence himself, there *is* a would-be redeemer in him, who keeps putting forward what looks like a message. But Lawrence is aware of that, he puts it in its place within the novel by means of Ursula's scepticism; the picture remains balanced.

All the same, by virtue of his juxtapositions Lawrence does provide us with insights we might well not have, if the novel had remained entirely within the 'German' tradition as I have outlined it. *Women in Love* is deeply indebted to German ideas, but it is also, that goes without saying, a particularly English novel; it marries something from the English world, especially an insistence on individuality and morality, with something from the German world that had better just be called mysticism, whatever the misunderstandings that may arise: antinomianism, the sense of all-embracingness, are two of its features. The *Blutbrüderschaft* which Rupert looks for between himself and Gerald is also the kind of relationship Lawrence must, I think, have looked for between himself and Germany: a combination of empiricism and 'mystical' beliefs. In his Englishness, moreover, Lawrence does often closely resemble 'English' Blake,[20] in whom a similar preoccupation with ultimately German ideas (Boehme) was apparent, and nowhere more closely than in relation to the lines from *Jerusalem*, in which the 'Only General and Universal Form' is identified with benevolence 'Who protects minute particulars, every one in their own identity'.[21] It is the combination of mystical union with enduring separateness here which places both Blake and Lawrence in a line of English writers who have made use of German ideas to produce something peculiarly their own. Apart from anything else, in the present political state of Europe this has a special value.

S O U R C E : *The German Tradition in Literature, 1871–1945* (Cambridge, 1965).

NOTES

1. See letter to Aldous Huxley, 27 Mar. 1928.
2. *Phoenix* (1936) pp. 308–13.
3. Ibid., p. 110.
4. *Women in Love*, ch. XIII.

5. *Women in Love*, ch. XXIII.

6. Letter to Aldous Huxley, 27 Mar. 1928.

7. *Women in Love*, ch. XIII.

8. Ibid., ch. XIII.

9. *Women in Love* in 1916, the *Elegies* between 1912 and 1922.

10. *Women in Love*, ch. XIII.

11. Ibid., ch. XXX.

12. Ibid., ch. XXIII.

13. Ibid., ch. XXXI.

14. Cf. Uwe Kitzinger, 'The Death of Ideology', in *The Listener*, 18 Jan. 1962.

15. *Women in Love*, ch. XXX.

16. Ibid., ch. XXX.

17. Ibid., ch. XXX.

18. Ibid., ch. XXX.

19. Ibid., ch. XXXI.

20. Contrary to Dr Leavis's disclaimer, in *D. H. Lawrence: Novelist* (1955) p. 12, although I am generally in agreement with his views on *Women in Love*.

21. Quoted in Joseph H. Wicksteed, *Blake's Vision of the Book of Job* (1910) p. 116.

Frank Kermode

LAWRENCE AND THE
APOCALYPTIC TYPES (1968)

I

WRITING novels is more like writing history than we often choose to think. The relationships between events, the selection of incident, even, in sophisticated fictions, the built-in scepticism as to the validity of procedures and assumptions, all these raise questions familiar to philosophers of history as problems relating to historical explanation.

One such problem is explanation by types. Types are obviously important in novels, for without them there would be no 'structure'. How do they work in history? How do we recognise, for instance, a revolution? The events of a selected series cease to look random when we assimilate them to other selected series which have been identified and classified under some such term as 'revolution'. Similarly for series which can be filed under 'crisis', or under 'transitional epoch'. There is the added complication that personalities involved in the events under consideration may very well have done the typing themselves, as revolutionaries generally do, and this means that historical like fictive events can in some measure be caused to occur in conformity with the types. Furthermore, since everybody's behaviour is indeterminately modified by the conviction that he is living through a crisis, it might be argued that history can, though with unpredictable variations, be prepared for such a conformity, even without the intervention of conscious theory. But the element of indeterminacy is so gross that we can perhaps forget this.

There are, very broadly speaking, two quite distinct and mutually hostile ways of considering 'typical' explanations. One is to assume that, with varying and acceptable degrees of 'displacement', histories and fictions cannot avoid conforming with types, so that the most useful thing that can be done is to demonstrate this conformity. However sophisticated and cautious the exponent of this doctrine may be, his thinking is likely, in the last analysis, to be sentimentally ritualistic and circular. He is nowadays much more likely to be a critic of fiction than an historian. Historians and modern theologians nowadays employ typology in a much more empirical way, a way consistent with a more linear notion of history.* The historian will agree that the discovery of a motive in some action or series of actions involves classifying it as belonging to a certain type. Unless that is done it will not appear that a motive has been discovered. Of course he will also, as a rule, agree that the material available is not always so classifiable; and so will the novelist. The distinction between these kinds of event is roughly that defined by Bultmann in respect of biblical history as a contrast between what is *historisch* and what is *geschichtlich*. The novelist, as a rule, has rather more interest than the historian in the latter, that is, he more completely ignores the multitude of events that might be supposed to have occurred along with the ones he chooses to treat as specially significant. His position is neatly put by Conrad: 'Fiction is history, human history, or it is nothing. But it is also more than that; it starts on firmer ground, being based on the reality of forms.' Forms are systematised typological insights; they are, or should be, always under very critical scrutiny, because they can tempt us into unjustified archaism.

The modern theologian is forced to understand the difference between sentimental or archaistic typology and the kind which is appropriate to a belief which has had to emigrate, like the Jews, from myth into history. He professes to use the old scriptural types only as indices of the contemporaneity of the New Testament, and not as elements in a miraculous plot, devised by the Holy Ghost, to keep Old and New Testaments, and the whole of history, in a condition of miraculous concord. Of course there are atavistic theologians as well as atavistic historians, literary critics, and novelists, though it is to me an interesting reflection

* Here I assume, perhaps wrongly, that we have as yet no 'structuralist' historians.

that modern theology got really deeply into de-mythologising at about the time when literary critics began to go overboard for mythology.

I will not pursue that, but ask why literary people should be so liable to this atavism. One reasonably simple explanation is that our immense scepticism, our deep concern with the nature of the tools we are using, is only one of the traditions to which we are heirs. Another is a tradition of mythological primitivism which has branches of many kinds: occultism, Frazerian Cambridge anthropology; and Freud and Jung. In the period which was formative for us there was also a fashionably circular historiography, provided by Spengler; a revival of primitive art; and, of course, a large and seminal literature which was in various ways primitivistic and favourable to archaic typologising. Thus, when novels are closest to history we may still ask whether their fidelity to certain types is wholly consistent with a just representation of human history.

II

I begin with this dogmatic introduction in order to make it clear in what relations I am considering D. H. Lawrence. Among the reasons why he continues to be thought of as a particularly important novelist is this: he believed himself to be living in a time of cosmic crisis, and partly justified this conviction by archaic typologising. History was for him a plot devised by the Holy Ghost, and 'scientific' explanations (which would first examine and then reject this as a fiction) he found hateful. Unlike George Eliot, a predecessor in The Great Tradition, he could not separate the intuition that he lived in the great age of transition from explanations devoid of empirical interest but interesting enough to all primitivists, and indeed historians of ideas. He knew a great deal (anti-intellectualists need to) and was exceptionally aware of the nature and history of his typologies; for example, he was a great student not only of mystery rituals but also of Apocalypse, and commentary on Apocalypse. This essay is about what he knew, and how it is expressed in various books, notably *Women in Love*.

In the 'Study of Thomas Hardy', which belongs in time to much the same period as *The Rainbow* and *Women in Love*, Lawrence observed that a man can only view the universe in the light of a theory, and since the novel is a microcosm, it has to reflect a micro-theory, 'some theory of being, some metaphysic'. Of course this metaphysic mustn't obtrude and turn the novel into a tract, nor must the novelist make himself a metaphysic of self-justification, and then 'apply the world to this, instead of applying this to the world', a practice of which he found a striking instance in the ascetic Tolstoy, whom he describes as 'a child of the Law'. The fact is that Lawrence was at the moment when he wrote that passage troubled about the 'metaphysic' of the work he had in hand. That he should use so curious an expression of Tolstoy – 'a child of the Law' – gives one a strong hint as to the character of that metaphysic.*

Lawrence was obsessed with Apocalypse from early youth, and he remembered the chiliastic chapel hymns of his childhood. During the war the apocalyptic coloration of his language is especially striking; sometimes it strongly recalls seventeenth-century puritanism. He considered the world to be undergoing a rapid decline which should issue in a renovation, and expected the English to have some part in this, much as Milton put the burden on God's Englishmen; Lawrence, however, dwelt more on the decadence, and seemed to think the English were rotting with especial rapidity in order to be ready. He spoke of the coming resurrection – 'Except a seed die, it bringeth not forth', he advises Bertrand Russell in May 1915. 'Our death must be accomplished first, then we will rise up.' 'Wait only a little while';

---

* It is worth remembering Lawrence's capacity for having things both ways. He balances his more extreme metaphysical and occult fantasies with a sophisticated pragmatism; the effect in his fiction is to have passages that jeer at Birkin's doctrines. If he had thought of it before Marshall McLuhan he might have called many of the speculations dealt with in this essay 'probes'. This hedging of bets I occasionally refer to, but it gets in the way of exposition, and the reader might like to re-introduce it into his reflections if he finds something that seems unexpectedly and positively absurd in my account of Lawrence's crisis-philosophy.

these were the last days, the 'last wave of time', he told Ottoline Morell. There would be a new age and a new ethical law.

The nature of Lawrence's pronouncements on the new age and the new ethic is such that he can very well be described as a 'moral terrorist', Kant's term for historians who think that the evident corruption of the world presages an immediate appearance, in one form or another, of anti-Christ. But he was also what Kant, in the same work (*The Disputation of the Faculties*) calls an 'abderitist', namely one who explains history in terms of culture-cycles. More specifically, and perhaps more recognisably, he was a Joachite.

Where Lawrence, who was to call himself Joachim in *The Plumed Serpent*, got his Joachitism from one can only guess. A possible source is Huysmans' *Là-Bas* ('Two of the Persons of the Trinity have shown themselves. As a matter of logic, the Third must appear'). But Joachitism is a hardy plant, and as Frank E. Manuel says in *Shapes of Philosophical History*, it was particularly abundant in the literature of the French decadence and so could have formed part of that current of occultist thinking to which Lawrence was so sensitive. The doctrine varies a bit, but broadly it postulates three historical epochs, one for each person of the Trinity, with a transitional age between each. The details are argued out of texts in Revelation.

It is hardly too much to claim that the vague and powerful assumptions we all make about historical transition have their roots in Joachitism; in Lawrence, however, the relation is much more specific. The war-time Hardy study speaks of our having reached an end, or a 'pause of finality' which is not an end. It is the moment of Transition. There has been an epoch of Law, and an epoch of 'Knowledge or Love', and out of the synthesis of the two will develop the new age, which will be the age of the Holy Spirit. As in some early Joachite sects, the sexual implications of this are especially important. Lawrence holds that the principle of Law is strongest in woman, and that of love in men (which is worth remembering when one considers Ursula and Birkin). Out of their true union in 'Consummate Marriage' will grow that ethic which is the product of Law and Love but is a

third distinct thing, like the Holy Ghost. Although there is every
sign that we have reached the point of transition, the art which
should reflect it has not yet been invented. Obviously the big
double novel he was working on was to be the first attempt at
this appropriate art.

Now I dare say that some admirers of Lawrence will go a long
way towards allowing one to speak of his thought, on sex and
other matters, as having a strong apocalyptic colouring, yet
draw the line at this very schematic and detailed application of
the idea. Yet it is, I think, incontrovertible. When Lawrence
spoke of 'signs' he did not mean only that everything was getting
very bad, he meant that there *were* apocalyptic images and signs
in the sky. The Zeppelin was one: 'there was war in heaven. . . .
It seemed as if the cosmic order were gone, as if there had come a
new order. . . . It seems our cosmos has burst, burst at last . . .
it is the end, our world has gone. . . . But there must be a new
heaven and a new earth.' This is from a letter to Lady Ottoline
Morell, in September 1915. A few days later he again calls the
Zeppelin 'a new great sign in the heavens'. When he came to
write the famous chapter 'Nightmare' in *Kangaroo* he again
remembered the Zeppelin, 'high, high, high, tiny, pale, as one
might imagine the Holy Ghost'.

In *Kangaroo* the Holy Ghost is patron of a new age which will
dispense with democracy and bosses and be dominated by 'verte-
brate telepathy' from a leader. As always in apocalyptic historiography, this renovation is preceded by a decadence; the 'new
show' cannot happen until there has been some smashing. Lawrence's image of the transitional smasher was the terrible 'non-
mental' mob, often symbolised by the troglodyte miner, one of
his recurrent figures and an object of hate and love, fear and
admiration. Continually reflecting on the apocalyptic types,
Lawrence produced his own brand of Joachitism, as distinctive
as that of Blake in *The Everlasting Gospel*, but easily identifiable,
just as one can readily see the conformity between his more
general apocalyptic thinking and the whole tradition. For
convenience one can identify three aspects of this, in addition
to the specifically Joachite notion of transition and crisis. They

are: the Terrors (the appalling events of *dies illa*, the last day); decadence and renovation, twin concepts that explain one's own discontent and one's own hopes for another Kingdom, somewhere; and finally what I call clerkly scepticism, the reluctance of the literate to credit popular apocalyptism in its crude forms, with consequent historiographical sophistications.

In Lawrence there is a very personal ambiguity in these matters; he was a clerkly writer, but the popular Apocalypse fascinated him just the same. He had a doctrine of symbolism which helped him to bridge this gap, and sometimes his allusions are so inexplicit that only if you are a naïve fundamentalist (in which case you probably won't be reading Lawrence) or are on the lookout (in which case you are reading abnormally) will you pick them up. A good example of this is the passage in *St Mawr*, which is in general an apocalyptic story, where Mrs Witt discusses with Lewis 'a very big, soft star' that falls down the sky. Lewis is led on to talk about the superstitions of his countryside, and finally to explain what the star means to him: 'There's movement in the sky. The world is going to change again.' When Mrs Witt reminds him of the physical explanation of shooting stars, mentioning that there are always many in August, he just insists that 'stones don't come at us out of the sky for nothing'. Whatever Lewis has in mind, Lawrence is certainly thinking of Revelation VI 13, 'And the stars of heaven fell unto the earth', which happens at the opening of the sixth seal, when 'the great day of his wrath is come'. Lawrence is explicit enough about the general apocalyptic bearing of the horse itself, and perhaps too explicit about the decadence and the possibility of a new show and Lewis's superior understanding of the situation, but in this little episode there is a set of variations on a hidden apocalyptic symbol which is in some ways even more characteristic.

What we have to see, I think, is that, explicit or inexplicit, this, the apocalyptic, is the chief mould of Lawrence's imaginative activity. In the work of the nineteen-twenties it grows increasingly explicit, for example in the Whitman essay, or in the study of Melville, where the sinking of the *Pequod* is called 'the doom of our white day'. There had always been a racial aspect to his

apocalyptic thinking, as we shall see; even in his essays on Dahl-
berg and Huxley's *Point Counter Point* he affirms the exhaustion
of the white racial psyche, the disintegration that will lead to a
new show. From 1923, mostly in letters to Frederick Carter,
he was offering elaborate interpretations of Revelation, based on a
study of conventional exegesis (which he despised) and on less
orthodox treatments, such as those of James Pryse, Madame
Blavatsky, and Carter himself. In 1924 he wrote some articles on
the subject, and in his last years worked hard on *Apocalypse*, his
own commentary.

In *Apocalypse* Lawrence acknowledges that the book of Revelation, and other parts of the Bible, with which he was saturated
in childhood, remained in his mind and 'affected all the processes
of emotion and thought'. But in the meantime he had come to
loathe it, and his long essay is an attempt to explain why, consciously and unconsciously, this 'detested' book could play so
large a part in his most serious work. It has to be separated from
mere vulgar credulity and subjected to a clerkly scepticism that
is still not mere rationalism. Years of labour went into Lawrence's
theory that the version we read in the Bible, the hateful book,
'Jewy' and 'chapel', meat for underdogs, was a horribly corrupt
version of an earlier work which must have related the ritual of
an authentic mystery religion. What he tries to do is to remove
the 'Judeo-Roman screen' and penetrate to the fundamental rite,
as it was represented in the imagery of the original pre-Christian
text. This rite would be a guide to 'emotional-passional knowledge'; the editorial sophistications stood for the non-vital
Christian universe. The original was quick, though the corrupt
version was dead. And of course Lawrence found in Revelation
his mystery ritual. There was the Great Mother, whom the
Jewish and Christian editors had dissociated into one good and
one bad, the Woman Clothed with the Sun and the Scarlet
Woman. There was the ritual descent into hell, and the rebirth.
And this *katabasis* was the type of the one the world was at
present undergoing. As in the mystery rite the contemporary
harrowing of hell is to be accomplished by a sexual act. In the
epoch of the Holy Ghost we shall revert 'towards our elementals',

as Lawrence put it in that curious homage to the Paraclete, *Fantasia of the Unconscious*; to Adam reborn, love will be a new thing; the man-woman relationship will be remade. But first there has to be death and rebirth.

Although his commentators pay very little and then only embarrassed attention to it, *Apocalypse* is ideologically a climax of Lawrence's work. But because he never ceased to feel that it was not enough merely to describe the crisis, the terrors, the death and rebirth, he wrote over the same years a novel, a novel which should be impregnated with this sexual eschatology. That novel was *Lady Chatterley's Lover*. As I tried to show in an essay published four or five years ago, that book enacts the sevenfold descent into hell and the climactic rebirth by sex. I shan't dwell on it now, because I want to discuss better books, and especially one in which the apocalyptic types have a peculiar historical force, namely *Women in Love*.

III

Ritual descent into hell, followed by rebirth – that is the character of Lawrence's transitional period. The reason why the world misunderstands what is happening is that it knows only a corrupt Apocalypse – it sees, with Mellors, that 'there's a bad time coming, boys', but thinks that the smashing-up will be a way of dislodging the proud, and setting the underdogs up instead. Actually the beneficiaries constitute an elect, isolate in a new consciousness, synthesising Law and Love. A mark of this elect will naturally be the new man-woman relationship; for the woman was law and the man love, and just as these two epochal ethics will be transformed in the third, so will the two Persons, Man and Woman, be, under the new dispensation, merged in a new relationship, and yet remain distinct. The obvious image for this sexual situation is the Trinity, of which the Persons are distinct but not divided. And this epoch of the Holy Ghost has no place for underdogs.

As we have seen, this programme, already implicit in the Hardy study, requires not only a new ethics and new philosophies of culture, but also its own art; so it is not surprising that the novels Lawrence wrote during the war have much apocalyptic figuration. *The Rainbow* came to represent the Old Testament (Law) and *Women in Love* the New Testament (Love). The rainbow at the end of the first novel is the symbol of the old Covenant; the apocalyptic climax of the second reflects the structure of the New Testament. *Women in Love* is an end, where *The Rainbow* was a beginning; it represents the destruction of the old, and enacts the pause before the new world. It projects a kind of Utopia; but it is subjected, like the rest of the apocalyptic material, to Lawrence's own brand of scepticism.

The Rainbow is deliberately rendered as a kind of Genesis. The opening passages have a sort of Blakean gravity, like the illustrations to Job – the gravity is patriarchal. Allusions to Genesis punctuate the book. The death of old Brangwen, drunk, after a flood, makes him a sort of distorted antitype of Noah. George Ford's extremely interesting book on Lawrence (*Double Measure*) makes these and other connections with Genesis, including the references to the coming together of the sons of God and the daughters of men, which establish a typical basis for Ursula. *The Rainbow* also contains some faint but characteristic premonitions of the Apocalypse to come: as when Anna sneers at the lamb-and-flag window of the church, calling it 'the biggest joke of the parish'. The lamb and flag constitutes a traditional icon of Apocalypse, but Anna is sneering at her husband's interest in such symbolism, as her daughter will later deride Birkin's more sophisticated Apocalypse. Women are sceptics, they cling, like Anna, 'to the worship of human knowledge', they hanker after the Law. In fact Brangwen is a sort of decadent typologist, with an underdog chapel Apocalypse; we are not surprised when we meet him briefly in *Women in Love* and find him grown insensitive, proletarian, obsolete.

The lamb-and-flag window is one of those glancing allusions, like the falling star in *St Mawr*, which show how these figures possessed Lawrence. The great chapter of the horses is more explicitly apocalyptic; Lawrence's discussion of the horse in *Apocalypse* establishes a direct connexion with Revelation; and in

the same section he once again quotes that text from Genesis,
earlier used in *The Rainbow*, about the sons of God visiting the
daughters of men, adding that according to Enoch these angels
had 'the members of horses'. The passage is extremely complicated, as always when Lawrence's imagination is fully extended
on this theme. These horses stand for the lost potency of white
civilisation (and specifically of England: there is a gloomy
patriotic element in Lawrence's eschatology); they also stand for
sexual terrors of the kind he associated with them in *Fantasia of
the Unconscious*. Of course sexual terror and racial decadence
were closely related subjects, as one sees most vividly in *Women
in Love*.

IV

In fact *Women in Love* exhibits all the apocalyptic types in their
Lawrentian version: decadence and renovation in a painful
transition or crisis, élitism, patriotic fervour, sex and mystery.
Its subject, like that of *Lady Chatterley*, is, basically, England,
and by extension the decline of 'white' racial culture to be un-
imaginably redeemed in a sexual mystery. The characteristic
pattern occurs with peculiar clarity in a letter of 1926: 'they've
pushed a spear through the side of my England', means, superficially, that the country round Nottingham had been ruined and
disfigured by 'miners – and pickets – and policemen' during the
great strike; but underneath there is the imagery of death and a
new love: dancing, disciples, a new 'England to come'. There is a
sort of Blakean patriotism, even in *The Rainbow*; but Ursula in
Women in Love, *is* England, for her, as for Connie, that other
sleeping beauty, there is a programme of renovation by sexual
shock. We find her, after the water-party, 'at the end of her line
of life', her 'next step was into death'. This death, she finds, is
preferable to mechanical life. But the death-flow of her mood is
interrupted by the arrival of Birkin. At once she hates him. 'He
was the enemy, fine as a diamond, and as hard and jewel-like,
the quintessence of all that was inimical. . . . She saw him as a
clear stroke of uttermost contradiction.' The life-flow of love

and the death-flow of law here clash. Birkin contradicts death, personal, national and cosmic. He himself often meditates on the necessary death of England: 'of race and national death' at the wedding party near the beginning, of the death of England when he and Ursula buy the old chair, of the necessary disappearance of England in the chapter 'Continental', when Gudrun sneers at him and calls him a patriot. But death is for him a preparation for the new life; so he must contain and overthrow Ursula's scepticism; and because she is England he must work the renovation on her body.

This intermittent equation of Ursula and England gives some indication of the means by which Lawrence matched his apocalyptic types with history. For *Women in Love* is an historical novel. Like *Middlemarch*, to which it owes so much, *Women in Love* is a novel about a modern crisis; and it deals with it, partly, by concentrating on the condition of women question, which, as George Eliot once remarked, had been from the time of Herodotus one of the most important symptoms of the state of a society. Unlike *Middlemarch*, however, Lawrence's novel contains no positive allusion to actual history. 'I should wish the time to remain unfixed', he wrote, 'so that the bitterness of the war may be taken for granted in the characters.' I shall postpone discussion of this radical difference of method, because the immediate need is simply to assert that *Women in Love* is nonetheless an historical novel, a book about a particular historical crisis. When Dr Leavis observes of Lawrence that 'as a recorder of essential English history he is a great successor of George Eliot', he is thinking primarily of *The Rainbow*; but he adds that '*Women in Love* has . . . astonishing comprehensiveness in the presentment of contemporary England (the England of 1914).' *The Rainbow* has 'historical depth', and studies the past in which the crisis germinated. *Women in Love* concerns itself less with evocations of a lost world than with a moment of history understood in terms of a crisis archetype. The random events of history assume the patterns of eschatological feeling and speculation.

'The book frightens me: it's so end of the world', said Lawrence in 1916. George Ford points out that among the early titles proposed for *Women in Love* were 'The Latter Days' and 'Dies Irae'. And this eschatological preoccupation touches everything in the book. Consider, for example, the social aspect. Lawrence's Apocalypse, as I have said, is élitist, and like the élite of the medieval Joachite sects, for instance The Brethren of the Free Spirit, his chosen ones exclude the profane from their mysteries. Birkin often remarks that people don't matter; or they matter only in so far as they may produce the terrors, the great mindless shove into the last days. The mood is reflected also in Lawrence's own letters and in *Kangaroo*. The mechanical mob has nothing to do with the true sexual mystery-religion of Apocalypse; it was in their name that the Jewish and Greek bottom-dogs corrupted the text of the original Revelation. They have a false, lesser mystery, no true *katabasis*, but merely a parody of it. These *profani*, destructive, even chthonic, were associated in Lawrence's mind with colliers, the 'blackened, slightly distorted human beings with red mouths' who work for Gerald. To Gudrun, who has an instinctive sympathy with their debased power – Lawrence writes several passages to make this point including the very fine one where the workmen lust after her in her fancy stockings – to Gudrun they are 'powerful, underworld men' in whose voices she hears 'the voluptuous resonance of darkness'; she desires them, related as they are to the kind of evil found in the water-plants of 'Sketchbook', and the decadence of Halliday's statue. If Ursula is the Magna Dea in her creative aspect, Gudrun is Hecate, a Queen of the Night. But in the renovated world there is to be no place for her, or for her underworld men.

The real descent into hell and rebirth Lawrence can signify only by sex. The purest expression of it is in *The Man Who Died*, but in some ways the love-death undergone by Ursula and Connie is a fuller image because it amalgamates heaven and hell, life-flow and death-flow, in one act. The act is anal. Lawrence is never explicit about it, whether in the novels or in the essays where one might have expected some explanation of the Holy Ghost's electing so curious an epiphany. But he has in mind what he takes to be the basic figure of the mystery behind revelation – this is the point, for Connie and Ursula and for England also, where life and death meet; when the shame induced by Law is defied and burnt out. 'How good it was to be really shameful. . . . She was free.' This participation in 'dreadful mysteries beyond the phallic cult', enacts death and rebirth at once, is decadent and renovatory at once.

As the literature shows, this is not easy to discuss. One cannot even distinguish, discursively, between the sex Gudrun desires from Loerke, which is obscene and decadent, and that which Ursula experiences with Birkin, which is on balance renovatory. The first comes straight out of Nordau, the second is darkly millennialist, again like that of some medieval sects in their Latter Days; yet in practice they presumably amount to almost the same thing. It is an ambivalence which may have characterised earlier apocalyptic postures, as Fraenger argues in his book on Hieronymus Bosch. Decadence and renovation, death and rebirth, in the last days, are hard to tell apart, being caught up in the terrors.

Does a new world – created in the burning out of sexual shame, in the birth from such an icy womb as that of the last chapters of Lawrence's novel – does such a world await the elect when the terrors of the transition are over? Do the elect rightly look forward to the epoch of the Holy Spirit? The myth in the book says yes. It says so throughout – in image after image and in a long series of antitheses: in 'Rabbit' and in 'Water-Party', in the water-weeds and butterflies, in Gerald's death journey to Gudrun's bed and in Birkin rolling naked in the pine-needles; in the flow of death and the flow of life, the imagery of *Fleurs du mal* and the rose of happiness. But the book also obscures the myth. Between the flow of life and that of death there is 'no difference – and all the difference. Dissolution rolls on, just as production does . . . it ends in universal nothing – the end of the world. . . . It means a new cycle of creation after. . . .' Birkin is glossing his earlier remark that Aphrodite 'is the flowering mystery of the death-process'. He cannot tell Ursula quite how their Aphrodite is dissociated from that process. And here he invites her scepticism.

As Magna Dea committed to continuance, as woman the voice

of Law, and as modern clerk Ursula is repeatedly the voice of that scepticism which always, in history, attends apocalyptic prophecy. When Birkin rants about the disappearance of England, she knows it cannot 'disappear so cleanly and conveniently'. It is part of the historical tension between myth and history (the long record of disappointed Apocalypse) or between what Birkin thinks of as life and death. The novel fights back at myth, and where the myth says yes, the novel and Ursula often say no. The novel, as a kind, belongs to humanism, not to mystery religion; or in terms of Worringer's contemporary distinction, it cannot, because of the society that produced it, abandon empathy entirely in favour of abstraction. Thus our white decadence can never take the obscenely abstract form of Halliday's statue. And Lawrence knew this. Whereas *The Rainbow*, which looks back to a pastoral Genesis, can end with the archetypal sign of the covenant, *Women in Love* must have a modern conclusion in which nothing is concluded, a matter of disappointed love, a pattern incomplete. It allows history some ground unconquered by the types.

'Has *everything* that happens universal significance?' It is Birkin's question, and the novelist's question always. For Birkin it arises out of the repeated assertion that Gerald's type is Cain. Gerald's shooting of his brother is to Gudrun 'the purest form of accident'. But Birkin decides that he 'does not believe there was any such thing as accident. It all hung together, in the deepest sense.' Hence the subsequent death of Gerald's sister, his own visit to the depths of the lake, the region of death, and finally his death in the ice, may be seen as pre-determined. At any rate Lawrence wants us to ask questions about the truth of the types in a novel. The New Testament shows them all fulfilled, in the 'fullness of time'. Can there be such a novelistic *pleroma*, in which no event is random? If so, all the apparent randomness of the book must have significance: cats, rabbits, jewels, floods. This kind of realism finds its *figura* in random event. So the mythic type returns powerfully to its ancient struggle with history. But Lawrence never in fact allowed history to lose altogether, even in *The Plumed Serpent*, even in the narrowly schematic *Lady Chatterley's Lover*. He headed dangerously

toward a typological predominance, and paid the price; the more
he asserted the fulfilment of preordained types, the less he could
depend on that randomness which leaves room for quickness
and special grace. Mrs Morel locked out of her house, experiencing
fear but burying her face in the lily – that is the kind of thing
that is lost. We still have it in *Women in Love* – in a relevance
altogether strange, in unique configurations. There are the naked
white men round the 'primitive', an image not subordinated to
the element of doctrine involved; or the eurhythmics and the
cows in 'Water-Party'. One of Lawrence's powers was a capacity
for stunning verisimilitude, a thing precious in itself – one thinks
of the passage in *The Rainbow* in which Will Brangwen picks
up the factory-girl at the music-hall. There are always untyped
graces of this sort in Lawrence; they belong to history, and they
are what all good novels ought to have. Lawrence never lost the
power, but it must have seemed that its relevance to what he was
doing progressively diminished.

Women in Love is the last novel in which he kept the balance.
Its radical type is Apocalypse, used as an explanation of the great
contemporary crisis; for 'it was in 1915 the old world ended' and
the great transition began. The great feat is to confront what
Auerbach calls 'the disintegration of the continuity of random
events' – reflected in the technique of Lawrence's novel – with
the unchangingness of the types, and to do it without sinking
into a verisimilar discreteness on the one hand, or into a rigid,
flux-denying *schema* on the other. *Women in Love* studies crisis
without unforgivably insulting reality. Its types do some of the
work which historians also do with types.

SOURCE: From 'Word in the Desert', the Tenth Anniversary
Number of the *Critical Quarterly*, x nos 1–2 (Spring–Summer
1968).

Colin Clarke

'LIVING DISINTEGRATION':
A SCENE FROM
WOMEN IN LOVE
REINTERPRETED (1969)

I

THE word 'disintegration' is used frequently in *Women in Love*
and almost always with a negative force; and this no doubt
accounts in part for the common assumption that throughout the
novel the disintegrative processes are conceived of as purely life-
destructive. The following reading, by H. M. Daleski, is representative:

Gerald's work in the mines and Gudrun's art are revealed as
'disintegrative', as an abuse of organic life; and the black sensuality of their relationship is productive of the violence which, in
the novel, is seen as an inevitable concomitant of *any* process of
'dissolution'. [Italics mine.][1]

But this will not do; violence is not merely destructive in *Women
in Love*. And the process of dissolution is positive quite as often
as not, or positive-negative. For the coming into being of the
true and 'original individuality of the blood' entails a disintegrating, or dissolving, of the 'dreary individuality of the ego'.
(I quote from 'Love Was Once a Little Boy'.)[2]
    The structure of this irony can be traced with special ease in the
following passage from the *Letters*:

They all want the same thing: a continuing in this state of disintegration wherein each separate little ego is an independent
little principality by itself. What does Russell really want? He
wants to keep his own established ego, his finite and ready-
defined self intact, free from contact and connection.[3]

Though Russell and Co. live and want to continue in a state of vicious disintegration – the body politic fragmented, reduced to component particles – it is, by implication, only some process of disintegration which can rescue them. For how is each to establish contact and connection again if not by the dissolution of his independent little principality – the hard, separate ego? In other words, the disintegrated state is at the same time a state of false integrity, implying as it does a fatal intactness of the established, finite self. Only through a submission to disintegration (or dissolution) can the disintegrated condition be superseded.

It is a token of Lawrence's Romantic lineage that his diagnosis of false integrity should be so bound up with the theme of belonging.

He was alone now, alone and immune in the middle of the waters, which he had all to himself. He exulted in his isolation in the new element, unquestioned and unconditioned. He was happy, thrusting with his legs and all his body, without bond or connexion anywhere, just himself in the watery world.

Gudrun envied him almost painfully. Even this momentary possession of pure isolation and fluidity seemed to her so terribly desirable that she felt herself as if damned, out there on the highroad.[4]

On the face of it the language might appear to endorse Gerald's immunity and apparent self-sufficiency. But a separateness that goes with an exultant sense of one's own advantage and entails sheer mobility and fluidity, no bond or connection of any kind, can only be suspect. This equating of fluidity and dissolution – a dissolving of the bonds that ought to link an individual to his human and natural environment – begins very early in the novel and is sustained throughout.

But equally the process of dissolution (or disintegration) may be life-enhancing, as when Ursula, though she feels 'the far-off awful nausea of dissolution' setting in within the body, reflects that 'To die is to move on with the invisible. . . . But to live mechanized and cut off within the motion of the will, to live as an entity absolved from the unknown, that is shameful and igno-

minious.'[5] In this instance dissolution, though painful and
nauseating, is on the whole a sign of life, a sign that here the
human spirit is in contact with the rhythms of living and dying.
The incapacity to dissolve or be transmuted, by contrast, is
conceived of as a mark of the isolated and mechanical state. The
truly integral spirit then preserves its integrity both by its resistance to dissolution and by its aptness to dissolve; and true
individuality is a matter of belonging.

But a distinction needs to be drawn here; for belonging may or
may not entail the acknowledging within oneself – and the incorporating – of *corruption*. Belief in the possibility of a 'paradisal
entry into pure, single being'[6] is kept alive throughout *Women
in Love* – together with a belief that self-sufficiency and belonging
presuppose a revitalising from the fountain of mystic corruption,
a communion with death. We are not allowed to rest for long in
either belief to the exclusion of the other and perhaps the finest
moments are those in which the two beliefs are forced to confront each other and to attest both their antipathy and their
affinities.

What it means to be replenished from the mystic source of
corruption is powerfully suggested in the episode in which
Hermione finds Birkin copying a Chinese drawing of geese.
With his intuitive awareness of the lotus mystery (in 'The Crown'
the lotus takes its place, along with the swan and the snake, as
one of the symbols of divine corruption)[7] he shows himself
capable of a kind of knowing that is quite beyond her scope. The
realisation of this destroys her; she is 'broken and gone in a
horrible corruption . . . gone like a corpse, that has no presence,
no connexion'.[8] Clearly we are not being allowed to adopt a
simple attitude to corruption or to dissolution. Hermione suffers
the ghastliness of dissolution (in the sense of decomposition)
because she refuses to dissolve (in the sense of become fluid,
yield to the flux). But the actual word 'dissolve' is not used in
this second sense. Whereas corruption is assigned a plural value
explicitly – 'entering their own blood like an inoculation of
corruptive fire', 'broken and gone in a horrible corruption' – the
word dissolution occurs only once and the burden of paradox

or ironical counterpointing is sustained by a synonym, 'flux'. The Chinese artist lives from a centre as the geese do, sustained by the world of water and mud. The fire flows into the goose's blood and in turn flows into the blood of the artist: barriers are dissolved. So there is connection, flux and centrality as opposed to isolation and corpse-like dissolution. Hermione battles to maintain her false integrity and pays for it with a squalid subjection to dissolution and corruption. This corruption is the mark of her inability to comprehend the corruptive fire, the lotus mystery. We may compare the later dissolution of Mr Crich. Nearer and nearer the process of reduction came 'towards the last knot which held the human being in its unity',[9] and yet this knot still remained 'hard and unrelaxed'. Like Hermione Mr Crich maintains the false integrity of the will and as a consequence is subdued to the dissolution he refuses to accept. The achievement of integrity, in short, is a matter of rendering justice to the corruptive agencies of nature as well as the paradisal.

II

I have suggested that some of the finest moments of the novel are those in which tribute is paid at one and the same time to both these agencies. A case in point is the episode at Willey Pond, at the beginning of the chapter 'Moony'. This episode is the most celebrated in the novel; yet it seems to have been widely misread, to judge by the commentaries that have been published (with the exception of that of Kinkead-Weekes: see above, p. 19). Critics appear to be unanimous that what the scene is centrally about is Birkin's hatred of the Magna Mater, the accursed Syria Dea; in hurling stones at the image of the moon he is reacting in fury against female arrogance – or tyranny, or possessiveness. But the whole incident has much more to do with integration and disintegration, the need to smash the false integrity of the ego in order to make possible the true integrity of the blood.

To understand the scene we need to attend carefully to what immediately precedes it. After Birkin's departure for France Ursula drifts into a spiritual condition that puts the reader in mind of Gudrun (and incidentally of Gerald). It is one of those moments in the story when the sisters seem to have a good deal in common: 'she was hard and indifferent, isolated in herself . . . she had no contact and no connexion anywhere'. We recall particularly the Gudrun of 'Coal-Dust', 'cold and separate', 'quite hard and cold and indifferent'. Altogether the passage prepares us very fully for the assimilation later of woman to moon: compare 'hard and indifferent' here and, further on, 'she wanted another night, not this moon-brilliant hardness'. And the early references to brightness and radiance serve the same purpose: 'But the strange brightness of her presence, a marvellous radiance of intrinsic vitality, was a luminousness of supreme repudiation.' So we are very ready to take the significance of the moon when it appears 'with its white and deathly smile'; at one level, at any rate, this is woman in a 'state of constant unfailing repudiation' – hard, indifferent, disconnected. And it is not only Birkin who is repelled. Ursula hurries on 'cowering from the white planet', and when she sees its image in the water 'for some reason she disliked it'. The moon is herself, but not a self she is pleased to recognise.

But Ursula's recoil from human society to some extent engages our sympathy also: 'she loved the horses and cows in the field. Each was single and to itself, magical.' Pure loneliness in these early paragraphs is made to seem both desirable and not desirable. To be separate and yet not coldly isolated, to be connected with another or others and yet retain one's singleness, to know specious individuality from true – these are the problems with which the chapter is centrally concerned.

Ursula, then, longs for true singleness but at this point seems only capable of isolation. Although she reflects that the animals 'were single and unsocial as she herself was' their magical singleness is in fact something she aspires towards rather than something she has achieved. So the significance of Birkin's stone-throwing would appear to be clear: it is an attack on that deathly supremacy of the ego that makes for mere separateness and indifference. 'And I wouldn't give a straw for your female ego – it's a rag doll', he says angrily in the discussion that follows. His violence renews the flow of life, which is at the same time a flowing in of darkness. The pure supremacy of light – the supremacy of the ego – gives way to a proper tension between light and dark: 'Darts of bright light shot asunder, darkness swept over the centre.' Emblematically Birkin's stoning of the moon brings about that singleness of being which later in the chapter he recognises as the main object of his quest:

. . . a lovely state of free proud singleness, which accepted the obligation of the permanent connexion with others, and with the other, submits to the yoke and leash of love, but never forfeits its own proud individual singleness, even while it loves and yields.

The image of the moon yields before the aggressive male yet never forfeits its singleness; the individuality of the ego gives way to a true individuality, though a precarious one. (There is a passage in the essay 'Love' which lends some support to this interpretation.[10] In 'Moony' as in the essay the rose is used as an image of the right kind of singleness: 'He saw the moon re-gathering itself insidiously, saw the heart of the rose intertwining vigorously and blindly.' The comparison of novel and essay is valid, I think, even though in the essay hard brilliance is the mark of a wholly *legitimate* otherness, as it is not in the novel.)

III

In case I appear to be labouring the obvious in this exegesis I had better point out again that though commentators have agreed in admiring the episode at the Pond wholeheartedly they have had nothing to say about what seems to me its central meaning. Their attention has all been given to a theme that is subsidiary to the one I have been discussing; they have been hypnotised by Birkin's reference to Cybele, 'the accursed Syria dea'. Middleton Murry began it all by claiming that Birkin, an incarnation of Lawrence himself, is endeavouring 'to annihilate the female insatiably demanding physical satisfaction from the man who cannot give it to her'.[11] And if we turn from Murry to Leavis we find a comment that scarcely adds anything positive, though it is not, like Murry's, merely wild: 'The possessiveness he divines in Ursula is what (though that, we may feel, is not all) he sees in the reflected moon. . . .'[12] And in Graham Hough's view 'the moon is the white goddess, the primal woman image, *das ewig weibliche*, by whom Birkin is obviously haunted'.[13]

True, Birkin has attacked the image of the Great Mother explicitly and virulently earlier in the novel, with reference to the arrogant pretensions of Ursula and Hermione, and his present invocation of Cybele obviously links this passage to the previous one. And we think, too, of Gudrun, for it is to a *magna mater* figure that Gerald does obeisance when he visits Gudrun in her room in Beldover.[14] For all that, the theme of female tyranny is strictly subordinate to the theme of female isolation, 'the cold white light of feminine independence' (to quote from *England, My England*). But this interpretation also needs to be qualified, for in the last analysis the episode is concerned with human isolation as such, of which feminine isolation is but the type. (And this certainly is what one might expect if one were to come to the novel direct from *Fantasia of the Unconscious*: 'The moon is the centre of our terrestrial individuality in the cosmos. . . . She it is who burns white with the intense friction of her withdrawal into separation, that cold, proud white fire of furious, almost malignant apartness, the struggle into fierce, frictional separation.'[15] If Birkin's reference to Cybele were excised, the episode would not lose greatly in point or in power; as parable it would remain intact, a dramatic rendering of the disintegration of the isolated female ego and the precarious achievement of true singleness.

Leavis and Hough, it is worth remarking, take it for granted that the shattered image of the moon returns to its original state: 'It does, of course, re-form finally'; 'as soon as he stops his stone-throwing the moon-image re-forms'. But if we consult the text this is what we find:

. . . until a ragged rose, a distorted frayed moon was shaking upon the waters again, reasserted, renewed, trying to recover from its convulsion, to get over the disfigurement and agitation, to be whole and composed, at peace.

No doubt we are aware with a part of our minds that the moon-image must eventually return to the static condition it was in prior to the stoning, but Lawrence's art contrives to prevent this knowledge from asserting itself as relevant. If his art did not do so, the scene would indeed spell 'ineluctable defeat' for Birkin. Leavis denies that in fact it does spell defeat; but he points to nothing that can be taken to be positive evidence for the truth of this assertion. And recently, in his analysis in *The Tragic Vision*, Murray Krieger has spelt out even more clearly the assumption that the return of the moon to its previous static state is part of the given meaning; indeed, for him it is central to the meaning. The moon returns 'to what Gide called "the terrifying fixity . . . the immobility of death" '. As evidence for this assertion he refers to the passage I have myself just quoted. His chapter ends like this:

As we witness Ursula's desire to monopolise Rupert, we are meant to wonder if one is ever totally free from the clutches of the Magna Mater. After all, at the crucial symbolic moment, Birkin, for all the fury of his stoning, could not keep the face of the moon from inevitably re-asserting itself on the still surface of the pond.[16]

This is merely the normal reading carried to an extreme.

In the discussion with Ursula that follows upon the stoning of the moon-image, Birkin tells her: 'I want you to drop your assertive *will*, your frightened apprehensive self-insistence, that is what I want.' This makes explicit a meaning that has hitherto been *im*plicit. The radiance of the moon is inescapable, just as Ursula's suffering is, or her 'state of constant unfailing repudiation'. And it is strongly implied that if she constantly suffers it is because of the constant presence and assertiveness of her own self: 'the strange brightness of her presence'; 'She herself was real, and only herself.' And this self-insistence or radiant assertiveness, which is at once triumphant and apprehensive, goes with an unfailing self-awareness. Ursula is oppressed with a sense that the moon is constantly watching her – in other words that she is being constantly watched by her own self. So when she overhears Birkin soliloquising it is significant that his first words should be 'You can't go away.... There *is* no away. You only withdraw upon yourself.'

IV

A useful gloss on this aspect of the meaning is Lawrence's review of Trigant Burrow's book *The Social Basis of Consciousness.*

As soon as man became aware of himself, he made a picture of himself. Then he began to live according to the picture.... What the analyst must try to do [is] to liberate his patient from his own image, from his horror of his own isolation and the horror of the 'stoppage' of his real vital flow.... Men must ... utterly break the present great picture of a normal humanity: shatter that mirror in which we all live grimacing: and fall again into true relatedness.[17]

When allowances have been made for the difference between fictional and non-fictional modes we can fairly claim that what is said in the review is also said in 'Moony'. We must 'shatter that mirror', 'break all this image business, so that life can flow freely'. For 'the true self is not aware that it is a self', is not divided: social or image consciousness is the enemy of true singleness.

The reading I have so far proposed is borne out, I believe, by what occurs in the remainder of the chapter. I cannot deal in detail here with Birkin's reflections on the African statuette, but I may at least remark that these reflections are concerned with nothing if not with the achievement of pure single being in the teeth of forces that make for disintegration and dissolution. If 'the moon is the white goddess, the primal woman image', and only or even primarily that, then Birkin's thoughts here have very little bearing on the episode by the Pond, which immediately precedes them and which they seem in intention at any rate to grow out of.

And in fact they do grow out of that episode, though not altogether directly. First (in the moon-stoning episode) there is an assertion of the need to dissolve and then (as always) a counter-assertion of the need to resist dissolution, an exposure of the monstrous threat to the soul's integrity that lies precisely in dissolution, disintegration and darkness. But the counter-assertion is already implicit in the moon-stoning scene itself; that is why we pass so easily to the discursive passage that follows, even though in the parable of the moon and how it yielded up its separateness before the influx of darkness the *word* dissolution is never used, and even though the African dissolution is, at the most obvious level, sinister, as the darkness with which the moon's image contends is not.

v

I pass now to the abortive proposal and its aftermath. Metaphors of light and radiance become frequent again with the re-entry of Ursula, and insist on the relevance of this latter part of the chapter to the scene at Willey Pond. Her father's violent attack on her is a kind of parody of Birkin's assault on the image of the moon; a parody, for Birkin's violence imposed itself on the reader as legitimate and necessary, whereas Brangwen's is mere bullying. Its immediate effect is to drive his daughter back into her bright hard isolation: 'She was so radiant with all things in her possession of perfect hostility.' In this condition she gangs up with Gudrun against the whole male sex.

They felt a strong, *bright* bond of understanding between them, surpassing everything else. And during all these days of blind *bright* abstraction and intimacy of his two daughters, the father seemed to breathe an air of death, as if he were destroyed in his very being. . . . They continued *radiant* in their easy female transcendency.

(This last looks back to 'The moon was transcendent over the

bare, open space, she suffered from being exposed to it.') Gudrun
is unable to distinguish between the two kinds of male violence,
Birkin's and Brangwen's, and she discusses the one as though it
were the other. Of Birkin she says: 'He cries you down. . . . And
by mere force of violence.' Soon enough, however, Ursula reacts
against Gudrun, whom she begins to suspect of an 'irreverence,
destructive of all true life'. Yet we are not left at the end of the
chapter with an Ursula who has been won over to Birkin's point
of view. 'She was not at all sure that it was this mutual unison in
separateness that she wanted. She wanted unspeakable intimacies.'
Though she is not radically corrupt as Gudrun is, Ursula too,
with her mistaken ideal of pure love and her mistaken desire for
intimacy, works against true singleness.

In short, the theme announced at the beginning of the chapter
is dominant to the end.

She believed that love far surpassed the individual. He said the
individual was more than love, or than any relationship. For him,
the bright, single soul accepted love as one of its conditions, a
condition of its own equilibrium. She believed that love was
everything.

It has been made clear throughout the chapter that there are *kinds*
of separateness and *kinds* of brightness, so that the significance of
'bright, single soul' inevitably registers itself as complex. The
phrase recognises for the last time the positive virtue in brightness or the impulse towards separateness, reminding us that this
impulse, which may make for indifference and isolation, is
precisely that which makes for true singleness or integrity. And
this is characteristic of a novel in which the sources of life are so
deeply and variously implicated with the sources of death.

VI

Our sense that in the account of Birkin's stoning of the moon's
image a great deal of the significance of the novel has been
concentrated in a rich and satisfying emblem is thoroughly

justified. What we particularly note is the perfect justice done to the activities of departure *and* coming together (to use the language of 'The Crown'), breaking down *and* creation. The more violent Birkin becomes the more the flakes of light struggle to achieve a paradisal serenity and unity; and neither is triumphant.

And departure is the opposite equivalent of coming together; decay, corruption, destruction, breaking down is the opposite equivalent of creation.

It may be granted that Birkin's violence has no immediate and obvious relevance to the activity of *decay* or *corruption*; and yet, intricately and variously, the language refers us back to numerous occasions where we have registered human or non-human activity as lethal and corruptive. 'Burst', 'exploded', 'white and dangerous fire', 'incandescent', 'not yet violated', 'violent pangs', 'white-burning', 'tormented', 'convulsive': one thinks how closely this vocabulary has been associated with Gerald and Gudrun – it is in these terms, partly, that Birkin has defined for Ursula that 'inverse process' of 'destructive creation' in which (at this moment in history – 'at the end of a great era or epoch') we all of us in some degree find ourselves involved. This is that rhetoric of disruption that Lawrence uses for his most equivocal purposes – a marvellously sensitive medium for suggesting, among other things, a quality of dangerous, frictional vitality. In the first version of the essay on Poe he claims that the great white race in America is 'keenly disintegrating, seething back in electric decomposition, back to that crisis where the old soul, the old era, perishes in the denuded frame of man, and the first throb of a new year sets in'.[18] The reader of that essay might well object that the paradoxes about 'living disintegration' are at least partly spurious, that we are in danger of being tricked by a ceaseless shifting between various senses of 'living', or 'vital'. The disintegration is living, we gather, in the sense that life is contained by it or concealed within it, as the pure death of winter conceals and prepares the way for spring; or, again, in the sense that what is disintegrating is itself alive, though in the process of dying; or finally in the sense that the death process is violent and convulsive, and violence is a form of energy and energy of life. In his monograph on *D. H. Lawrence as a Literary Critic* David Gordon writes:

The critic's prophetic reading of Dostoevsky and Poe is more ambiguous [than his reading of Hawthorne, Melville, and Whitman]. *The Idiot* and 'Ligeia' are profound exposures of the bankruptcy of the egoistic love-ideal. But Lawrence wavers as to whether the artistic impulse that informs them is truly physical and sensual or merely nervous and intellectual, as to whether it is the needed reduction *of* the ego or merely reduction *within* the ego.[19]

True; and yet an equivalent ambiguity or wavering, an ambivalence of attitude towards the reductive processes, is precisely the *strength* of the fiction, very often. Certainly it does much to account for the power of *Women in Love*. Wilson Knight has observed finely that Lawrence endeavours in this novel 'to blast through... degradation to a new health'.[20] And the conditions for that health are located ambiguously in all four lovers; the damned are not set over in any simple way against the elect. For it is never safe to assume (as critics habitually do assume) that what is being said about destructiveness and corruption on the surface is *all* that is being said; almost certainly, beneath the surface, significant qualifications are being made. There is, for instance, that superbly evocative account of Beldover in the chapter 'Coal-Dust'. On the one hand the familiar distinction of the living and the mechanical would seem to encourage a very simple attitude of rejection:

She hated it, she knew how utterly cut off it was, how hideous and how sickeningly mindless. Sometimes she beat her wings like a new Daphne, turning not into a tree but a machine.

On the other hand the fatal callousness of miner and machine corresponds to a quality of ruthlessness which has already been proposed as no less life-enhancing than life-destructive.

Gerald watched him closely.

'You think we ought to break up this life, just start and let fly?' he asked.

'This life. Yes I do. We've got to bust it completely. . . .'[21]

The two men don't, of course, mean the same thing by 'break up', or 'bust'; the incipient excitement we sense in Gerald is stirred by a prospect of *mere* destructiveness, a kind of abandon that is very different from what Birkin has in mind. But the fact that the two kinds of destructiveness are so unlike while yet being alike is just what is characteristic of this novel, and just the kind of irony we need to be alert to in the later passage about Beldover. To begin with, we note how the strident and mechanical quality of the miner's life ('The sense of talk . . . vibrated in the air like discordant machinery') is modified by a deeper and darker rhythm, no less destructive but far richer: 'In their voices she could hear the voluptuous resonance of darkness, the strong, dangerous underworld, mindless, inhuman.' This resonance is much closer to what Lawrence called 'the rich centrality of the self'. We have a sense of involuntary process at the deeper levels of the psyche. And the effect is not merely to indicate the quality of life which the machine is destroying but to invest the mechanical process itself with a paradoxical but genuine vitality. The machine takes over something of the age-old glamour of coal, and its mysterious cruelty is half-sanctioned and half-repudiated. If Gudrun, suffering from her fascination and resisting, is nevertheless compelled by the callousness and disruptiveness, this is a token of her vitality as well as of something worse. (In the next chapter, 'Sketch-Book', her 'stupor of apprehension' as she contemplates the water-plants resembles Birkin's sensuous vision of the lotus-mystery, as well as being different from it. As in *Antony and Cleopatra* the ooze here is the source of an evident phallic energy: the water-plants are 'surging', 'rigid, naked', 'thick and cool and fleshy'.) If the Beldover colliers are half-automatised, it is also true that the dark, disruptive force which they mediate is an elemental life-energy. And finally, if Ursula is unresponsive to these equivocal resonances, if at this stage in the story she shows no faculty for this knowledge in corruption (effectively she is not present in the scene, though at the beginning we know her to be at Gudrun's side), then so much the worse – as well as the better – for her. We will go hopelessly astray in our reading of the novel if we assume that, quite simply, Lawrence spoke here for life and growth as against mechanism and the flux of corruption.

So, given Birkin's disintegrative violence at the Pond, we need not be surprised to find that his *explicit* repudiation of the awful African process (later in the chapter) does not in the event represent the whole truth about him. When he engages in a wrestling match with Gerald, for instance, the two men commit themselves so utterly in the combat as to go 'beyond the limits of mental consciousness' – like the savage woman in labour. The experience the men share, it is fair to say, is equivalent to that mystical death which the Africans must have undergone 'thousands of years' ago, when 'the relations between the senses and the outspoken mind' broke, 'leaving the experience all in one sort mystically sensual'. In short, the events in 'Moony' are concerned with *living* disintegration. If earlier, at Breadalby, Birkin had annihilated Hermione with 'corruptive fire – fire of the cold-burning mud', he destroys the false individuality of Ursula now with an energy which, again, is burning and disruptive – distinguishable from the African sun-destruction and yet analogous to it. So the fragments of the moon, 'falling back as in panic, but working their way home again persistently', image a process at once reductive and integrative, peace-loving and violent. In effect two traditions of Romanticism – distinct concepts of belonging or ideals of self-sufficiency – are compelled to confront each other here and in the novel at large: the paradisal and the demonic. And in the confrontation neither is affirmed at the expense of the other. In *Women in Love* English Romanticism becomes for the first time fully self-conscious.

SOURCE: *River of Dissolution: D. H. Lawrence and English Romanticism* (Routledge, 1969).

NOTES

1. *The Forked Flame* (1965) p. 181.
2. In *Reflections on the Death of a Porcupine* (Philadelphia, 1925; reprinted Bloomington, 1963) p. 180.
3. *The Collected Letters of D. H. Lawrence*, ed. Harry T. Moore, 2 vols (1962) I 360.
4. *Women in Love*, ch. IV.
5. Ibid., ch. XV.
6. Ibid., ch. XIX.
7. 'The Crown' first appeared in 1915 and was later included in *Reflections on the Death of a Porcupine*.
8. *Women in Love*, ch. VIII.
9. Ibid., ch. XXI.
10. In *Phoenix* (1936, reprinted 1961) pp. 153 ff.
11. *Son of Woman* (1931, reprinted 1936) p. 118.
12. *D. H. Lawrence: Novelist* (London, 1955; New York, 1956) p. 180.
13. *The Dark Sun* (1956).
14. Daleski makes this point (op. cit. p. 158).
15. *Fantasia of the Unconscious* (New York, 1922; London, 1923).
16. Murray Krieger, *The Tragic Vision* (1960).
17. See *Phoenix*, pp. 377–82.
18. *The Symbolic Meaning*, The Uncollected Versions of *Studies in Classic American Literature*, ed. Armin Arnold (London, 1962; New York, 1962) p. 116.
19. David Gordon, *D. H. Lawrence as a Literary Critic* (New Haven, Conn., 1966) p. 115.
20. 'Lawrence, Joyce and Powys', in *Essays in Criticism*, XI (Oct. 1961) 408.
21. *Women in Love*, ch. V.

SELECT BIBLIOGRAPHY

OF books devoted exclusively or in part to Lawrence's fiction, apart from those represented in this anthology, mention may be made of the following:

Mark Spilka, *The Love Ethic of D. H. Lawrence* (Indiana U.P., 1955; Dobson, 1958).

Graham Hough, *The Dark Sun* (Duckworth, 1956; Capricorn, 1959).

Eliseo Vivas, *D. H. Lawrence: The Failure and the Triumph of Art* (Northwestern U.P., 1960; Allen & Unwin, 1961).

Keith Sagar, *The Art of D. H. Lawrence* (Cambridge U.P., 1966).

Laurence Lerner, *The Truthtellers: Jane Austen, George Eliot, D. H. Lawrence* (Chatto & Windus, 1967).

The following essays are useful:

Angelo P. Bertocci, 'Symbolism in *Women in Love*', in *A D. H. Lawrence Miscellany*, ed. Harry T. Moore (Southern Illinois U.P., 1959).

William Walsh, 'Ursula in *The Rainbow*', in *The Use of Imagination* (Chatto & Windus, 1959; Barnes & Noble, 1961).

A. L. Clements, 'The Quest for Self: D. H. Lawrence's *The Rainbow*', in *Thoth*, III (Spring 1962).

Robert L. Chamberlain, 'Pussum, Minette, and the Afro-Nordic Symbol in Lawrence's *Women in Love*', in *Publications of the Modern Language Association of America*, September 1963.

Eldon S. Branda, 'Textual Changes in *Women in Love*', in *Texas Studies in Literature and Language*, VI (1964).

A second discarded chapter of *Women in Love*, portraying Ursula and Gudrun, and essentially another version of the opening chapter as we know it, has been published with an introduction by George H. Ford: see ' "The Wedding" Chapter of D. H. Lawrence's *Women in Love*', in *Texas Studies in Literature and Language*, VI (1964). According to Ford, 'The Wedding' chapter, from certain indications in the manuscript, seems to have been written earlier than the 'Prologue' and linked on to it at a later date.

For a full bibliography of Lawrence criticism see the checklist of Maurice Beebe and Anthony Tommasi in *Modern Fiction Studies*, V (Spring 1959) i. In his bibliography at the end of *The Art of D. H. Lawrence* Keith Sagar has collected a few items missing from that checklist and has added some of those which have appeared since 1959.

NOTES ON CONTRIBUTORS

COLIN CLARKE, Reader at the University of East Anglia, is the author of *Romantic Paradox: An Essay on the Poetry of Wordsworth* (1962).

H. M. DALESKI is a member of the English Faculty at the Hebrew University, Jerusalem.

GEORGE H. FORD is the author of *Keats and the Victorians* (1962) and *Dickens and his Readers* (1965). He has co-edited *The Dickens Critics* (1962) and *The Norton Anthology of English Literature*. Currently he is Chairman of the Department of English at the University of Rochester.

S. L. GOLDBERG, Professor of English at the University of Melbourne, is author of *The Classical Temper: A Study of James Joyce's 'Ulysses'* (1961) and *Joyce* (1962).

RONALD GRAY, Fellow of Emmanuel College and Lecturer in German in the University of Cambridge, is author of *Goethe the Alchemist* (1952), *Kafka's Castle* (1956), *Brecht* (1961), *An Introduction to German Poetry* (1965) and is the editor of *Kafka* in the Twentieth-century Views series.

FRANK KERMODE is Lord Northcliffe Professor of English at University College, London. His books include *Romantic Image* and *The Sense of An Ending*.

G. WILSON KNIGHT is the author of numerous books on Shakespeare and other themes, including *The Wheel of Fire* (1949, reprinted 1961), *The Golden Labyrinth: A Study of British*

Drama (1962), *The Saturnian Quest: A Chart of the Prose Works of John Cowper Powys* (1964).

JULIAN MOYNAHAN is a member of the English Department at Princeton University. He is the author of a novel, *Sisters and Brothers* (1960), and a frequent contributor to journals and newspapers in America and England.

JOHN MIDDLETON MURRY was the author of *The Problem of Style* (1921), *Keats and Shakespeare* (1926) and other works of criticism. He founded the *Adelphi* 'for Lawrence' in 1923, but the two men quarrelled and Lawrence rarely wrote for it. After the publication of *Son of Woman* (1931) Murry continued throughout the rest of his life to turn out commentaries on Lawrence. Apart from *Reminiscences of D. H. Lawrence* (1933), see in particular *Between Two Worlds* and *Love, Freedom and Society* (1957).

ROGER SALE teaches English at Amherst College.

INDEX

CASEBOOK SERIES

D. H. Lawrence:
The Rainbow and *Women in Love*

Casebook Series

GENERAL EDITOR: A. E. Dyson

Jane Austen: *Emma* DAVID LODGE
T. S. Eliot: *The Waste Land* C. B. COX AND A. P. HINCHLIFFE
D. H. Lawrence: *Sons and Lovers* GĀMINI SALGĀDO
D. H. Lawrence: '*The Rainbow*' and
  '*Women in Love*' COLIN CLARKE
Marlowe: *Doctor Faustus* JOHN JUMP
John Osborne: *Look Back in Anger* J. RUSSELL TAYLOR
Pope: *The Rape of the Lock* JOHN DIXON HUNT
Shakespeare: *Antony and Cleopatra* J. RUSSELL BROWN
Shakespeare: *Hamlet* JOHN JUMP
Shakespeare: *Julius Caesar* PETER URE
Shakespeare: *Macbeth* JOHN WAIN
Shakespeare: *The Merchant of Venice* JOHN WILDERS
Shakespeare: *The Tempest* D. J. PALMER
Shakespeare: *The Winter's Tale* KENNETH MUIR
Yeats: *Last Poems* JON STALLWORTHY

IN PREPARATION
William Blake: *Songs of Innocence and*
  Experience MARGARET BOTTRALL
Emily Brontë: *Wuthering Heights* MIRIAM ALLOTT
Joseph Conrad: *The Secret Agent* IAN WATT
Dickens: *Bleak House* A. E. DYSON
Donne: *Songs and Sonnets* ANNE RIGHTER
George Eliot: *Middlemarch* PATRICK SWINDEN
T. S. Eliot: *Four Quartets* BERNARD BERGONZI
Henry Fielding: *Tom Jones* NEIL COMPTON
E. M. Forster: *A Passage to India* MALCOLM BRADBURY
Ben Jonson: *Volpone* JONAS BARISH
Keats: *The Odes* G. S. FRASER
Milton: '*Comus*' and '*Samson Agonistes*' STANLEY FISH
Shakespeare: *Henry IV* Parts I and II G. K. HUNTER
Shakespeare: *Henry V* MICHAEL QUINN
Shakespeare: *King Lear* FRANK KERMODE
Shakespeare: *Measure for Measure* C. K. STEAD
Shakespeare: *Othello* JOHN WAIN
Shakespeare: *Richard II* NICHOLAS BROOKE
Tennyson: *In Memoriam* JOHN DIXON HUNT
Virginia Woolf: *To the Lighthouse* MAURICE BEJA
Wordsworth: *Lyrical Ballads* ALUN JONES
Wordsworth: *The Prelude* W. J. HARVEY